ROUTLEDGE LIBRARY
NAZI GERMANY AND TH

Volume 10

NAZI PROPAGANDA

NAZI PROPAGANDA

The Power and the Limitations

Edited by
DAVID WELCH

Routledge
Taylor & Francis Group

LONDON AND NEW YORK

First published in 1983

This edition first published in 2015
by Routledge
2 Park Square, Milton Park, Abingdon, Oxon, OX14 4RN

and by Routledge
711 Third Avenue, New York, NY 10017

Routledge is an imprint of the Taylor & Francis Group, an informa business

British Library Cataloguing in Publication Data
A catalogue record for this book is available from the British Library

ISBN: 978-1-138-79664-5 (Set)
eISBN: 978-1-315-75774-2 (Set)
ISBN: 978-1-138-80394-7 (Volume 10)
eISBN: 978-1-315-75336-2 (Volume 10)
Pb ISBN: 978-1-138-80396-1 (Volume 10)

Publisher's Note
The publisher has gone to great lengths to ensure the quality of this reprint but points out that some imperfections in the original copies may be apparent.

Disclaimer
The publisher has made every effort to trace copyright holders and would welcome correspondence from those they have been unable to trace.

Printed and bound by CPI Group (UK) Ltd, Croydon, CR0 4YY

Nazi PROPAGANDA

THE POWER AND THE LIMITATIONS

Edited by DAVID WELCH

CROOM HELM
London & Canberra
BARNES & NOBLE BOOKS
Totowa, New Jersey

© 1983 David Welch
Croom Helm Ltd, Provident House, Burrell Row,
Beckenham, Kent BR3 1AT

British Library Cataloguing in Publication Data

Nazi propaganda
    1. Nationalsozialistische Deutche Arbeiter-Partei
    — Party work   2. Propaganda German
    I. Welch, David
    303.3'75'0943   DD253.25
    ISBN 0-7099-2736-3

First published in the USA 1983 by
BARNES & NOBLE BOOKS
81 ADAMS DRIVE
TOTOWA, NEW JERSEY 07512

Library of Congress Cataloging in Publication Data

Main entry under title:

Nazi propaganda.

    Bibliography: p.
    Includes index.
    Contents: Introduction / David Welch — Hitler's
impact on the lower middle class / Lothar Kettenacker —
Goebbels and the function of propaganda / Richard
Taylor — [etc.]
    1. Nationalsozialistische Deutsche Arbeiter-Partei-
Party work. 2. Propaganda, German. I. Welch, David
DD253.25.N39 1983   943.085   83-8739
ISBN 0-389-20400-5

Printed and bound in Great Britain

CONTENTS

TABLES AND FIGURES

Tables

Figures

1 INTRODUCTION

David Welch

> Propaganda, propaganda, propaganda. All that matters is propaganda.
> — Adolf Hitler[1]

The rise and fall of National Socialism is understandably one of the most closely studied issues in European history. Historians have been at great pains to explain why millions of Germans voted for the NSDAP in free elections and how such a regime could eventually acquire such an extensive European Empire. This book attempts to understand such questions in the light of a detailed examination of Nazi propaganda, both in terms of its theory and practice.

Although Nazi propaganda has only recently come to receive the attention of historians commensurate with its importance, the degree of consensus about the effectiveness of Nazi propaganda is quite revealing. Historians of widely different political persuasions and approaches have testified to the crucial role it played in mobilising support for the Nazis. In his study of Nazi propaganda, Z.A.B. Zeman asserted that the growth of the NSDAP from 'insignificant beginnings' into a truly mass-movement 'was largely due to the skilful exploitation of propaganda techniques . . . Although the theory and practice of Nazi propaganda were derivative to a certain extent . . . its cumulative effect has never been surpassed'.[2] Martin Broszat, on the other hand, has persuasively argued that 'the originality of the Party did not consist in its intellectual equipment, but in the manner in which it propagandised and fought for ideas represented by others. It was the dynamics of the Party, its parades, the ceremonial blessing of banners, the marching columns of the SA, the uniforms, the bands, etc., which captured the imagination of the masses.'[3]

Similarly, East German historians, although approaching the subject from a different ideological point of view, have also stressed the importance of propaganda. In the standard East German text dealing with this period, Wolfgang Ruge noted: 'The fascist party developed a propaganda apparatus whose activities far eclipsed all previous heights of the demogogy of German imperialism. The insidious methods it employed to influence the masses, fastened on to the social crisis and the nationalist sentiments of the broadest strata of the population.'[4]

However, despite this general consensus, it has been rightly argued that the functions and assumed effectiveness of Nazi propaganda have not been examined sufficiently closely and critically in the past.[5] This volume will not attempt to outline the historical development of Nazi propaganda, nor will it prescribe the secrets of propaganda success. The most rewarding method of understanding the phenomenon of propaganda is not, I feel, through the study of the rhetorical and psychological tricks employed, but rather through the analysis of the total social context, conceiving the whole as a dynamic field of stresses and strains wherein the forces of propaganda play their part. The aim of this book then, based on detailed examinations of specific aspects of Nazi propaganda, is to enhance our understanding of National Socialism by revealing both its power and limitations.

Before discussing briefly what propaganda meant to the Nazis themselves, I would first like to identify two common misconceptions connected with the study of propaganda. There is a widely held belief that propaganda implies nothing less than the art of persuasion, which serves only to change attitudes and ideas. This is undoubtedly one of its aims, but often a limited and subordinate one. More often, propaganda is concerned with reinforcing existing trends and beliefs; to sharpen and focus them. A second basic misconception is the entirely erroneous conviction that propaganda consists only of lies and falsehood. In fact it operates with many different kinds of truth — from the outright lie, the half truth, to the truth out of context. Moreover, as Terence Qualter has rightly pointed out, many writers on the subject see propaganda as essentially appeasing the irrational instincts of man, and this is true to a certain extent, but because our attitudes and behaviour are also the product of rational decisions, then propaganda must appeal to the rational elements in human nature as well.[6] The preoccupation with the former ignores the basic fact that propaganda is ethically neutral — it may be good or bad. In all political systems policy must be explained, the public must be convinced of the efficacy of government decisions, and rational discussion is not always the most useful means of doing this, particularly in the age of 'mass man'.[7] Therefore, in any body politic, propaganda is not, as is often supposed, a malignant growth, but is an essential part of the whole political process.

There can surely be little doubt that one of the most crucial factors contributing to the Nazis' rise to power was the skilful use of propaganda; certainly the Nazis themselves were convinced of its effectiveness. In *Mein Kampf*, Hitler devoted two chapters to the study and practice of propaganda. Hitler was not an original theorist of propaganda techniques, but while a student in Vienna he learnt the art of stimulating the hopes and fears of his audience into positive action. In his early writings he referred to the Austrian Marxists in Vienna, 'who knew how to flatter the masses'. Profoundly influenced by British propaganda in the First World War, Hitler was firmly convinced that propaganda was a powerful weapon in the hands of experts. By appointing Joseph Goebbels Head of Party Propaganda (*Reichspropagandaleiter*) in November 1928, Hitler found his expert. From now on the emphasis was to be on the expert. However, one must necessarily turn back to *Mein Kampf* where Hitler laid down the broad lines along which Nazi propaganda was to operate. In the following extract Hitler assessed his audience as follows:

> The receptive powers of the masses are very restricted, and their understanding is feeble. On the other hand, they quickly forget. Such being the case, all effective propaganda must be confined to a few bare essentials and those must be expressed as far as possible in stereotyped formulae. These slogans should be persistently repeated until the very last individual has come to grasp the idea that has been put forward.[8]

According to Hitler, propaganda for the masses had to be simple, it had to aim at the lowest level of intelligence, and it had to be reduced to easily learned slogans which then had to be repeated many times, concentrating on such emotional elements as love and hatred. Thus, unlike the Bolsheviks, the Nazis did not make a distinction in their terminology between agitation and propaganda. In Soviet Russia, agitation was concerned with influencing the masses through ideas and slogans, while propaganda served to spread the Communist ideology of Marxist-Leninism.[9] Hitler, on the other hand, did not regard propaganda as merely an instrument for reaching the Party elite, but rather as a means for the persuasion and indoctrination of all Germans. This distinction led E.K. Bramsted to conclude that propaganda for the Nazis 'had not a specific, but a total validity'.[10] The main objective then of Nazi propaganda in both opposition and government was to unify the German people behind a single thought and purpose. In turn this belief in the invincibility of one's own cause could be used as a weapon to undermine the power of one's enemies.

In some ways propaganda is easier in opposition than in power, and Goebbels proved a skilful orchestrator of the Party's propaganda resources. But propaganda alone can never change social and political conditions; it acts in conjunction with other factors, like organisation. National Socialist propaganda did not destroy Weimar democracy, although it did undermine it. What distinguished the NSDAP from other political parties was its ability, consistently maintained throughout its development, to merge the themes of traditional German patriotism with Nazi ideological motifs. This unification of German patriotism and Nazi ideology allowed Hitler, in Jay W. Baird's words to 'forge a compelling weapon against what he termed the 'immorality of Weimar rationalism', the symbol of cultural decadence, racial impurity, and Jewish putrefaction'.[11] In fact Hitler felt that the importance of propaganda would decline once the Party gained political power. In this respect organisation would eventually replace propaganda.[12] Not surprisingly, given Goebbels' success in master-minding the NSDAP's victory in 1933, he disagreed with Hitler's distinction between propaganda and organisation. Goebbels believed that propaganda would be just as necessary in power, not only to mobilise mass support for the new *Völkischer Staat* but also to maintain a heightened level of enthusiasm and commitment to the new regime.

It was during the beginning of 1933 that Goebbels was making final plans for a Propaganda Ministry that would assume control over all aspects of mass-communications. However, because Goebbels was so involved in the forthcoming elections on 5 March, it was decided to delay announcing the creation of this new Ministry until after the Nazi's success was guaranteed. Eventually Goebbels was appointed Reich Minister for Popular Enlightenment and Propaganda (*Reichsministerium für Volksaufklärung und Propaganda* – RMVP) by Presidential decree on 13 March. In June Hitler was to define the scope of the RMVP, making Goebbels responsible for 'the spiritual direction of the nation'. Not only did this vague directive provide Goebbels with room to out-manoeuvre his critics within the Party, it also gave the mark of legality to what was soon to be the Ministry's complete control of all that mattered most in the functioning of the mass media in the Third Reich.

From the outset Goebbels reaffirmed the importance of successful propaganda. In a revealing address to representatives of the press on 15 March 1933, he declared:

I see the establishment of this new Ministry of Popular Enlightenment and Propaganda as a revolutionary act of government because the new government has no intention of abandoning the people to their own devices and locking them up in an airless room. This government is, in the truest sense of the word, a people's government . . . The name of the new Ministry tells us quite clearly what we mean by this. We have founded a Ministry for Popular Enlightenment and Propaganda. These two titles do not convey the same thing. Popular enlightenment is essentially something passive: propaganda, on the other hand, is something active. We cannot be satisfied with just telling the people what we want and enlightening them as to how we are doing it. We must replace this enlightenment with an active government propaganda, a propaganda that aims at winning people over. It is not enough to reconcile people more or less to our regime, to move them towards a position of neutrality towards us, we want rather to work on people until they are addicted to us . . .[13]

Once in power Goebbels stressed the importance of co-ordinating propaganda with other activities. Propaganda in a totalitarian police state must address itself to large masses of people and attempt to move them to a uniformity of opinion and action. But the Nazis' understood that propaganda is of little value in isolation. To some extent this explains why Goebbels impressed on all his staff the imperative neccessity of constantly gauging public moods. He therefore regularly received extraordinarily detailed reports from the Secret Police about the mood of the people. To assure themselves of continued popular support was an unwavering concern of the Nazi leaders, and of Goebbels in particular.

By the outbreak of the Second World War the Propaganda Ministry had complete control of all the media of information. The population had therefore been unable for several years to relate what they saw, or heard, or read, to alternative sources. Writers in a pluralist society tend to view propaganda as a separate entity from other functions of leadership, even as something of which to be rather ashamed. Propaganda in Nazi Germany, on the other hand, was only an additional power weapon, albeit an indispensable function of the *Völkischer Staat* (hence the open advertisement of 'propaganda' in the title of Goebbels' ministry). The criterion in regard to truth was simply whether 'truth' at a given time would serve the best interests of the state. Addressing his staff in the RMVP during the war, Goebbels declared: 'There must be absolute certainty that words are followed up by corresponding events. Propaganda does not have anything to do with truth! We serve truth by serving a German victory.'[14] Goebbels was expressing the view that in the Third Reich, the propaganda machinery served an ideal higher than truth, namely the National Socialist *Weltanschauung*. However, Goebbels was careful not to tell all lies; he was master at distorting the truth. All the same both Goebbels and Hitler appreciated the burden that a war would place on the Nazi propaganda machine. In a society where the illusion at least of a monolithic unity between leadership and people had to be preserved at all costs, the war presented considerable strains on the political system. The manner in which it responded to these tensions would depend on the Propaganda Ministry's efficiency in forging an effective link with the regime's leadership and the credibility of propaganda itself. I have argued elsewhere that propaganda during this period had not only to convince the German people of their own cause and invincibility, but abroad it needed to win over neutral nations and at the same time undermine the enemy's spirit of resistance.[15] In fact Nazi propaganda became so intrinsically linked to German military success that defeat after Stalingrad found propaganda in a difficult position. Goebbels' response was to retreat more and more into the mythical and irrational elements of National Socialist doctrine, which failed increasingly to survive reality during the last years of the Third Reich.

It has been said of Nazi propaganda that it was a crucial bridge between 'objective' circumstances and the mass conversion to what has often appeared an irrational and contradictory doctrine. In the first chapter in this volume, Lothar Kettenacker demonstrates the extent to which Hitler's propaganda in opposition represented the true aspirations of the German middle class, or more specifically, the petit-bourgeoisie (*Kleinbürgertum*). Dr Kettenacker also provides a valuable examination of recent historiography dealing with this fascinating relationship. The creation of the 'Führer-myth' has always been credited to Goebbels' manipulatory talents. Kettenacker argues that the Propaganda Minister's success was only possible because of the tremendous reception given to his adulation of the Führer by ordinary Germans. Richard Taylor takes this a stage further and, with the benefit of his extensive research carried out in European and American archives, re-examines the basic concepts and appeal of Nazi propaganda by analysing Goebbels the propagandist and the political function of propaganda in the National Socialist system of government.

The next two chapters look at architecture and film propaganda during the Third Reich. These were aspects of Nazi propaganda which were of particular interest to Hitler and Goebbels. Jochen Thies shows that it was Hitler's abtruse understanding of art and history which allowed a grandiose architectural vision to take shape in a building programme that was intended to symbolise German superiority and her imperial ambitions. My own contribution analyses the role of film propaganda in the schools and youth organisations and leads me to the conclusion that cinema was the perfect medium for combining both entertainment and propaganda. By disguising its intent such propaganda was able to exert and maintain a considerable influence over German youth, so that consequently a uniformity of opinion and action developed with few opportunities for resistance.

Martin Broszat has recently suggested the need for a broadening of our concept of resistance to the Nazi regime.[16] Taking up this theme, Stephen Salter notes that although coercion played an increasingly important role in the 'containment' of the German working class during the war, workers' informal protests and attempts to defend their interests *can* be classified as a form of resistance. Drawing on substantial primary sources used in his forthcoming doctoral thesis on the subject, Salter outlines the main influences on workers' moral and work-discipline and assesses its political significance. Similarly, by discussing Nazi propaganda channelled through official women's agencies promoting thrifty practices and the skilful use of German substitutes, Jill Stephenson demonstrates that propaganda clearly failed to persuade the German housewife to identify herself with a cause which was manifestly not in her interests. As such, Dr Stephenson reveals the limitations of propaganda when its message was unpalatable.

Goebbels maintained that the purpose of propaganda was to persuade the audience to believe in the viewpoint expressed by the propagandist. But if propaganda is to be effective it must, in a sense, preach to those who are already partially converted. Writing before the Second World War, Aldous Huxley observed:

> Propaganda gives force and direction to the successive movements of popular feeling and desire; but it does not do much to create these movements. The propagandist is a man who canalises an already existing stream. In a land where there is no water, he digs in vain.[17]

It has been said of National Socialism that it lacked international appeal. Z.A.B. Zeman concluded his work on Nazi propaganda by stating that the Nazis thought of propaganda abroad as a mere extension of propaganda at home: 'this meant that the contents and the eccentricities of Nazi agitation in Germany were translated, indiscriminately on the international plane'.[18] In order to test this view and to provide a more informed picture, two case studies attempt to show how Nazi propaganda operated in the occupied territories of Western Europe. In the case of the Netherlands, Gerhard Hirschfeld shows that Nazi propaganda only played a decisive role with the ranks of the local fascist movement. In general it failed to persuade most sectors of Dutch society to either 'collaborate' or indeed to co-operate with the German authorities. François Garçon comes to a similar conclusion in his study of Nazi film propaganda in France. He argues that despite concerted Nazi efforts to utilise the cinema for their own ends, French film makers managed not only to resist in a restrictive creative environment, but actually eliminated German cultural and technical influence from their work. Finally, Ian Kershaw reappraises the conventional view that Nazi propaganda *must* have been successful. He concludes by suggesting that the effectiveness of propaganda was dependent upon its ability to build on an existing consensus. Its success was guaranteed wherever it could identify Nazi aims with values which were unquestioned.

The importance of propaganda in the politics of the twentieth century should not be underestimated. However, because propaganda has come to have prejorative connotations, the term 'propaganda' is too often devalued in its usage. Divested of these associations, the study of propaganda will reveal its significance as an intrinsic part of the whole political process in the twentieth century. E.H. Carr has written that 'Power over opinion is therefore not less essential for political purposes than military and economic power, and has always been associated with them. The art of persuasion has always been a necessary part of the equipment of a political leader.'[19] This volume offers an appreciation of both the power and limitations of propaganda. Not only do the essays tackle aspects of Nazi propaganda that have been neglected in the past, but each contribution is written by an acknowledged expert in his/her field. Together they demonstrate the disproportionate role assigned to propaganda in one of the most highly politicised societies in contemporary European history . . . and perhaps serve as a timely reminder for tolerance and understanding in our own times.

Notes

1. J. Fest, *Hitler* (London, 1974), p. 187.
2. Z.A.B. Zeman, *Nazi Propaganda* (Oxford, 1973), p. 32.
3. M. Broszat, *German National Socialism* (Santa Barbara, California, 1966), p. 62, quoted in R. Bessel, 'The Rise of the NSDAP and the Myth of Nazi

Propaganda', *The Wiener Library Bulletin*, vol. XXXIII, nos. 51/2 (1980), p. 21.

4. W. Ruge, *Deutschland von 1917 bis 1933* (East Berlin, 1967), p. 354.

5. Cf. Bessel, 'The Rise of the NSDAP', p. 22. I am greatly indebted to the author for my introductory remarks.

6. T.H. Qualter, *Propaganda and Psychological Warfare* (New York, 1962), p. 63.

7. I am grateful to George Boyce for drawing my attention to the fact that in recent years, for example, the British public have been reminded on more than one occasion of the 'Dunkirk' and now the 'Falklands spirit'; it has been asked to consider 'who governs Britain'; it has been assured that the rate of price increases can be reduced 'at a stroke'; and it has been guaranteed that the 'pound in your pocket' has not, and will not, decrease in value.

8. A. Hitler, *Mein Kampf* (London, 1939), p. 159.

9. The distinction dates back to Plekhanov's famous definition: 'A propagandist presents many ideas to one or a few persons; an agitator presents only one or a few ideas, but presents them to a mass of people.'

10. E.K. Bramsted, *Goebbels and National Socialist Propaganda 1925-45* (Michigan, 1965), p. 454.

11. J.W. Baird, *The Mythical World of Nazi War Propaganda, 1939-45* (Minneapolis, 1974), p. 4.

12. For a discussion of this, see D. Welch, *Propaganda and the German Cinema, 1933-45* (Oxford, 1983), pp. 40-2.

13. Speech to representatives of the press, 15 March 1933 taken from WTB (*Wolffs Telegraphisches Büro*) press agency report of 16 March 1933 deposited in the Bundesarchiv, Koblenz).

14. W. von Oven, *Mit Goebbels bis zum Ende* (2 vols., Buenos Aires, 1949-50), vol. 1, p. 32.

15. D. Welch, 'Nazi Wartime Newsreel Propaganda' in K. Short (ed.), *Film and Radio Propaganda in World War II: A Global Perspective* (London, 1983), p. 201.

16. M. Broszat, 'Resistenz und Widerstand. Eine Zwischenbilanz des Forschungsprojekts' in M. Broszat *et al.* (eds.) *Bayern in der NS-Zeit IV. Herrschaft und Gesellschaft im Konflikt Teil C* (Munich, 1981), pp. 691-709.

17. A. Huxley, 'Notes on Propaganda', *Harper's Magazine*, vol. 174 (December, 1936), p. 39.

18. Zeman, *Nazi Propaganda*, p. 178.

19. E.H. Carr, *The Twenty Years' Crisis, 1919-39* (New York, 1964), p. 132.

2 HITLER'S IMPACT ON THE LOWER MIDDLE CLASS

Lothar Kettenacker

The important facts about the Third Reich, a mere twelve years in a national history covering more than a thousand years, have all been established: the breakdown of Weimar democracy, Hitler's seizure of power, the rivalry of his vassals behind a façade of unparalleled uniformity, the road to war, genocide and unconditional surrender.[1] Indeed, hardly any period in Germany's history has been scrutinised to the same extent. There is certainly more than ample evidence for a jury to reach its verdict. Nevertheless, the debate about the phenomenon of National Socialism and the character of Hitler's regime is still raging with no sign of coming to an end. There is no other event — and this was altogether more of an event than a period — of which it can be said with more justification that history is one thing and what you make of it another. In no small measure interpretations are coloured by political attitudes due to the proximity of the Second World War and the momentous consequences it entailed. Still, historians are genuinely puzzled by the ambiguity of their evidence and often cannot agree on whether to stress the reactionary intentions or the modernising effects.[2] Even the terminology is in dispute:[3] while some authors would argue that Germany experienced the most extreme form of fascism, there are others who point to the singularity of the 'Hitler-movement' which had, in spite of all similarities, a much more devastating impact on world history than Mussolini's Italy. It is because of the incriminating nature of what happened in Germany, and not in Italy, that so many theories on fascism have emerged.[4]

They tend to emphasise certain aspects to the exclusion of others and none of them should be trusted as the sole key to understanding German history between 1933 and 1945, though taken together they probably furnish quite a reliable picture of the many facets of the Third Reich. No doubt, if attention is focused, as in the case of the Marxist model,[5] on the last years of the Weimar Republic the promises that a Nazi takeover held for agrarians and industrialists seemed to cast Hitler in the role of a saviour of capitalism. However, the Nazi movement, or rather *Hitlerbewegung*, as it was appropriately labelled at the time, had already become a political force in its own right by the time the conservative elites tried to come to terms with its leader. Surely, the higher echelons in the civil service, the army and industry would have fared much better under an authoritarian regime established by General von Schleicher. At the end of the day they were as much the victims of Hitler's rule (von Schleicher as early as 1934) as were the lower middle classes whose unswerving loyalty to the 'Führer' was crucial for his electoral successes before 1933 and the relative stability of his regime afterwards. If one is prepared to make great play of the illusory belief amongst the upper classes that they could use the 'Bohemian lance-corporal' then it is only fair to give due credit to Hitler who was by far the superior manipulator. He was certainly not the agent of capitalism or any other economic system.[6] On the contrary, he would use any device which suited his plans for the next stage of his ambitions: before 1933 he seemed to embrace the idea of a corporate state which was most popular among farmers, artisans and small businessmen; afterwards he was quick to drop such plans in favour of rapid rearmament for which he required the support of heavy industry and the established governmental machine.

In most theories on fascism the impact of Hitler and his propaganda are grossly underrated. Why is this? First of all, it is assumed that history cannot be explained in terms of personalities: they may wield all kinds of power but are devoid of 'explanatory power', a favourite term of those who are attracted to the theoretical approach. No wonder it has taken a whole generation of sophisticated research for someone to rediscover that there is no better way to describe Hitler's rule than the term 'autocracy'.[7] What appeared to be self-evident at the time is now regarded as another controversial theory. There is no denying that Hitler's personality was indeed of a most mediocre brand. Yet this is the very secret of his success, as Fest has revealed in his brilliantly conceived biography.[8] To say that the 'Führer' was the 'representative individual' of the Germans in general, goes too far;[9] too many members of the bourgeoisie and the working class were disgusted by him. It is the purpose of this chapter to show that he was more specifically the mouthpiece of the German lower middle class, the *unterer Mittelstand* in sociological terms, or more to the point, the *Kleinbürgertum* (petit-bourgeoisie).

Equally, propaganda in politics has been dismissed all too easily as unworthy of serious attention: it is ideology put into practice for public consumption, in other words something which does not really matter for those like Hans Mommsen whose overriding concern is to detect administrative structures amounting to, or else failing to achieve, a political system of some duration.[10] What ordinary people between the wars felt, sensed or thought, to what degree they were receptive to propaganda, appears to be of no consequence, unless, of course, economic promises are made. Only economic interests *vis-à-vis* society are judged to be rational, and in this sense political, whereas spiritual demands on the state can be brushed aside as almost irrelevant. In this perspective there is no place for the small man, the *kleine Mann* in the eyes of Hans Fallada,[11] whose beliefs, hopes and illusions are only proof of his *falsches Bewusstsein* (false consciousness) caused by the rejection of his 'proper' place in society. If this dubious assumption were accepted; all middle-class historians embracing the cause of the working class could be accused of the same deviation. Historical responsibility for the right cause or the wrong decision is, of course, no privilege of the educated classes. Hitler, for one, took propaganda very seriously as he admits quite openly in *Mein Kampf*; it was to appeal to instinct rather than to intellect, to prejudice rather than to knowledge, to the masses rather than to the individual.[12] The *Hitlerbewegung* was the 'mobilisation of the *declassé*'[13] and as such much more successful than the traditional political parties who promised to redress genuine and specific grievances. The total rejection of the so-called Weimar system meant that Hitler was never expected, at least not by his followers, to do better within the framework of the existing constitution. Instead he was allowed to play around with negative and positive images, to create a world of political fantasies which were as real as bad dreams. However, this was not out of tune with a society which lived in constant suspense brought about by sudden defeat, unexpected revolution, *coups d'état*, rapid inflation, ostentatious advertising and consumerism and, finally, world economic depression followed by mass unemployment — all in quick succession. Most of Hitler's rhetoric, themes like the Bolshevist danger, the injustice of Versailles, the world Jewish conspiracy, were hardly of immediate concern to the typical Nazi voter, such as the small-town Protestant artisan under 30,[14] far away from the twilight world of Berlin, whose apprehensions were, nevertheless, real in the sense that they were welded into a politically effective instrument for the purposes of undermining the Republic. Therefore, and for no other reason, the strange relationship between the ordinary man and his extraordinary alter ego in the person of the 'Führer' requires further investigation.

It was in his chapter on *Kriegspropaganda* (War Propaganda)[15] that Hitler revealed for the first time how little he thought of his fellow citizens. The model he admired was the *Greuelpropaganda* (atrocity propaganda) disseminated by the Northcliff Press, of which British liberals were to be ashamed in later years and which contributed to the slow realisation of German atrocities committed in the Second World War. Indeed, he compared political propaganda to commercial advertising: exaggerations and outright fabrications are all right as long as they are believed. If the Imperial army was supposed to be the 'school of the nation' it was the war which moulded Hitler and forged the link between him and his voters in later years. Tracing the roots of National Socialism is a dubious exercise because there is no clear point of departure. What matters is the vulgarisation of certain philosophical and political assumptions, especially those so-called 'ideas of 1914',[16] as a means of strengthening both the fighting morale of the troops and the home front. During the First World War propaganda was slightly more sophisticated than in the Second, though not necessarily more successful, in that the emphasis was on pseudo-intellectual justifications of Germany's political culture rather than on denouncing the enemy, to the dismay of Hitler who was greatly influenced by it none the less. It is significant that so many German academics felt called upon to make their contribution to the war effort instead of leaving psychological warfare to the professionals. Hitler's personal resentment of the bourgeois world which refused to recognise his 'genius' as an artist received a new quality and a new meaning because it could now be directed against Germany's enemies who were conspiring to frustrate her aspirations to historical greatness.

Before the war Hitler tried to maintain his precarious social position by his hostility towards working-class politics. His weakness for the opera was quite genuine, but it also served to prove to himself that he had not lowered his aesthetic standards regardless of his miserable existence. During the war he came to identify the left as the enemy from within who denounced all territorial claims and tried to drag the country down the road to a shameful peace. His opposition to bourgeois capitalism, be it amongst the enemies abroad or civilian war profiteers at home, as well as to the war-weary left, coincided with that of the lower middle class who were strongly represented in right-wing associations, particularly the *Vaterlandspartei* (the German Fatherland Party).[17]

Perhaps the most decisive of Hitler's experiences, the one crucial precondition of his later success, was his distinguished war service. He took part in all the major battles on the Western front and received his first decoration when his regiment of over three and a half thousand men was reduced, in December 1914, to just over 600 within four days.[18] The war might have crippled others, both physically and psychologically, but for Hitler it was a great boost to his ego. At the beginning he was a failed artist, a bohemian with no fixed address or income, at the end of it he could claim to be one of those unknown war heroes who had returned to a country shattered by defeatism and revolution and headed by a new leadership unworthy of the army's sacrifice. His career as the most outspoken representative of his generation as well as of his social class was to begin. The terms of reference and the rhetoric of his early speeches were clearly those of the frustrated soldier who felt cheated by the outcome of the war. His explanation for Germany's misery was an easy one: world Jewry had conspired to bring down the Reich. Hitler's early speeches reveal that his pathological anti-semitism served a political purpose before it became predominantly racist: the 'Jew' typified everything the war veteran had learned to loathe, the profiteering bourgeois capitalist who made a fortune from the war, as well as the left-wing journalist and intellectual whose reservations about Germany's official war aims had helped to undermine public morale.[19] International democracy, liberalism and Bolshevism, all commandeered by Jews, were let loose to sap Germany's independent strength. The means to strangle her was the peace treaty, the 'shame of Versailles', into which Germany was tricked. All those who had accepted Versailles were either Jews or *Judentzer*, i.e. agents of international Jewry, like Matthias Erzberger. Hitler's propaganda was one of pure hatred which was all the more effective because it was directed not against anonymous forces but against the Jew as the personally responsible and recognisable perpetrator. His language became most abusive and insulting when he referred to the Jews and their alleged machinations. It seems that his *idée fixe* about the Jews was not taken too seriously by his early audiences, especially in Bavaria where strong language is part of the tribal culture; to some extent it was good entertainment to go to one of Hitler's mud-slinging performances.[20] After all, it was a totally new experience to see common prejudice expressed with so much spite and *sang-froid*. No doubt his popularity was increased in Bavaria by the fact that the object of his venom was 'red Berlin', the seat of the central government as well as the Government of Prussia, or rather of those politicians who, as he saw it, had sold Germany's honour to the Allies and were trying to keep the nation in a state of weakness and subjection. It must be added that a great many of the pre-1924 Nazi rallies took place in Munich beer cellars, in an atmosphere of drunkenness and drum-beating nationalism.

Apart from the principle of *semper aliquid haeret*, it can safely be said that on the whole Hitler's message was most favourably received by the half-educated, yet self-righteous lower middle class, such as artisans, shopkeepers, low grade employees and civil servants.

It is true that Hitler was courted by certain quarters of Munich society; hostesses in particular seemed to have been thrilled by the presence of this notorious rabble-rouser with an Austrian sense of deference.[21] Most of the prominent participants in the failed *Putsch* of 9 November 1923 were also clearly middle class in origin.[22] But this does not say much about the impact of Hitler's propaganda. After all, most of the leadership of the political left was drawn from the same background. Taken as a whole, the propertied and educated classes (*Bildungs- und Besitzbürgertum*) stayed aloof, at least up to 1924. So did the mass of the working class.

The main result of Hitler's propaganda campaign up to his honourable confinement in Landsberg was the recruitment of his *alte Kämpfer*, the old Party hands, whose devotion to the cause of a 'conservative revolution' was indispensible in later years, at least up to 1933. The SA, his Praetorian guard (*Schutz-Abteilung*), helped to shape the popular image of the NSDAP more than any programme, the image of youthful radicalism displaying an *élan vital* totally lacking among the established parties. The percentage of party members between 18 and 30 was twice as high as in the SPD. Peter Merkl, who has examined a fairly representative sample of early Nazis, concludes: 'German youth set up the stormladders against the republic and helped one of its false alternatives, the Nazi party, to power.'[23] Indeed, no other party in Weimar Germany was able to stage its rallies with the same youthful activism and idealism, flag-waving, marching, singing and rough camping.[24] Hitler was the incarnation of the new militant nationalism of the war veterans, freecorps members and would-be soldiers who could not reconcile themselves to defeat and to the civilian life-style of a democratic and competitive society. They could easily be persuaded that politics was just another form of warfare. In fact, Hitler's attacks on the leading figures of the left and in the Centre Party were more vitriolic than German wartime propaganda levelled against enemy statesmen.

However, all of Hitler's radical rhetoric against Versailles and the Jews was not enough if power was to be gained at the ballot box, an attempt he resolved to make after the failure of his coup. Now a mass movement had to be launched all over Germany.[25] There can be no doubt that two ideological concepts were of fundamental importance for Hitler's success in mobilising disaffection: the idea of the *Volks-*

gemeinschaft based on the principle laid down in the party programme of 1920 – *Gemeinnutz geht vor Eigennutz* (Common good before the good of the individual) and the myth of the charismatic 'Führer',[26] the great leader who rose from the ranks in order to save the German *Volk* from the corrupt 'system' imposed by the victors. The lower middle class was the most fertile ground for this kind of message. According to the official statistics of the NSDAP even before 14 September 1930 membership amongst the *Mittelstand*, i.e. including farmers and civil servants, amounted to 61 per cent rising to 73 per cent of the party officials.[27] Not only had the lower middle class expanded rapidly during and after the war owing to the increase in bureaucracy and the rising demand for employees in industry and commerce, but there was also a widespread feeling amongst its members that their economic and spiritual interests were not sufficiently taken into account by the traditional parties.[28] Hitler's propaganda was specific-ally designed to appeal to such sentiments. His movement, he wrote, was not to embrace the satisfied and contented sections of society, in other words the bourgeois elements of the middle class, but 'those plagued by misfortune and restlessness, those who are malcontent and disaffected'.[29] In normal times the utterly disaffected groups form but a minority of society; in Weimar Germany this was not the case.

The *Kleinbürger* felt most strongly that he represented the 'average German', yet he was unable to identify either with the new men at the top, be it in politics, industry or the arts, or with the mass of the working class. Fears of social degradation as well as frustrated ambi-tions led to large-scale disaffection amongst the members of the *Mittel-stand* which was bound to be exacerbated in times of economic depres-sion. Their man was Adolf Hitler who had himself experienced what it meant to be an aspiring artist and social *declassé*; espousing national causes was an escape from the problem of settling for a life below one's social expectations. Hitler admitted quite openly that he belonged to the social milieu which rose into the lower middle class – his father being a petty Austrian customs official – and was most anxious not to revert to its proletarian origins.[30] Anton Drexler, a locksmith who founded the *Deutsche Arbeiterpartei* (later NSDAP), claimed the right for all working men, provided that they were skilled and resident, to be regarded as members of the middle class.[31]

Moeller van den Bruck, author of *Das Dritte Reich* and greatly admired by the leadership of the Association of Commercial Employees, spelled out the same message: 'Whoever wants to be a proletarian, is one'[32] as though adherence to the working class was a state of mind rather than a fact of social life. This might be classified as an inadequate perception of social reality, or *falsches Bewusstsein*, but it can nevertheless be made most effective by means of propaganda. Theodor Geiger, one of the first sociologists to explore the relationship between the mentality of the lower middle class and National Socialism, stresses the point that false ideologies might very well be typical of the collective mentality of certain sections of society which have not yet identified their own position *vis-à-vis* society as a whole.[33] This is certainly true of the German lower middle class after the war which tended to regard itself as *pars pro toto*, though not of society, but of the nation or rather the *Volk*. The war had caused a steady erosion of middle-class living standards, especially among the lower echelons. According to Jürgen Kocka's pioneering research the narrowing gap between the incomes of the salaried class and the wage-earners precipitated a process of 'proletarisation' of the lower middle class which in many cases had only just emerged from the ranks of the working class.[34] The wartime trend towards the left amongst white-collar organisations was reversed after the revolution which brought social democracy and its allies into power; the NSDAP was not a party known for its appreciation of middle-class anxieties.

The initial attitudes towards the Nazi Party of the so-called old, more established *Mittelstand*, i.e. artisans, small retailers and farmers, were more reserved in view of the latter's alleged pledge to socialism; the name 'National Socialist Workers' Party' certainly was no recommendation and it took some time, as well as a worsening of the economic situation, for people to realise that neither the party name, nor its programme meant much to Hitler.[35] Even when the great majority of the old *Mittelstand* rejected the Hitler movement it became quite clear that young artisans were already drawn to Nazi slogans. Opposition from the older generation was not based on liberal or democratic principles either. On the contrary, the concept of strong leadership and the idea of a corporate state shielded from class conflict formed the core of the artisan's beliefs: he wished to remain 'master' in his own house and, if the latter happened to be a small family business, to be able to keep the trade unions at bay. He did not look upon himself as an ordinary factory worker, but as a skilled craftsman, regardless of whether he was self-employed or working for somebody else.[36] A great many statistics concerning membership of the NSDAP are clearly misleading, because people like Anton Drexler, the founder of the party, classified themselves as *Handwerker* (craftsman) rather than *Arbeiter*, (worker) though to all intents and purposes their lot was exactly the same as that of the working class. Up until the Chancellorship of Heinrich Brüning, who introduced a measure of protectionist legislation, none of the Weimar governments had cared to develop a genuine programme for the benefit of the traditional *Mittelstand*, because politics were overshadowed by the fight against inflation in the face of limitless reparation demands and the conflict between industry and labour.

Nor had the Republic much to offer as far as the spiritual needs of ordinary people were concerned: no pomp and circumstance, no royal family above party squabbles, no colonial empire left where Teutonic virtues could be displayed. Above all, no strong, respected government which could enforce social harmony. With the steady erosion of a previously privileged position *vis-à-vis* the working class the desire to maintain the social *status quo* grew more intense. The more the objective foundations of the social fabric were undermined the more they were underpinned by ideological defence mechanisms. Moeller van den Bruck's pleading for a conservative revolution was hailed as the true goal of German politics by the association of commercial employees. A somewhat outdated concept of humanist education, a watered-down version of the much-admired model provided by the *Gymnasium*, served to prop up the image of social respectability in adverse times.[37] A new kind of popular nationalism was fostered centred on the *Volk*, the nation as a *Gemeinschaft* (community) bonded together by blood, soil and heritage, rather than a *Gesellschaft* (society) divided into classes and interest groups. The intense identification with the nation's fortunes during the war was to continue in times of peace and was to be achieved by the same means of military discipline and heroism. Hans Speier has pointed out that the concept of *Volk* was rather vague unless defined by its negative connotations, by its antagonism towards (1) the reactionary nationalism of the land-owning and entrepreneurial class, (2) the 'atomising' effects of liberal democracy with its alleged emphasis on superficial consumerism, and (3) the Marxist notion of permanent class struggle.[38] Consequently, the 'decent' member of the *Mittelstand* with no grudge in his heart against his fellow German and no shares in his pocket was the genuine representative of the *Volksgemeinschaft* (Community of the People), whose voice in politics had, as it were, been drowned on the stock-exchange. Rainer Lepsius has argued that here was a new type of popular nationalism emerging from the middle ground of society that was more perniciously extreme than anything before 1914.[39] The *Mittelstand* claimed to articulate the ethical code of the whole of society (*Normalmoral*) by which Weimar Germany

was measured and found wanting. It was exactly this antiliberal prejudice of the common man to which Hitler was to appeal in later years in
order to justify his policy of persecution, of cleansing Germany of the
Jews, gypsies, mentally handicapped and others who were seen to con-
taminate the purity of the *Volk*. There is no more telling term to
describe this mentality than the Nazi reference of the *'gesundes Volksempfinden'* (a healthy-minded people), the 'healthy', in actual fact
utterly prejudiced 'common sense', by which everything not in line
with party doctrine could be branded as 'un-German'.

Once Hitler had distanced himself from the socialist wing within his
party and thereby strengthened his position not only as the chief
propagandist, but also as undisputed 'Führer', there was no ideological
barrier left which would stop the lower middle class from swelling the
ranks of the movement.[40] There might still be reservations about the
means and methods which the Nazi Party applied to further its aims;
about the conduct of the storm-troopers, the pacts made with the
Communist Party from time to time, but these were overcome when
the economic depression led to further a polarisation of German society
and when Hitler was seen to shake hands with the gentlemen politicians
of the right at Bad Harzburg in October 1931. Full use could now be
made of Nazi anti-semitism to gain the support of small shopkeepers
who suffered from the competition of the large department stores in
Jewish hands. Farmers, too, were now more favourably disposed
towards Hitler and his demand for more living space, a slogan which
also gained acceptance among the more respectable economists after
the collapse of international trade.[41]

Nevertheless, the most effective propaganda topic remained Hitler's
claim that he would bring about the *Volksgemeinschaft*, the true harmony of classes, instead of a mere nationalisation of the means of
production. Too many white-collar workers and petty officials were
already employed by local or central government authorities without
feeling in any way spiritually uplifted and convinced that this was the
answer to all their grievances. Too many self-employed artisans and
retailers resented the intrusion by an ever-increasing bureaucracy.
Before Hitler set about establishing his one-party state it was anyone's
guess how social reconciliation was to be achieved in practical terms;
the Weimar 'system' was an easy target for abuse. In what may well
have been one of his most effective speeches, leading to the elections of
31 July 1932, he poured ridicule on parliamentary decision-making;
every faction of society – shopkeepers, farmers, landlords, tenants,
Catholics, Protestants – had to be represented by their own lobby with

the ensuing result of chaos and impotence. 'All these efforts', he claimed, 'to divide the nation into classes, estates, professions and denominations and to lead them to economic prosperity bit by bit can now be said to have utterly failed'.[42] New research into the social background of Nazi voters reveals that, compared with other parties during the last years of the republic and given the particular impetus of the Protestant lower middle class, the NSDAP did after all come nearest to a people's party embracing all sections of society, employees and workers, farmers and officials, housewives (especially among the first-time voters), Catholics and Protestants, young and old.[43]

Admittedly, the party was least successful in Catholic regions and strongholds of the Social Democrats. But this does not prove that democratic values had taken root in those parts of Germany. Apart from the ideological antagonism expressed by the leadership this was due in large measure to the existence of a *juste milieu* established by long-standing traditions and loyalties.[44] Catholics and Social Democrats had their own *Volksgemeinschaft*, both as an ideological claim and a well-tested social environment. The relationship between Church and State in Italy, Austria, and Spain is ample evidence that there was no intrinsic dichotomy between fascism and the Catholic way of life, as long as a *modus vivendi* could be found which left the organisational network of the Catholic Church untouched. Once the local establishment in Bavaria had been won over the party made considerable inroads even before March 1933.[45] Nor was the working class immune to the appeal of the Nazi Party and its promise to secure full employment and social harmony. Even before the great landslide of September 1930 nearly every fifth party official (18.5 per cent) was of working class origin,[46] which was roughly the same percentage as those drawn from the peasantry who are usually more identified with National Socialism. The unions did not rise to the support of their leaders when the free labour movement was crushed and brought into line with the new set-up.[47] One day before Hitler launched this course of action he gave his pledge to one million people assembled at the Tempelhof aerodrome in Berlin that he would eradicate all class snobbery towards the working man. In the midst of the depression he announced the end of all class conflict, promised work for everyone, emphasised the dignity of manual labour and hinted at the introduction of a national labour service in order to discipline the sons and daughters of the upper classes.[48]

Of course, this did not mean very much in practical terms: full employment was to be achieved by rapid rearmament, not by a change in the economic order. Yet the impact of Hitler's speeches on the working man should not be underrated: the idea that what mattered was the socialisation of man rather than of machines.[49] All previously conceived schemes for the protection of the *Mittelstand* were dropped − not one department store was closed − once power was firmly secured and Hitler had set his eyes on more ambitious goals for which the collaboration of the traditional elites in government and industry were clearly indispensible. Nevertheless, the spread of the party organisation into all walks of life and the constant launching of new ventures created many new openings for an aspiring class of hitherto frustrated clerks, petty officials, unemployed professionals and the like. Thus it would be totally misleading to focus attention on the meagre results of special legislation for the *Mittelstand*.[50] It can safely be assumed that the staging of the *Volksgemeinschaft* at public occasions, the social dynamism produced by new career patterns and, last but not least, the imposition of a corporate superstructure based on the leadership principle, carried more weight with the lower middle class than any specific economic measures.

If the NSDAP was commonly referred to as the *Hitlerbewegung* before 1933 the regime that emerged afterwards had all the hallmarks of what one might call the *Führerstaat* (Leader State). It would be misleading to think that Hitler's personal rule extended to all levels of Government and all regions of the Reich. For that he was much too lazy, quite apart from the neo-feudal leadership principle which left the regions or *Gaue* in the hands of his trusted vassals.[51] What it means is that he did decide all the major issues in foreign policy which was in keeping with the image of himself as a second and superior Bismarck; it meant, moreover, that the myth of the infallible leader under the protection of providence was the most important asset for the stability of his regime. The degree of national − *not* social − cohesion which Germany achieved after 1933, almost within months of the Nazi take-over, was mainly due to the charisma of the Führer and *Reichskanzler* who was held in much higher popular esteem than his party. While the ideology of the *Volksgemeinschaft* helped to win elections and eventually to seize power the Führer-myth proved to be the most successful propaganda instrument to prepare the German population for the endurance and hardship of the years to come. The sudden loss of the monarchy in 1918, for which Germany was in no way psychologically prepared, had left a vacuum which was now filled by Hitler, the up-to-date *Volkskaiser*. Throughout the 1920s dissatisfaction with Berlin politics and democracy in general expressed itself in hopes for the advent of a strong national leader who would put an end to the non-sense of parliamentary decision-making. This explains the quasi-religious symbolism of the day of Potsdam[52] as the coming of the new political Messiah who received the blessing of the last representative of the old monarchy.

The creation of the Führer-myth has always been credited to Goebbels' manipulatory talents.[53] However, the success of the new minister for *Propaganda und Volksaufklärung* (Propaganda and Popular Enlightenment) was only possible because of the tremendous and unexpected response to his adulation of the Führer by ordinary Germans. This is the conclusion reached by Ian Kershaw who has explored the response of the *vox populi* to Hitler's charisma more thoroughly than anybody before him. There can be no doubt that the enthusiasm for the new Chancellor was very genuine. Regarding the public celebration on the occasion of his forty-fourth birthday, within months of his accession to power, Kershaw writes: 'Apparently the efforts of clever propaganda, which in itself could not achieve all this, were greeted by a marked psychological disposition for adoring Hitler.'[54] That this could be sustained and even intensified must in the first place be attributed to the undeniable achievements of his govern-ment in domestic and foreign affairs. What has been overlooked is that Hitler's immense popularity can also be explained by the representative character of his mentality: he was and remained the most outspoken petit bourgeois of his time, regardless of the fact that he himself used the term in a derogatory sense.

Post festum et bellum many foreign observers wondered whether the country of Mozart and Beethoven, Goethe and Schiller had not deser-ved better leadership than that exercised by a half-educated bohemian. However, if ever it has been true that people get the leadership they deserve, the average German philistine did find his *alter ego* in Adolf Hitler, who exclaimed that it was the Germans' greatest fortune to have found him.[55] If this claim could in any way be substantiated it would be further proof that it was Hitler who was the first casualty of the Führer-myth, as Martin Broszat argues, and not the German people, as Sebastian Haffner would have it.[56] There is not the slightest doubt that his commonplace views on such subjects as art and architecture, bureaucrats and intellectuals, academic learning and the like were widely shared by the half-educated classes in Germany. Every small town *pater familias* was deeply moved by the miraculous accord of his personal views with those of the Great Leader: in his heart of hearts he always knew that abstract art was rubbish, that intellectuals were unreliable bedfellows, that most diplomats were fools, that women were destined to raise children, that sport and not bookish learning was the way to control youngsters and so on.[57] One of the most revealing aspects of Hitler's personality as the 'representative individual' are his aesthetic views. After all, he saw himself as an architect by vocation. Goebbels often praised the modesty of the Führer in his personal demands. It would be more appropriate to say that he felt most at home in surroundings which can only be described as *'kleinbürgerlich'* (petit bourgeois). This at least is the verdict of Hermann Rauschning who was somewhat taken aback by the common taste displayed in the interior of Hitler's mountain retreat near Berchtesgadan (before it was redesigned). 'The great popular orator', he observed, 'in these surroundings was reduced to the insignificance of the petit bourgeois.'[58] The impression of his personal quarters in the old Imperial Chancellery was no different. He also liked to be surrounded by his old cronies who had to suffer his monologues until the early hours of the morning.[59] It is no contradiction that he loved to design grandiose schemes for official buildings, notably for Berlin, or rather *Germania* the metropolis of the new world power: they were daydreams of a provincial megalomaniac with a weakness for the opera. The historical greatness and uniqueness of the Third Reich demanded architecture on a monumental scale.[60] The millenial character was nowhere more explicit than in Hitler's *ex-cathedra* lectures on German art and architecture, which was meant to last for thousands of years, in other words, to be immortal, everlasting: *'Grösse'* (size) and *'Jahrtausende'* (thousand years) are the most recurrent epithets.[61] It goes without saying that modern art did not meet these criteria at all: it was decadent, unhealthy if not pathological, at best unworthy of the German genius. Hitler revelled in pouring ridicule on those artists who were devoted to modern styles. On 10 July 1938 he compared the unique achievements of the Third Reich — chiefly schemes and designs as a matter of fact — with the alleged decadence of Weimar culture, the period of *'dadaistische Lärmerzeuger, kubistische Gipsformer oder futuristischer Leinwandfärber'* (Dadaist loudmouths, Cubist plasterers or Futurist decorators).[62] No doubt, he expressed exactly what most of Germany sincerely felt, but did not dare to say in public. It was the essence of the *gesundes Volksempfinden* not to be ashamed of these sentiments any longer.

Hitler realised that politics, too, could be manipulated so as to serve as an outlet for the strong feelings and frustrations of the common man. His habit of arguing with foreign statesmen from the rostrum and making a mockery of their warnings was deeply gratifying for the average German who loved to be compensated for defeat and a humiliating peace. For once their was somebody at the helm who was not pushed around by foreign diplomats or by his own counsellors; instead, he kept everybody guessing and was seen to wield power like a medieval emperor. He would emerge from any crisis he faced with flying colours as the events of June 1934 appeared to prove, when his authority was challenged by the frustrated SA leadership which was pressing for revolutionary change. After all, the Nazi takeover did not lead to an immediate exchange of elites. It was more reassuring to see the government machine being purged and controlled by new men at the top than to risk inefficiency and chaos brought about by a completely new set-up. Recent research has shown that Hitler's bloody methods of dealing with his old guard enhanced his popularity rather than compromising it, as one might have thought.[63] The code of petit bourgeois respectability was reaffirmed throughout the ranks of the SA. Those who were not shot had their records checked for any misdemeanour in the past and faced degradation and expulsion. Hitler announced that the national revolution had come to an end, to the great relief of those who had remained uneasy about the 'bolshevist' elements within the party. There was no awareness amongst the mass of supporters that the criminal character of the regime was revealed as much by its means as by its ends and that the methods in this instance were signals for worse to come. Hitler had got away with it before when he publicly defended the murders of Potempa without in any way compromising his electoral chances.[64]

There is then a direct link between the blood-bath of Bad Wiessee (where the SA were 'purged') and the holocaust which the chief perpetrator in both cases, Himmler, drew attention to when addressing high SS leaders in Posen on 4 October 1943.[65] To have sustained the horror of the Final Solution, he said, and to have remained 'decent' — with the exception of human weaknesses — was a glorious achievement, though never to be recorded. The SS had the moral right, accruing from its duty to the German people, to exterminate the Jews. But, of course, no one was entitled to help himself to a single fur coat, watch, Mark or even a cigarette. He then went on to elaborate on the most important virtues of the SS-men, such as loyalty, obedience, bravery and honesty. On a philosophical level this frame of mind can be attributed to the pernicious distinction between *Staatsmoral* and *Privatmoral* which permitted a total perversion of common morality in the name of *Realpolitik*. However, social psychology is probably a better guide to the understanding of the incomprehensible. The collective mentality of the lower middle class was more the product of German political culture in general, than of any particular philosophical tradition: it was open to political and ideological manipulation and at the same time was narrowly defined by a petit bourgeois code of moral respectability; what counted was professional ethos, the rest was outside the scope of personal responsibility. One might argue that this mental disposition was not confined to the lower middle class. Indeed, Erich Fromm discovered on the eve of the Nazi seizure of power that outside the party political spectrum 25 per cent of a certain sample of KPD and SPD members could be classified as halfway or completely authoritarian.[66] Amongst the *Mittelstand* there were no opposing influences emanating from the leadership. On the contrary, the tendencies inherent in a most susceptible mentality were further strengthened by means of an ideological superstructure and by Adolf Hitler, a master of propaganda.

Notes

1. Here attention should be drawn to the English translation of Martin Broszat's pioneering study *The Hitler State. The Foundation and Development of the Internal Structure of the Third Reich* (London, 1981). A somewhat different interpretation is given by Klaus Hildebrand, *Das Dritte Reich* (Munich, 1979) who focuses on foreign policy and therefore, more than Broszat, on Hitler's personal decision-making. This is a most useful textbook of the whole period including both the historiography and a detailed bibliography.

2. Cf. Karl Dietrich Bracher, *Zeitgeschichtliche Kontroversen* (Munich, 1976), pp. 62-78.

3. Cf. Hildebrand, *Das Dritte Reich*, p. 139; see also his contribution, 'Monokratie oder Polykratie? Hitlers Herrschaft und das Dritte Reich' in Gerhard Hirschfeld and Lothar Kettenacker (eds.), *The 'Führer State': Myth and Reality* (Stuttgart, 1981), pp. 73-97.

4. See the bibliographical note in the annex to Stanley G. Payne, *Fascism* (Madison/Wisconsin, 1980); also bibliography in Hildebrand, *Das Dritte Reich*, pp. 202.

5. Cf. Wolfgang Wippermann, *Faschismustheorien* (Darmstadt, 1976), pp. 11-55; Eike Henning, 'Zum Verhältnis von Industrie und Faschismus in Deutschland' in Reinhard Kühnl (ed.), *Texte zur Faschismusdiskussion* (Hamburg, 1971), pp. 140-63. Critical assessment by Heinrich August Winkler, 'Die "neue Linke" und der Faschismus: Zur Kritik neomarxistischer Theorien über den Nationalsozialismus' in Winkler (ed.), *Revolution, Staat, Faschismus* (Göttingen 1978), pp. 65-117.

6. This is rightly stressed by Hildebrand in 'Monokratie oder Polykratie?'; also Henry A. Turner Jr. 'Hitlers Einstellung zur Wirtschaft und Gesellschaft vor 1933', *Geschichte und Gesellschaft*, vol. 1 (1976), pp. 89-117.

7. Eberhard Jäckel, 'Hitler und die Deutschen. Versuch einer geschichtlichen Deutung' in Karl Corino, *Intellektuelle im Bann des Nationalsozialismus* (Hamburg, 1980); see also Hildebrand, 'Monokratie oder Polykratie'.

8. Joachim C. Fest, *Hitler* (Frankfurt am Main, 1973), pp. 20ff.

9. J.P. Stern, *Hitler: The Führer and the People* (London, 1975), pp. 9-22.

10. Cf. Hans Mommsen, 'Hitlers Stellung im nationalsozialistischen Herr-schaftssystem' in Hirschfeld and Kettenacker (eds.), *The 'Führer State'*, pp. 43-72 or his epilogue to the German translation of David Schoenbaum, *Die braune Revolution* (Munich, 1980), pp. 352-68 where he questions the revolutionary impact of the regime.

11. The title of his novel – *Kleiner Mann, was nun?* (Berlin, 1932) – incapsulates Fallada's concern for the common man at a time of economic crisis and intellectual confusion. The novel provides a very apt description of German small town milieu on the eve of the Nazi seizure of power.

12. See Adolf Hitler, *Mein Kampf* (Munich, 1937), p. 198.

13. David Schoenbaum, *Hitler's Social Revolution* (New York/London, 1967), p. 17.

14. Cf. Ibid., p. 35.

15. Hitler, *Mein Kampf*, pp. 193-204.

16. Cf. Klaus Schwabe, *Wissenschaft und Kriegsmoral* (Göttingen, 1969), pp. 21ff.

17. Dirk Stegmann, *Die Erben Bismarcks. Parteien und Verbände in der Spätphase \des Wilheminischen Reiches* (Köln, 1970), pp. 497-519; see also George E. Etue, 'The German Fatherland Party' (PhD thesis Berkeley/California, 1959) and for the pre-1914 period: Geoff Eley, *Reshaping the German Right* (New Haven/London, 1979).

18. See Hitler's description of the first major battles in his letter to Ernst Hepp, 5 February 1915, in Eberhard Jäckel and Axel Kuhn (eds.), *Hitler. Sämtliche Aufzeichnungen 1905-1924* (Stuttgart, 1980), pp. 64ff.

19. Ibid., *passim*.

20. Cf. Georg Franz-Willing, *Ursprung der Hitlerbewegung 1919-1922* (Preussisch Oldendorf, 1974), pp. 217-52; Fest, *Hitler*, pp. 186-230.

21. See the memoirs of Ernst Hanfstaengl, *Zwischen Weissem und Braumen Haus* (Munich, 1970), pp. 48-52.

22. Cf. Harold J. Gordon, *Hitler and the Beer Hall Putsch* (Princeton, 1972), pp. 464-85; Ernst Deuerlein, *Der Hitler-Putsch. Bayerische Dokumente zum 8./9. November 1923* (Stuttgart, 1962).

23. Peter H. Merkl, *Political Violence under the Swastika* (Princeton/London, 1975), p. 13.

24. Cf. Sebastian Haffner, *Anmerkungen zu Hitler* (Munich, 1978), p. 35.

25. Dieter Orlow, *The History of the Nazi Party* (2 vols., Newton Abbot, 1971-3), vol. I, pp. 128-84.

26. See Wolfgang Horn, *Führerideologie und Parteiorganisation in der NSDAP, 1919-1933* (Düsseldorf, 1972), pp. 209ff.; Martin Broszat, 'Soziale Motivation und Führer-Bindung im Nationalsozialismus' in Wolfgang Michalka (ed.), *Nationalsozialistische Aussenpolitik* (Darmstadt, 1978), pp. 92-116.

27. Robert Ley (ed.), *Parteistatistik* (Archive of the Institut für Zeitgeschichte in Munich, Munich, 1935); vol. I, p. 70 and vol. II, p. 164.

28. Cf. Jürgen Kocka, *Klassengesellschaft im Krieg. Deutsche Sozialgeschichte 1914-1918* (Göttingen 1973).

29. Hitler, *Mein Kampf*, p. 364.

30. Ibid., p. 22.

31. Herbert Michaelis and Ernst Schraepler (eds.), *Ursachen und Folgen* (3 vols., Berlin, 1958ff.), vol. III, pp. 212ff.

32. Quoted by Hans Speier, *Die Angestellten vor dem Nationalsozialismus* (Göttingen, 1977), p. 103.

33. Theodor Geiger, *Die soziale Schichtung des deutschen Volkes* (Stuttgart, 1932), p. 78.

34. Kocka, *Klassengesellschaft im Krieg*, pp. 71-6.

Hitler's Impact on the Lower Middle Class 27

35. Cf. Heinrich August Winkler, 'Vom Protest zur Panik: Der gewerbliche Mittelstand in der Weimarer Republik' in Hans Mommsen, Dietmar Petzina and Bern Weisbrod (eds.), *Industrielles System und politische Entwicklung in der Weimarer Republik* (Düsseldorf, 1974), pp. 778-91.

36. As to the manipulation of these attitudes by the Nazi Regime see Adelheid von Saldern, *Mittelstand im Dritten Reich* (Frankfurt/New York, 1979).

37. See Speier, *Die Angestellten*, particularly his chapter 'Die Funktion der Bildung', pp. 102-9.

38. Ibid., p. 123.

39. Rainer Lepsius, *Extremer Nationalismus* (Stuttgart, 1966), p. 13.

40. For the systematic campaign to win the support of the *Mittelstand* see Karl Dietrich Bracher, *Die deutsche Diktatur* (Köln, 1969), pp. 166-83; for the regional level: Jeremy Noakes, *The Nazi Party in Lower Saxony* (London, 1971), pp. 121-38; as for farmers in particular: Horst Gies, 'R. Walther Darré und die nationalsozialistische Bauernpolitik in den Jahren 1930-1933' (Phil. Diss. Frankfurt am Main, 1966) as well as John E. Farquharson, *The Plough and the Swastika. The NSDAP and Agriculture in Germany 1928-1945* (London/Beverly Hills, 1976).

41. Cf. Hans-Erich Volkmann, 'Die NS–Wirtschaft in Vorbereitung des Krieges' in Wilhelm Deist et al. (eds.), *Ursachen und Voraussetzungen der deutschen Kriegspolitik* (Stuttgart, 1979), pp. 177-89.

42. Speech on record: 'Appell an die Nation' (15 July 1932), in Max Domarus (ed.), *Hitler. Reden und Proklamationen*, (3 vols., Munich, 1965), vol. I, p. 116.

43. Jürgen W. Falter, 'Wer half der NSDAP zum Sieg?' in *Beilage zu Das Parlament*, B28-9, p. 19; also though less outspoken because of the implications for the working class Heinrich August Winkler, 'Mittelstandsbewegung oder Volkspartei? Zur sozialen Basis der NSDAP' in Wolfgang Schieder (ed.), *Faschismus als soziale Bewegung* (Hamburg, 1976), pp. 97-118.

44. Cf. Karle Rohe's research into the voting pattern in the Ruhr area: 'Vom alten Revier zum heutigen Ruhrgebiet. Die Entwicklung einer regionalen politischen Gesellschaft im Spiegel der Wahlen' in K. Rohe and H. Kühr (eds.), *Politik und Gesellschaft im Ruhrgebiet* (Königstein, 1979), pp. 21-73; also: W. Böhnke, *Die NSDAP im Ruhrgebiet 1920-33* (Bonn/Bad Godesberg, 1974).

45. Elke Fröhlich, 'Die Partei auf lokaler Ebene. Zwischen gesellschaftlicher Assimilation und Veränderungsdynamik' in Hirschfeld and Kettenacker (eds.), *The 'Führer-State'*, pp. 194-227.

46. Ley (ed.), *Parteistatistik*, vol. II, p. 164.

47. Cf. Bracher, *Diktatur*, pp. 235ff. and Karl Rohe, *Das Reichsbanner Schwarz-Rot-Gold* (Düsseldorf, 1966), pp. 110ff.

48. Domarus (ed.), *Hitler. Reden und Proklamationen*, vol. I, pp. 259-64 (1 May 1933).

49. This is what he said to Herrmann Rauschning, *Hitler Speaks* (London, 1940), p. 192; as to the impact of this idea see Haffner, *Anmerkungen zu Hitler*, p. 50.

50. Heinrich August Winkler, 'Der entbehrliche Stand. Zur Mittelstandspolitik im Dritten Reich' in *Archiv für Sozialgeschichte* vol. 17 (1977), pp. 1-40. This view has now been challenged by von Saldern, *Mittelstand im Dritten Reich*, pp. 236ff.

51. See Hans Mommsen, 'Hitler's Stellung im nationalsozialistischen Herrschaftssystem' in Hirschfeld and Kettenacker (eds.), *The 'Führer-State'*, pp. 43-72 as well as Peter Hüttenberger, *Die Gauleiter* (Stuttgart, 1969).

52. As to the manipulation of the myth of Prussia see Manfred Schlenke, 'Nationalsozialismus und Preussen/Preussentum' in Otto Büsch (ed.), *Das Preussenbild in der Geschichte* (Berlin/New York, 1981), pp. 247-64.

53. Cf. Ernest K. Bamsted, *Goebbels and National Socialist Propaganda 1925-45* (Michigan, 1965), pp. 189-229.

54. Ian Kershaw, *Der Hitler-Mythos: Volksmeinung und Propaganda im Dritten Reich* (Stuttgart, 1980), p. 53.

55. Hitler's speech at the annual party rally at Nuremberg on 13 September 1936: Domarus (ed.), *Hitler*, vol. I, p. 643.

56. Introduction by Martin Broszat to Kershaw, *Hitler-Mythos*, p. 14.

57. See entries in Domarus (Index) under 'Kulturreden', 'Intellektuelle', 'Diplomaten', 'deutsche Frau', 'Hitlerjugend' etc.; see also Henry Picker (ed.), *Hitler's Tischgespräche im Führerhauptquartier* (Stuttgart, 1976).

58. Hermann Rauschning, *Hitler Speaks* (London, 1940), pp. 22ff and 66.

59. See introduction to Picker (ed.), *Hitlers Tischgespräche*, pp. 9-54.

60. Cf. Jochen Thies, *Architekt der Weltherrschaft* (Düsseldorf, 1976), pp. 62-104; also the chapter on Hitler's taste in George L. Mosse, *The Nationalization of the Masses* (New York, 1975).

61. See Hitler's speeches in Domarus (ed.), *Hitler*, Index, p. 2284: 'Kulturreden'.

62. Ibid., vol. I, p. 878.

63. Kershaw, *Hitler-Mythos* pp. 72-81; also: Mathilde Jamin, 'Zur Rolle der SA im nationalsozialistischen Herrschaftssystem' in Hirschfeld and Kettenacker (eds.), *Führer-State*. pp. 329-60.

64. Cf. Paul Kluke, 'Der Fall Potempa', *Vierteljahreshefte für Zeitgeschichte* vol. 5 (1957), pp. 279-97.

65. *Der Prozess gegen die Haupkriegsverbrecher* (IMG), (Nürnberg, 1948), vol. 29, Doc. No. 1919-PS, esp. pp. 145f.

66. Erich Fromm, *Arbeiter und Angestellte am Vorabend des Dritten Reiches*, ed. by Wolfgang Boss (Stuttgart, 1980), p. 37.

3 GOEBBELS AND THE FUNCTION OF PROPAGANDA

Richard Taylor

> Propaganda is an inalienable and vital function of the modern state.
>
> — Goebbels, 1934[1]

There can be few politicians or statesmen in the twentieth century, or, indeed, in any previous century, who have attracted the obloquy that has been heaped upon Hitler's Minister for Popular Enlightenment and Propaganda, Joseph Goebbels.

In the literature on Goebbels the epithets associated with his name range from 'a great scoundrel'[2] or 'a spider . . . in the middle of the spreading web'[3], through 'the bacillus'[4] and 'The Sorcerer's Apprentice'[5] to an 'agent of Lucifer',[6] the 'demon of a dictatorship',[7] 'Mephistopheles'[8] and 'Judas Iscariot'.[9] An early account of his family life has his wife, Magda, as the 'Devil's companion' (*Gefährtin des Teufels*) but the English translation has toned down the description of Goebbels from the 'Devil' to mere *Evil Genius*.[10]

Given the general standard of much of the more popular literature on National Socialism and the Third Reich the general tenor of these epithets is perhaps not surprising. What is surprising, however, is that so much of the more serious, even the more academic literature has fallen under the shadow of such emotionally charged vocabulary. To describe the man who was probably the most overt, and arguably also the most important, exponent of propaganda in history in such terms is at best a moral judgement and at worst a journalistic ploy. It is not however a historical judgement. A historian will of course make moral judgements but he will make them as a human being, for historians (or most of them!) are also human beings. But his task as a historian is neither to condemn nor to justify: it is merely to explain. Condemnation and justification may be signs of moral strength, even acts of moral bravery, but they are also acts of historical cowardice for they stand in the way of historical explanation. While the literature on Goebbels is rich in examinations of the psychological consequences of his physical disabilities, or in anecdotes about the lengths to which his Ministry went to conceal his limp from the general public (and here Goebbels had something at least in common with the perceived arch-enemy Roosevelt!) it is much thinner indeed on serious scholarly attempts to explain precisely what Goebbels thought he was doing. Even the best works on Nazi propaganda, such as Herzstein's *The War That Hitler Won*,[11] or Heiber's introduction to the two-volume German edition of the speeches,[12] do not, in the final analysis, really confront the fundamental question that a historian must ask about Goebbels and his role in the Third Reich. That question is, quite simply: what, as Reich Minister for Popular Enlightenment and Propaganda, was Goebbels' view of the political function of propaganda in the National Socialist system of government?

Any historian has to face the difficulties involved in separating fact from fiction. The historian of propaganda confronts the added problem of distinguishing fact from propaganda and in the case of Goebbels this problem is particularly acute. The source materials available to us are limited: the destruction of the Propaganda Ministry building in Berlin by RAF bombing in late 1944 has deprived historians of what would have been a veritable treasure-house of material. Such Propaganda Ministry files and records as do survive are either fragmentary, such as those in the *Bundesarchiv* in Koblenz,[13] or inaccessible (at least to Western historians), such as those in the *Zentrales Staatsarchiv der DDR* in Potsdam, or both. The all-important minutes of Goebbels' daily meetings with his staff, preserved in Potsdam, have been edited and made available through the painstaking efforts of Willi A. Boelcke[14] but *The Secret Conferences of Dr. Goebbels* cover only the war years, when the Minister was concerned with action rather than with words, practice rather than theory, and to read the theory into the practice would be at best a risky undertaking.

Another official source survives in almost complete form: the various reports on civilian morale and public opinion conducted by the Security Service (*Sicherheitsdienst* or SD)[15] of the SS and later, under cover, by the RMVP itself.[16] These too are confined to the war period and, while they provide a fascinating impression of popular attitudes and the effects of propaganda, they tell us nothing about the intentions or the aspirations of Goebbels or his Ministry.

Beyond the Ministry files and the official reports there are the more personal records, the interviews with survivors from the period and the memoirs of those involved. Memory, however, is fallible, especially in political circumstances that have changed beyond all recognition.[17] What we might term the 'I was only obeying orders' syndrome has in any case done a great deal (if not as much as the demand for commercially profitable sensationalism) to accentuate the demonisation of Goebbels. Thus, while all memoir materials present difficulties for the historian, memoirs of the Third Reich create particular problems. Useful as background material, as the flesh that fills out the bones, but the historian must find a more reliable and authentic source for the skeleton of his explanation.

Probably the most widely known and quoted source for students of Goebbels is the vast collection of diaries that he left behind him. Unlike most diarists, however, Goebbels did not confide his innermost personal thoughts to his daily journal. On the contrary, the Goebbels diaries were conceived as a message to future generations and designed as a source for historians of the Third Reich. The diaries are a public rather than a personal testament: they are the Propaganda Minister's propaganda for propaganda. That is why Goebbels the busy politician could find time to be Goebbels the conscientious diarist: as Bullock has remarked, 'Goebbels was an astute as well as an ambitious politician.'[18] Lochner estimates that, even at the height of the war the daily entries 'in some cases took up as many as eighty-five typewritten pages,'[19] an achievement that would defeat most people in full-time unemployment! As the organisation of the Third Reich weakened, so the importance of propaganda in the political system at large increased and this shift in the balance is reflected in the diaries.[20] It is a shift that Goebbels was well aware of: as Trevor Roper remarks, 'To the end, he could distinguish the objective truth from his own propaganda.'[21] It is also a curious inversion of Hitler's argument in *Mein Kampf*:

> If propaganda has imbued a whole people with an idea, the organisation can draw the consequences with a handful of men. Propaganda and organisation, in other words, supporters and members, thus stand in a certain mutual relationship. The better the propaganda has worked, the smaller the organisation can be, and the larger the number of supporters, the more modest the number of members can be, and vice versa: the poorer the propaganda is, the larger the organisation must be, and the smaller the host of followers of a movement remains, the more extensive the number of its members must be, if it still hopes to count on any success at all.[22]

It was of course Hitler's intention that propaganda was to give way to organisation and not that organisation would then ultimately give way once more to propaganda. The Goddess of History, whom Goebbels was to denounce as a 'whore out for money',[23] was to prove Hitler a mere fallible mortal.

For our source materials we are left then with the speeches that Goebbels made as Propaganda Minister. An excellent two-volume edition of these, edited by Heiber, was published in German in 1971-2[24] but has never been translated into English. It is a curious omission: the diaries, the conferences, but not the speeches and yet, in Bullock's widely shared view: 'Goebbels was second only to Hitler as a mob-orator.'[25] It is not, however, either the effectiveness or the aesthetic qualities of the speeches (if indeed we can pass definitive judgement on either) that concern us here: it is their contribution to our understanding of Goebbels' view of the political function of propaganda in the modern state. The speeches are important because they represent a direct and living contact, indeed the only direct and living contact, between the Propaganda Minister and his audience: they are themselves examples of propaganda in action and at first hand and they therefore constitute a fusion of both the theory and practice of propaganda.

There are no doubt many of Goebbels' numerous speeches that would shed light on the question under discussion but in this essay I want to concentrate specifically on three speeches that Goebbels delivered shortly after assuming his responsibilities as Minister for Popular Enlightenment and Propaganda on 13 March 1933. In his new task he had three major media at his disposal: the press, the radio and film; and in the latter half of March 1933 he took care to address representatives of all three of these potential political weapons. On 15 March he addressed representatives of the press.[26] Ten days later he spoke to the managerial staff of German radio in the *Haus des Rundfunks*[27] and on 28 March in the Kaiserhof he turned to film workers.[28]

In these speeches Goebbels' concern was primarily three-fold: first, to allay the fears of his audience, partly by flattery and partly by trying to establish some common ground; secondly, to build upon that by trying to develop a bond of sympathy with his audience; and thirdly, to communicate his ideas on the role of the Propaganda Ministry in the Third Reich. Each of the three speeches comprises a clever blend of these three concerns.

Let us look first at the flattery. In his speech to the representatives of the press Goebbels remarked:

I know very well the very important role that the press plays nowadays in public life. This instrument is the seventh great power that is better suited than any other to shape and to influence public opinion for or against a government.[29]

But to those working in the German radio he said first of all that, 'I hold radio to be the most modern and the more important instrument of mass influence that exists anywhere,'[30] and then continued: 'I am also of the opinion – and one shouldn't say this out loud – I am of the opinion that in the long term radio will replace newspapers.'[31] To his film audience, Goebbels was less flattering, but then his speech of 28 March is more disjointed than the other two and shows every sign of having been put together in haste. This is perhaps why he addressed film workers again on 19 May 1933[32] and why they had to wait until 9 February 1934 before being told that film was 'one of the most modern and far-reaching media that there is for influencing the masses'.[33] By that time, presumably, film workers with long enough memories would assume that any similarity between that remark and the remarks made about radio almost a year earlier were purely coincidental.

Having flattered his audience, Goebbels' next concern was to assert his own legitimacy as the new Minister by establishing some common ground. To the press representatives he claimed: 'I believe that I can present myself to you as a colleague, as it were, because I do not come to the press as an innocent but am myself from the press.'[34] After generalising about the role of his new Ministry, Goebbels returned to the specific functions of the press and again presented a reassuring common front with his audience:

I do not regard the banning of newspapers as a normal or an ideal state of affairs although I was the first among us to have the right to ban certain sections of the press. If opposition papers claim today that their issues have been forbidden, they can talk to me as a fellow-sufferer. There is, I think, no representative of any newspaper who can claim to have had his newspaper banned fifteen times as mine was.[35]

Goebbels, then, was 'one of them' and he used this common bond to gain a sympathetic understanding, if not active support, for measures that would otherwise have been unpalatable:

Nonetheless, as I say, the banning of papers is neither a normal nor an ideal state of affairs. On the contrary, I am of the opinion that the press must help the Government. The press may also criticise the Government but it should not do it in order to misrepresent the

Government to the people. The Government will use all possible measures against such attempts. They simply will not arise. No-one need be in any doubt that we should recognise them straight away. We shall know the right time to act.[36]

The carrot had a stick behind it after all.

The press, according to Goebbels, had twin tasks: 'the press must not merely inform: it must also instruct',[37] but it is clear that he intended instruction to play a greater part than information:

> You too will consider ideal a situation in which the press is so finely tuned that it is, as it were, like a piano in the hands of the Government and on which the Government can play, a situation in which it is an enormously important and significant instrument of mass influence that the Government can make use of in the work for which it is responsible.[38]

The task of the press was to explain Government policy to its readers in accordance with Government instructions which would be conveyed at the daily press conferences held by the Propaganda Ministry. The press had the freedom to criticise but only within stringent limits that rendered that criticism impotent and that freedom illusory: in effect the press was to become, whatever else Goebbels wanted to call it, a transmission belt in the engine of Government propaganda:

> You may of course criticise the Government but in the process you should not lose sight of the Government's interest and you must ensure that the one is properly weighed against the other. You must not merely ensure that the Government's measures are communicated to the people because the Government has a thousand other means of doing that: you must also view it as your major task to make the Government's measures intelligible to the people. For this reason I view the press conference that takes place here every day somewhat differently from what has gone on before. You should obviously get your information here but you should also get your instructions. You should not only know what is happening but also what the Government is thinking and how you can most usefully explain this to the people. We want to have a press that works with the Government, just as the Government wants to work with the press.[39]

The carrot has become a mailed fist.

Goebbels was none the less well aware that the carrot was infinitely preferable to the mailed fist. What is more he knew that, at least in the early stages of the National Revolution, the Government really did need the press as much as, if not more than, the press needed the Government. From his own experience he argued that the propaganda of previous governments had been counterproductive and from this he concluded: 'A government that wishes to conduct propaganda must gather round it the most able brains in mass public influence and resort to the most modern methods to achieve this mass influence.'[40] In this the Nazis were naturally to benefit from their past experience:

> If we look at the work that lies behind us and at the unparalleled successes we have achieved even in the past few weeks, we must attribute this mainly to the fact that as a young revolutionary movement we gained a virtuoso mastery of all the means of modern mass influence, and that, rather than directing propaganda from a baize table, we, as true popular leaders, have come from the people and have never lost intimate contact with the people. I think that one of the most important advantages of the new Government propaganda consists in the fact that the activity of the men who have hitherto been responsible for National Socialist propaganda can now be made to bear fruit for the new state.[41]

There was then to be a considerable degree of continuity but, with the ambivalence that characterises so many of the early steps of the Third Reich, there was also to be a revolutionary break with some at least of the aspects of the past. The National Revolution was after all to be carried through by the party that called itself not only 'National' but 'Socialist' as well:

> There can no longer be any doubt that since 30 January a National Revolution has been carried through in Germany . . . I see the establishment of this new Ministry of Popular Enlightenment and Propaganda as a revolutionary act of government because the new Government has no intention of abandoning the people to their own devices and locking them up in an airless room.[42]

This curious analogy is the first real hint of what Goebbels regards as the political function of propaganda in the National Socialist system of government and, in particular, its essential role in the initial process of *Gleichschaltung*, of co-ordinating the political will of the nation with the aims of the state:

> This Government is, in the truest sense of the word, a People's Government. It derives from the people and it will always execute the people's will. I protest most passionately against the notion that this Government is the expression of some reactionary will and that we are reactionaries. We could reintroduce domestic service or the three-class franchise for we have the power to do it. But we have no intention of doing so. There is nothing more alien to this Government than that sort of thing. We want to give the people what belongs to them, albeit in a different form than has been the case under parliamentary democracy.
>
> I see in the newly established Ministry for Popular Enlightenment and Propaganda a link between Government and people, the living contact between the National Government as the expression of the popular will and the people itself. In the past few weeks we have experienced a growing political coordination [*Gleichschaltung*] between the policy of the Reich and the policy of the Länder and I see the first task of this new Ministry as establishing a coordination between the Government and the whole people. I do not believe that we have reached our goal when, if I may use one of those old-fashioned expressions, we have a 52% majority in Parliament. A government that faces the great and far-reaching tasks that the present Government faces could not survive for long and could not find the popular support it needs for these far-reaching measures if it were satisfied with this 52% majority. It must rather see its task as making all the necessary propaganda preparations to win the whole people over to its side in the long term. If this Government is now resolved never to yield – never under any circumstances – then it has no need of the dead power of the bayonet: it will not be satisfied for long with the knowledge that it has 52% behind it while terrorising the other 48%, but will in contrast see its next task as winning over that other 48% to its own cause.[43]

Clearly the role of propaganda was to be central: indeed the new state could not function without it, because propaganda was to fill the hitherto existing void between government and people. Instead of the exercise of popular pressure on government from below through the democratic parliamentary forms of the Weimar Republic, the Third Reich was to offer a system in which the Government through propaganda – in press, radio, film and elsewhere – told the people what it was doing and why they should agree with it. Hence, as we have already seen, 'the new Government has no intention of abandoning the people to their own devices and locking them up in an airless room'[44] where the masses are not politically mobilised. Hence, for instance, also:

> The task of the press cannot be merely to inform, rather the press has above and beyond that the much greater task of instructing. It naturally has the task of making clear to the people what the Government is doing but it must also explain why the Government is doing it, why the Government is forced to act in a certain way and no other.[45]

Although Goebbels had earlier in the same speech identified the press as the 'seventh great power' it is now clear that he intended it to be not a third estate but a mere single cog in the Government's propaganda machine.

Goebbels intended his propaganda to be an active force welding the nation together into a single whole:

> We have founded a Ministry for Popular Enlightenment and Propaganda. These two titles do not convey the same thing. Popular enlightenment is essentially something passive: propaganda, on the other hand, is something active. We cannot therefore be satisfied with just telling the people what we want and enlightening them as to how we are doing it. We must replace this enlightenment with an active government propaganda that aims at winning people over. It is not enough to reconcile people more or less to our regimen, to move them towards a position of neutrality towards us, we want rather to work on people until they are addicted to us, until they realise, in the ideological sense as well, that what is happening now in Germany not only must be accepted, but can be accepted.[46]

The people must not only tolerate what the Government does, it must actively and wholeheartedly support its every action: the people must be mobilised into a total commitment to the National Socialist state – and this could be more profitably achieved through propaganda than by force of arms. Goebbels remarked: 'unlike previous governments, we have no intention of calling on the bayonet'.[47]

Goebbels explained precisely the qualities that he thought were required of the propagandist, First, though, he had to rescue the concept of propaganda from its pejorative connotations:

> Propaganda — a much maligned and often misunderstood word. The layman uses it to mean something inferior or even despicable. The word 'propaganda' always has a bitter after-taste. But, if you examine propaganda's most secret causes, you will come to different conclusions: then there will be no more doubting that the propagandist must be the man with the greatest knowledge of souls. I cannot convince a single person of the necessity of something unless I have got to know the soul of that person, unless I understand how to pluck the string in the harp of his soul that must be made to sound. It is not true that propaganda presents merely a rough blueprint; it is not true that the propagandist does no more than administer complex thought processes in rough form, in a raw state, to the mass. Rather the propagandist must know not just the soul of the people in general but he must also understand the secret swings of the popular soul from one side to another. The propagandist must understand not only how to speak to the people in their totality but also to individual sections of the population: to the worker, the peasant, the middle class. He must understand how to speak to both the South German and the North German, he must be able to speak to different professions and to different faiths. The propagandist must always be in a position to speak to people in the language that they understand. These capacities are the essential preconditions for success.[48]

It is clear from this section of his speech that Goebbels regarded propaganda as an all-embracing activity. The successful propagandist had to know his audience both as individuals or individual groups ('the South German and the North German . . . different professions and different faiths'), to modulate his appeals accordingly (he must 'get to know the soul of that person . . . understand how to pluck the string in the harp of his soul'), for the purpose of the National Socialist propagandist was to weld these disparate elements into a united nation.

The only measure of propaganda was the extent to which it achieved this purpose:

> No aesthete can pass judgement on the methods of propaganda. A binding judgement can only be passed on the basis of success. For propaganda is not an end in itself but a means to an end. We are

setting up here a Propaganda Ministry that does not exist for its own sake and thus represent an end in itself, but one which is a means to an end. If we achieve our end through this means, then the means is good; in any case whether or not it meets strict aesthetic requirements is thus terribly irrelevant. But, if this end is not achieved, then this means will have been a bad one. The purpose of our Movement was to mobilise people, to organise people and to win them over to the idea of the National Revolution. That end — and even the most ill-disposed person cannot argue with this — has been achieved and so the verdict has been passed on our propaganda methods. The new Ministry has no other purpose than to place the nation firmly behind the idea of the National Revolution. If that end is achieved, people can condemn me: that would make absolutely no difference if the Ministry and its workers had achieved their purpose. If that end is not achieved, then I could prove that my propaganda methods have satisfied all the laws of aesthetics but in that case I ought to have been a theatre director or the director of an academy of art rather than the Minister of a Ministry of Propaganda and Popular Enlightenment.[49]

The aim of Goebbels' Propaganda Ministry was not just success but *total* success:

Coordination between the Revolutionary Government and the people will require tireless labour. I am absolutely certain that this coordination cannot be achieved in two weeks or so, or in two months or perhaps in two years, but I am convinced that our work will be directed so that this coordination is increasingly achieved. I am however also convinced that the methods that we employ must eventually convince even the most reserved and malevolent that the political course we have embarked on is the correct one.[50]

It was, as Goebbels himself was the first to recognise, a massive and daunting task.

Once the necessary flattery is cast aside it is clear, even from his speech to press representatives, that Goebbels felt radio to be the central medium for the co-ordination between individual citizen and nation. Radio was unique in possessing the immediacy that would allow listeners to feel that they were participants in the great occasions of state, such as the Opening of the *Reichstag* or the Thanksgiving at Potsdam:

Anyone who is really unbiased must concede that the radio propaganda conducted by the men of the Government of National Revolution in the weeks since 30 January has been exemplary. The consequences predicted by the knowalls, that listeners would switch off their sets, have not occurred. On the contrary, millions of new listeners have emerged and this is because the Government did not produce its radio propaganda in a vacuum, in the radio headquarters, but in the atmosphere-laden halls of mass gatherings. In this way every listener has become a direct participant in these events. I have visions of a new and topical radio, a radio that really takes account of the *Zeitgeist*, a radio that we shall purge of all mustiness and hypocrisy and a radio that is also aware of its great national responsibility. I have visions of a radio that really enables every individual listener to participate in great national events.[51]

It was to this end, in repeatedly staged 'National Moments' (*Stunden der Nation),* that events like the Führer's speeches were broadcast simultaneously throughout the Reich, bringing street and café life to a standstill but identifying the individual citizen with the nation, making him feel that he belonged to the national community (*Volksgemeinschaft*). In his speech to radio representatives, Goebbels remarked: 'As the piano is to the pianist, so the transmitter is to you, the instrument that you play on as sovereign masters of public opinion.'[52] In the new age dawning 'The individual will be replaced by the community of the nation (*die Gemeinschaft des Volkes*)'[53] and Germany was to be rescued from the nadir to which it had sunk during the Weimar Republic. Had it not been for the National Revolution, Goebbels argued: 'Germany would have become completely Swissified, a nation of hotel porters and bowing waiters, a nation having no political sense whatsoever that had lost any idea of its own historical significance.'[54]

In his speeches on radio and film Goebbels added little to the basic ideas expressed in his speech to the press. What he did add was largely confined to further illustrative examples appropriate to the medium concerned. In both his speech on radio, and his first speech on film, for instance, he cited Eisenstein's *Battleship Potemkin* as a model to be emulated.[55] The meat of his argument did not, however, change even if its packaging was different: 'The new Ministry has no other purpose than to place the nation firmly behind the idea of the National Revolution.'

For Goebbels, then, propaganda was to be the oil that lubricated the machinery of state. It was, through 'simplicity, force and concentration'[56] to ease the path of Government policy through 'explaining' it to the people in a manner that would not merely 'inform' them but also 'instruct' them in their proper reaction. It was to 'execute the people's will' by telling the people what that will was, rather than 'abandoning them to their own devices'. In his speech on radio Goebbels observed rather ominously that, 'I do not consider it an ideal situation that twenty parties have existed in Germany: one is quite enough.'[57] There was, he argued, 'nothing at all that is not tendentious. The discovery of the principle of absolute objectivity is the privilege of German university professors – and I do not believe that university professors make history.'[58] National Socialists, however, did make history and Goebbels was determined to be one of them. His aim was nothing less than a complete identification between the people, both as individuals and as a mass, and the Government of National Revolution and its ideals. Implicit in his aim, and later more explicit, was a growing role for propaganda in all aspects of state activity. As war loomed so the early analogy became more and more appropriate: 'The Propaganda Ministry has the job of effecting a spiritual mobilisation in Germany. It is therefore in the spiritual field the same as the Defence Ministry is in the field of military protection.'[59]

The logical consequence of Goebbels' view of the function of propaganda is, not surprisingly perhaps, that the Propaganda Minister will have a central, and eventually a commanding, role in the National Socialist system, for propaganda lies at the heart of all contact between Government and people, indeed at the heart of all political activity.

Elsewhere Goebbels observed that 'In propaganda, as in love anything is permissible which is successful.'[60] It is, perhaps fortunately, not the purpose of this essay to investigate the extent to which he was successful in orchestrating German public opinion and effecting a *Gleichschaltung* between people and government. It is a tempting question but the research that will perhaps one day enable us to approach an answer with some degree of authority is only just beginning to be done.[61] For the moment we can say merely that Goebbels moved towards the realisation of his views on the political function of propaganda only in the closing stages of the war when he became Reich Plenipotentiary for the Total War Effort. But then it was too late. The total war speech of 18 February 1943 was an ideal: but when the audience of thousands in the Berlin *Sportpalast* screamed their assent to Goebbels' ten questions it was a staged ideal, unattainable in reality, for outside the stadium in the real world people were more dubious. In December 1943 the Security Service (SD) reported this popular anecdote:

> Dr. Goebbels is bombed out in Berlin. He rescues two suitcases, leaves them on the street and goes back into the house to get some other things. When he comes out again the suitcases have been stolen. Dr. Goebbels is very unhappy. He cries and moans. Someone asks him why the suitcases were so valuable and he replies: 'One had the revenge weapon in it and the other final victory.'[62]

Perhaps though Goebbels did after all have the last word, when he remarked some ten years earlier that 'In the final analysis the people are always even more astute than their government.'[63]

Notes

1. From a speech to the 1934 Nuremberg Rally, reprinted in *Der Kongress zu Nürnberg vom 5. bis 10. September 1934. Offizieller Bericht über den Verlauf des Reichsparteitages mit sämtlichen Reden* (Munich, 1934), p. 138.

2. Louis P. Lochner (ed.), in his Introduction to *The Goebbels Diaries* (London, 1948), p. xv.

3. H. Heiber, *Goebbels* (London, 1973), p. 120. An anti-semitic Nazi poster of 1924 depicts a Jewish businessman very much in this role as *Der Drahtzieher* (the string-puller); see Z.A.B. Zeman, *Nazi Propaganda* (2nd edn, London, 1973), pl. I. Curiously enough, this image was in turn based on a Bolshevik anti-capitalist poster of 1919 by Viktor Deni; see B.S. Butnik-Siverskii (ed.), *Sovetskii plakat epokhi Grazhdanskoi voiny, 1918-1921* (Moscow, 1960), pp. 164, 598.

4. Heiber, *Goebbels*, p. 349.

5. The title of Ch. 2 of C. Riess, *Joseph Goebbels. A Biography* (London, 1949), pp. 26-49.

6. R.E. Herzstein, *The War That Hitler Won* (London, 1979), p. 111, though, to be fair to Herzstein, it should be noted that he is here offering not his own interpretation but a characterisation of Goebbels' view of his own demise.

7. The title of W. Stephan, *Joseph Goebbels. Dämon einer Diktatur* (Stuttgart, 1949).

8. Lochner, *Goebbels Diaries*, p. xxii.

9. The title of Ch. 7 on Heiber, *Goebbels*, pp. 78-90.

10. E. Ebermayer and H. Roos, *Gefährtin des Teufels: Leben und Tod der Magda Goebbels* (Hamburg, 1952). The English translation has been packaged as 'The life and death of Joseph Goebbels – the mastermind of propaganda who directed a nation to destruction'; see the front cover of Ebermayer and Roos, *Evil Genius* (London, 1973).

11. See n. 6 above.

12. H. Heiber (ed.), *Goebbels Reden* (2 vols., Düsseldorf, 1971).

13. I am grateful to the Nuffield Foundation for funding my visit to Koblenz. The scattered Ministry papers found in the *Bundesarchiv* (BA) R55 series relate mainly to Personnel, Finance and Legal Divisions. The *Findbuch* is invaluable, as indeed it needs to be, because the papers cover matters ranging from a subsidy of 50,000 RM in 1937 to Thos. Cook & Son, London, to advertise Germany as a suitable holiday destination (R55/509), through guidelines for state funerals

(R55/510) and a proposal to establish a fashion academy (*Reichs-Modewerbe-Akademie*) in 1941 (R55/941), to such matters as Leni Riefenstahl's expenses for the Olympics films (R55/503, 1327-8) or the mobilisation of artists for the war effort in 1944 (R55/660). Perhaps the most valuable parts of the collection are the in-house newsletter, *Nachrichtenblatt des RMVP*, for 1939-45 (R55/436-41, 1347) and the morale and public opinion reports, *Tätigkeitsberichte*, for 1943-5 (R55/601). For an excellent introduction to these and other materials see Balfour's 'Note on Sources' in his *Propaganda in War 1939-45* (London, 1979), pp. 446-50.

14. W.A. Boelcke (ed.), *Kriegspropaganda 1939-1941: Geheime Ministerkonferenzen im Reichspropagandaministerium* (Stuttgart, 1966) and '*Wollt Ihr den totalen Krieg?' Die geheimen Goebbels-Konferenzen 1939-1943* (Stuttgart, 1967). A selection has been translated into English as: *The Secret Conferences of Dr. Goebbels. October 1939-March 1943* (London, 1970).

15. The SD documents are held in the BA R58 series covering the Reich Security HQ (*Reichssicherheitshauptamt*) and comprise the following: *Berichte zur innenpolitischen Lage* (October-December 1939), *Meldungen aus dem Reich* (December 1939-June 1943), *SD-Berichte zu Inlandsfragen* (June 1943-July 1944) and the parallel run of *Meldungen wichtiger staatspolizeilicher Ereignisse* (August 1941-November 1944). A selection has been published in H. Boberach, *Meldungen aus dem Reich* (Neuwied, 1965). Regrettably this volume has still to be translated into English.

16. For details of the *Tätigkeitsberichte*, see n. 13 above and Balfour, *Propaganda in War*, pp. 449-50.

17. Compare, for instance, the account of the film *Triumph des Willens* (*Triumph of the Will*) given by its director in: *Hinter den Kulissen des Reichsparteitag-Films* (Munich, 1935) with that she gave in M. Delahaye, 'Leni et le loup: entretien avec Leni Riefenstahl', *Cahiers du Cinéma*, (September 1965), p. 46, both cited in R. Taylor, *Film Propaganda: Soviet Russia and Nazi Germany* (London, 1979), Ch. 13.

18. From Alan Bullock's Preface to H. Heiber (ed.), *The Early Goebbels Diaries. The Journal of Joseph Goebbels from 1925-1926* (London, 1962), p. 13.

19. Lochner, *The Goebbels Diaries*, p. xiv.

20. See especially the collection: H.R. Trevor Roper (ed.), *The Goebbels Diaries: The Last Days* (London, 1978)

21. Ibid., p. xvii.

22. A. Hitler, *Mein Kampf* (Munich, 1933), pp. 653-4. This translation is based on that by Ralph Manheim (London, 1969), p. 530.

23. In a radio speech of 28 February 1945, quoted in Heiber, *Goebbels Reden*, vol. 2, p. 435.

24. Heiber, *Goebbels Reden*. Vol. 1 covers the years 1932-9 while vol. 2 deals with the wartime period.

25. Bullock, Preface, in Heiber, *Early Goebbels Diaries*, p. 8. Trevor Roper also refers to his 'shameless brilliance as a mob orator'; see Trevor Roper, *Goebbels Diaries: The Last Days*, p. xv.

26. BA R43/II 1149, pp. 25-9.

27. Heiber, *Goebbels Reden*, vol. 1, pp. 82-107.

28. C. Belling, *Der Film in Staat und Partei* (Berlin, 1936), pp. 27-31.

29. BA R43/II 1149, p. 25.

30. Heiber, *Goebbels Reden*, vol. 1, p. 91.

31. Ibid.

32. Belling, *Der Film*, pp. 31-7.

33. Quoted in E. Leiser, *Deutschland, erwache! Propaganda im Film des Dritten Reiches* (Reinbek bei Hamburg, 1968), pp. 40-1.

34. BA R43/II 1149, p. 25.

35. Ibid., p. 27a.

36. Ibid., p. 28.
37. Ibid.
38. Ibid.
39. Ibid.
40. Ibid., pp. 28-28a.
41. Ibid., pp. 25a-26.
42. Ibid., p. 25.
43. Ibid., pp. 25-25a.
44. Ibid., p. 25.
45. Ibid., p. 25a.
46. Ibid.
47. Ibid., p. 26a.
48. Ibid., p. 26.
49. Ibid., pp. 26-26a.
50. Ibid., p. 26a.
51. Ibid., p. 27a. He went on to note that, 'If television is one day invented, the whole nation should also be able to watch as these events take place.'
52. Heiber, *Goebbels Reden*, vol. 1, p. 106. Goebbels had employed this musical analogy in his speech to the press; see n. 38 above.
53. Ibid., p. 82.
54. Ibid., p. 85.
55. Ibid., p. 94; Belling, *Der Film*, p. 27.
56. BA R43/II 1149, p. 28a.
57. Heiber, *Goebbels Reden*, vol. 1, p. 87.
58. Ibid.
59. Ibid., p. 90.
60. Boelcke, *Kriegspropaganda*, p. 21.
61. The best published example is I Kershaw, *Der Hitler-Mythos. Volksmeinung und Propaganda im Dritten Reich* (Stuttgart, 1980).
62. *SD-Berichte zu Inlandsfragen*, No. 191, 27 December 1943, p. 20a. BA R58/191.
63. Heiber, *Goebbels Reden*, vol. 1, p. 83.

4 NAZI ARCHITECTURE – A BLUEPRINT FOR WORLD DOMINATION: THE LAST AIMS OF ADOLF HITLER

Jochen Thies

It was generally agreed by those who knew Hitler that during his last weeks as Chancellor he was obsessed with architectural planning. Apparently one of his favourite pastimes was to visit daily a model of Linz that had been constructed for him in the bunker of the Reich Chancellery. He preferred to go there by night, following the depressing reports from the Front suggesting that the Third Reich was coming to an end. Hermann Giesler, like Albert Speer an architect, and the latter's rival, has recounted these scenes in considerable detail. As Hitler stood by the model, the sun's position was simulated by movable spotlights, and the construction of the building was clearly picked out by the light and shade, which gave the wooden and cardboard buildings the appearance of reality.

As Soviet troops neared Berlin, Hitler was busy developing plans for his parents' burial place in Linz and for his own place of retirement on the banks of the Danube. Linz, he had already made clear, was to be the new European centre of culture, and many paintings and sculptures appropriated from the occupied countries of Europe were to be exhibited here. All in all, Hitler intended making the town a sort of German Budapest, as well as a serious rival for Vienna, which he despised. Linz was, after all, the town in which he had spent an important part of his youth. His friends from those days, like Adolf Kubizek, a class-mate, claim that even as a young man Hitler was planning such a transformation for the town. Indeed, some of his comrades during the *Kampfzeit* years, such as the photographer Heinrich Hoffman and the Nazi Party's Foreign Press Chief 'Putzi' Hanfstaengl, both write in their memoirs that as well as Linz Hitler had similar plans for other towns like Munich, Nuremberg and Berlin.[1] What is worthy of note, however, is that all this coincided with the political testament that he had set out in *Mein Kampf* in 1925-6. In this document, the 37-year-old Hitler outlined the quest for world domination that he would attempt to put into practice during the early years of the Second World War. In fact his reflections on architecture in *Mein Kampf* go hand in hand with his political ambitions, for he refers to a building programme that would have been unequalled even in ancient Egypt or Rome.

Thus in *Mein Kampf*, Hitler speaks of a 'mission' bequeathed to the German people whereby they would form the basis of a political State designed to protect and secure civilisation. This 'mission' was deliberately set high since Hitler believed that history showed that the greater the struggle, the more spectacular the results. Only the purest and strongest race would be able to take up the challenge and assume this role. The penultimate sentence of the Epilogue to *Mein Kampf* reads: 'A State which, in an epoch of racial adulteration, devotes itself to the duty of preserving the best elements of its racial stock must one day become ruler of the Earth.'[2]

In writing *Mein Kampf* Hitler not only outlined a world view to which he held unwaveringly for over 20 years but in addition developed a series of theoretical and practical ideas about the kind of building programme that would do justice to this inherited world empire. He was to repeat these ideas on numerous occasions after he assumed power in 1933, especially in the so-called 'Art Speeches' he made during the Nuremberg Party Rallies. According to Hitler there were no architectural styles, there is only an eternal art which must always return to the formal elements of the buildings of antiquity. To understand this theory of architecture, it must be remembered that for him antiquity was more or less synonymous with the German race. According to this theory, as the Romans and the Germans merged into one 'original race', Germany had a two-thousand-year history as a world power. The theory indicates the aspirations behind Hitler's building programme: monumentality and record dimensions were what really interested him. Within such terms of reference the forums, temples, baths and circuses of the ancient world formed a genealogical relationship with their successors, the medieval cathedrals and palaces. But thanks to the technical possibilities of the twentieth century, Hitler would now surpass even these buildings. It was his abtruse understanding of art and history which allowed such an architectural vision to take shape. In the following passage from *Mein Kampf*, for example, he maintains:

> the geopolitical importance for a movement of a vital physical centre . . . cannot be overemphasized. The existence of such a place, imbued as it must be with the enchanted and magical atmosphere that surrounds a Mecca or Rome, can alone in the long run give a movement that strength which resides in its inner unity and in the

acknowledgement of a leadership embodying that unity.[3]

The Nazi dictator thus saw himself not merely as Führer of the Third Reich but an amalgum of Augustus and Mohammed as well!

On 31 January 1933, shortly after he had been sworn in as Chancellor, Hitler delivered a lengthy monologue to a group of faithful comrades in the reception room in the Reich Chancellery. It is a situation that would be repeated many times in the *Führerhauptquartier* during the long evenings throughout the Second World War. The speech was already familiar: the key battle for world domination was about to begin, it would be fought between the white Aryan and the coloured and mongol races hiding under the mantle of Bolshevism: 'Today, therefore, let the greatest Germanic race revolution in history begin.'[4] Linked to this was a planned building programme that would do justice to such a grandiose political plan. Thus almost immediately, the failed architect who fell short of the entry requirements to the Vienna Academy, announced the rebuilding of a new Reich Chancellery in Berlin. It was completed in 1939, a few months before the outbreak of war. Although Hitler regarded even this new building as a provisional Chancellery to be replaced by another building by 1950 at the latest, it is nevertheless, a good example of what, during the Third Reich, became known as 'Representation Architecture' (*Repräsentationsarchitektur*).[5] Only three days later on 3 February 1933 Hitler made his real intentions clear at a meeting with the Commanders in Chief of the Army and Navy, by indicating that one of the most pressing tasks of German foreign policy was the creation of new 'living-space' in the East and the ruthless 'Germanification' of this. A year later, when the crisis between the *Reichswehr* and the SA came to a head, these intentions were repeated at a similar meeting, with the stipulation that the new army should be prepared for offensive warfare within eight years.[6]

At first glance it would appear that Hitler's expansionist ideas were largely shelved until the 'Hossbach-Protokoll' of November 1937. However, if one examines the 'secondary theatres of war' (*Nebenkriegsschauplätze*) during this period, then it is clear that Hitler never lost sight of his intentions. Indeed, his activities in the field of architecture are the best proof of this. Although there are still some gaps in our knowledge, it is known that Hitler supported the concept of *Blitzkrieg* and that both he and his military leaders were well aware that the Nazi's best chance of winning the European war was if they could avoid fighting a battle of attrition as in the First World War. In other words, the expansionist phase of the Third Reich should and must be brief. Since the planning stage of their building schemes covered ten to fifteen years and involved considerable preparatory work, it made good sense to prepare for the final military victory. A number of Hitler's remarks lead one to conclude that he believed that Germany would be free from all military involvement by 1950, therefore it is important to establish whether any important decisions bearing his signature were taken in the areas of town planning or *Repräsentationsarchitektur* other than the 15-year plan mentioned above. In fact Hitler made a key speech at the 1935 Nuremberg Party Rally when he recommended a large-scale building programme as a therapy against bad times, hoping to convince the nation that their current problems were only temporary. Hitler had already expressed similar sentiments when introducing the Enabling Act in 1933, saying that it was precisely in times of limited political power that the survival instinct of a nation had to find even greater cultural expression: blood and race, he concluded, should once more be the source of artistic expression.[7]

Joseph Goebbels, who had first commented on Hitler's architectural ideas in a diary entry during the summer of 1926, repeated similar observations in another entry of 3 February 1932: 'In his leisure hours the Führer is busy with plans for a new Party Building as well as a grandiose reconstruction of the Reich capital. His programme is all ready and it never fails to surprise me the expert manner in which he can tackle so many issues.' Rauschning, Otto Strasser, Dietrich, Frank, the Prince of Schaumburg-Lippe as well as Schwerin von Krosigk, the Reich Finance Minister, have all substantiated Goebbels' observations for the period immediately before and after the assumption of power. They confirm that architecture and town planning had always been of the utmost importance to Hitler.[8]

In the late summer of 1933 the frustrated architect got his first opportunity to present his informed intentions for the rebuilding of Berlin to a circle of experts. Due to a quarrel between the city fathers and the railways, Hitler was able to act as mediator in the talks which began on 19 September 1933. As they dragged on for months they afforded him the chance to explain his ideas. He talked about erecting a Triumphal Arch and a Congress Hall for 250,000 people.[9] Later, in 1936, he handed Albert Speer two sketches of both projects, saying: 'I drew these designs ten years ago. I've always kept them because I never doubted that one day I'd build them. And now shall we carry them out?'[10] Speer succeeded in reducing the capacity of the Domed Hall down to 180,000 people, however its interior would still be seventeen times greater than that of St Peter's. By 1939 the preparatory work was underway on the building site and the granite ordered.

Hitler's most important advisor in the field of architecture in the period just before and after 1933 was Paul Ludwig Troost, who died at the beginning of 1934. His wife Gerdy was one of the few people allowed to speak openly against Hitler without falling into disgrace. Troost, well known to a small circle of experts as the interior designer of liners was responsible for, among other things, the building on the Königsplatz and the House of German Art in Munich, whose foundation stone had already been laid by 15 October 1933. His critics have described the picture gallery, which ironically survived the war un-damaged, as a stranded liner on account of its unfortunate proportions. The locals, on the other hand, refer to it as the 'sausage temple' (*Weisswursttempel*) because of its useless façade of columns. It is further proof that nothing came to Hitler's hopes that these buildings would give Germans a new feeling of power. Even though it cannot be denied that Troost had a certain influence on Hitler it must be said that the Dictator had his own concept of building long before even Speer came into contention. Hitler's activities in this field began long before he had entrusted an established architect in his entourage. In September 1941 he was to say about the early Vienna years: 'I lived in palaces during those years – at least in spirit; it was during this period that the vision to rebuild Berlin came to me.' Nearer the truth was perhaps the remark of his personal adjutant Fritz Wiedemann, whom Hitler was later to expel from his entourage by making him Consular General in San Francisco. He described Hitler as the real master builder of the Third Reich. Even Speer came to realise this during his imprisonment in Spandau, as his diary entries testify.[11]

The redevelopment of the major German cities came into force in the summer of 1936 when Hitler appointed Albert Speer to carry out these plans. Speer received his official contract in January of the following year, together with the resounding title of 'Inspector General of Buildings for the Renovation of the Federal Capital'. Further titles, albeit without the formal powers, soon followed for Hermann Giesler in Munich, Konstanty Gutschow in Hamburg and Roderich Fick in Linz. In Nuremberg, where buildings in the grand style had been under construction since 1935, matters were in the hands of a local adminis-trative body for the Nuremberg Party Congress Site. But here too Speer was responsible for most of the projects, apart from the Congress Hall, for which Ludwig Ruff and his son Franz were the architects.

There is unquestionably a close link between the rapidly increased tempo of building activity and Hitler's success in international affairs during this period. In 1936, for example, Germany was the host to the Olympic Games in Berlin, which afforded the regime much favourable propaganda and to some extent offset the muted criticism of their campaign against political opponents and Jews at home. Abroad, the occupation of the Rhineland in March 1936 had long since been forgotten, proving to Hitler that the Western powers would accept occasional 'weekend coups' on the part of the Third Reich. On 24 April 1936 at the opening of the Crössinsee *Ordensburg*, one of the future elite schools, Hitler said: 'I am convinced, and proudly so, that there is no people in the world better than the Germans . . . where is the race who can single-handedly oppose us?'[12] As far as sport was concerned Hitler was right, for at the Berlin summer Olympics the host nation won more medals than any other nation, including the USA and Jesse Owens.

Hitler was now in his element. He had long since given up his work room and the clumsy study. Cabinet meetings were held only sporadically and soon ceased completely. The Führer's favourite place to stay was now Obersalzberg, to where he would summon delegations from the towns undergoing redevelopment. If a meeting was necessary to discuss these plans then the delegation would simply be transferred by aeroplane to Berlin and the models would travel by road. For his own journeys between Berlin and Munich, Hitler favoured an open car. En route he would frequently stop to look over architecturally interesting sights and to give advice on future projects. Further towns were added to this already large-scale building programme so that within a short time almost all the 50 or so regional capitals (*Gauhauptstädte*) were incorporated in the project.

Whether one looks at the site of the Party Congress at Nuremberg or at the model which is all that remains of the Domed Hall in Berlin, or whether one reads the sketches for the Party High School at the Chiemsee, one cannot miss the pseudo-religious cult of Hitler. Despite its gigantic dimensions, the architecture always emphasised Hitler's position and the all-pervasive presence of the Führer. He was to discover, at the time of his electioneering, the possibilities that the aeroplane lent – mornings in Königsberg, midday in Bremen and perhaps evening in Augsburg; his 'plane gliding in the evening sky with the cabin lit up over the masses of heads below. The same mood of reverential awe that Leni Riefenstahl's films of the *Parteitag* conveyed was to be found at the Harvest Festival which Hitler attended every year on the Bückeberg near Hannover. There he would stand like Moses on top of a mountain visible for miles around, accepting the hommage of the North German country folk who numbered about one million. In the NSDAP High School to be set up on the banks of the Chiemsee, a broadcasting station was planned to enable Hitler to send radio messages all over the world; and only he was to have access to this observatory. Many people tried to give Hitler the status of 'Superman' (*Übermensch*) but this of course was not always done in the most tasteful way. It was decreed, for example, that the Führer's tribune in Nuremberg should have a *concealed* gutter which would prevent rain water from collecting in the overhead canopy and inadvertently soaking him.

Nuremberg was undoubtedly the most imposing of all the huge building complexes that had been started since 1935.[13] With a proposed surface area of 10 kilometres x 6 kilometres it gave the observer the impression of having strayed into Babylon or Assur. The stadium in particular conveyed this feeling as it was to hold 405,000 people – that is double the capacity of the largest sports stadium today. When, in the spring of 1937, Speer pointed out to Hitler that the measurements of the playing field did not correspond to Olympic standards, his reply was most revealing: 'Quite unimportant. In 1940 the Olympic Games will be held in Tokyo, but after that they will find a permanent home in Germany and in this stadium. Then we will decide the measurements of the sports ground'. Other problems like the shape of the oval stadium, which Speer believed might produce psychological discomfort and whether sporting events would be visible from the upper rows, were directly related to the size of the project. Therefore near a little village in the Franconian-Jura mountains, these problems were tested by building a temporary grandstand of approximately the same size and structure out of a hillside. The results proved positive enough for the project to go ahead. Thus, when war broke out, the foundations for the 'German Stadium' were already being dug – Hitler, in fact, had laid the cornerstone on 9 September 1937. Today, on the spot where the huge arena was to have stood, there is now a lake surrounded by a recreation area.

Together with the Congress Hall designed to hold 60,000 people and still under construction in 1943, the Zeppelin Field and the Marchfield deserve special mention. The former was conceived as a gathering place for political leaders and the Reich Labour Service (*Reichsarbeitsdienst*) at party conferences which Hitler believed would continue for the next 800 years. It included 250,000 standing places and 70,000 seats. The Marchfield, intended as a reference to the war god Mars, and bearing in mind the introduction of compulsory service in March 1935, was to have held 500,000 people. Within this enormous tract, an interior area of 610 metres x 955 metres was set aside to enable the *Wehrmacht* to demonstrate its drills and manoeuvres.

South of Nuremberg a series of buildings were planned for Munich which were also designed to break with historical precedent and defy imagination.[14] Foremost was the new Central Railway Station, whose foundations were discovered during roadworks in the summer of 1979. The station hall together with its forecourt was destined to be the largest steel-frame structure in the world, covering an area six times greater than St Peter's, on which it was modelled. The charming silhouette of the city would have been overshadowed, for apart from the huge diameter of the hall which measured 378 metres, the dome would have had a height of 136 metres – 37 metres higher than the towers of the Munich Frauenkirche. Leading from the station's forecourt was to be an east-west axis 6.6 kilometres long and 120 metres wide. At the end of this was to be the new symbol of the city, a victory column 214.5 metres high. Hitler, who had suggested the project, ordered work to begin in late 1946 to be completed by January 1950. It was to be decorated with a frieze 11 metres high depicting scenes from the *Kampfzeit*, and topped by an eagle with a wingspan of 33 metres.

The forerunner of these examples of 'Building in the New Reich', as a Nazi magazine launched on a large scale was called, can be said to be Hamburg. Here the Elbe river bank was to be redeveloped for about 50 kilometres and the town centre was to be shifted several kilometres west.[15] On Hitler's orders, the show-piece was to be the construction of a gigantic suspension bridge across the Elbe, which was deliberately designed on a grander scale than its model in San Francisco. The bridge's pylons alone were to have been 180 metres high and to create space for the ramps the residential suburb of Othmarschen was to have been uprooted, had the bridge been completed. (Until a few years ago, the remains of one of the bridge's original pylons, used to test the effect of different types of stone cladding, could still be seen in the Hamburg dock area.) Preparations were also underway for the construction of a skyscraper to house the NSDAP Regional Headquarters. The building was originally planned to rise high above the Empire State Building, at the time the highest in the world. However, because of the unsuitable sub-soil its projected height had to be reduced by 250 metres. At night, a gigantic neon swastika was to have guided ships entering the Elbe from the Deutsche Bucht.

On 10 February 1939 at the opening of Speer's new Reich Chancellery in Berlin, Hitler explained to the Wehrmacht Command his reasons for planning such construction projects: he wanted to instil in the nation the feeling

> that it [was] not second-rate, but the equal of any other people on earth, even America. To cite one example, this is why I have ordered this great bridge to be built in Hamburg. You will perhaps ask: 'Why don't you build a tunnel?' I don't consider a tunnel useful. But even if I did, I would still have the largest bridge in the world erected in Hamburg, so that any German coming from abroad or going abroad or who has the opportunity to compare Germany with other countries must say to himself: 'What is so extraordinary about America and its bridges? We can do the same.' This is why I am having skyscrapers built which will be just as 'impressive' as the American ones.[16]

The sentiments that Hitler expressed to his officers while leading them through the Chancellery in 1939 were strikingly similar to passages from *Mein Kampf* and to his famous Offenburg speech in November 1930.[17] In 1918, according to Hitler, the people who were numerically the largest in Europe, had lost their position of political power. In his opinion the Germans were not only potentially the strongest nation in Europe, but practically in the whole world. The purpose behind these remarks become clearer in a speech he made to a Nazi Elite School (*Ordensburg*) in Vogelsang near Cologne in April 1937. Here, before local party leaders, Hitler argued that a major conflict with the Western democracies would be inevitable. He concluded by saying that he hoped that this conflict would not break out immediately, but in a few years time – the longer the better![18]

That Hitler held unwaveringly to these ideas can be further illustrated by an address given to his generals in January 1938, which was recorded by one of those present.[19] Hitler explained the necessity of acquiring new territory with force. Then followed Hitler's revealing comparison, which is only now being fully understood as a result of recent research: when one looked at the world's ruling nations – the British, the French, the Americans – then it was clear that 40-50 million pure-blooded citizens of each of these nations controlled vast expanses of land and millions of other people in the world. However, Hitler continued, there was one race, tightly knit by a common language and blood, which occupied a large part of central Europe. The

German people, he declared, with a population of 110 million, would one day dominate the world. As late as 1943, Goebbels was still confirming in his diary that Hitler had not deviated from this view: 'The Führer expresses his unshakeable belief that the Reich will one day rule all of Europe . . . From that point the way to world domination is practically mapped out. The ruler of Europe will seize world leadership.'[20]

There is no doubt that from 1937 onwards the military leaders were fully aware of the consequences of Hitler's policies. A glance at the building programme alone reveals the inevitable direction that would have to be taken in order to pay for these schemes. For example, the redevelopment of the five 'Leader Cities' (*Führerstädte*) Berlin, Nuremberg, Munich, Hamburg and Linz, which Hitler insisted had to be completed by 1950, could not have been borne by Nazi resources. Such programmes could only have been implemented after the annexation of extensive overseas territories. One must bear in mind that Germany was also carrying out a massive rearmaments programme at this time, with each section of the armed forces making ever increasing demands. Massive battleships were being built, colonial units were being drawn up on a large scale and vehicles developed for use in the tropics.[21] People must have wondered at all this, for the German public was told that it was for the Danzig Corridor, the Sudetenland and the annexation of Austria.

Alongside the military, the *gleichgeschaltet* (co-ordinated) Nazi press was also being informed of Hitler's new foreign policy targets. On 10 November 1938 the Führer addressed representatives of the press and told them that numerical strength and the innate qualities of a people were decisive factors in world history. In his opinion the Germans were the most superior race on earth. Hitler then produced figures to substantiate this claim. He pointed out that although the USA had 125 million inhabitants there were not even 60 million left when one deducted immigrants and racially inferior groups. His grotesque statistical game then cited the USSR, where he claimed there were only 55 million genuine Russians, and the British Empire with only 46 million true British followed by the French Empire with 37 million Frenchmen. On the other hand, Hitler found great comfort in the fact that by 1940, 80 million people of one race would be living in Germany.[22]

While in the summer of 1939 demolition work was beginning for the projected buildings, Jews had to leave their homes in the wake of the Holocaust.[23] Workers' towns were being built and thousands of people were working on these projects alongside Speer and other prominent architects. Hitler's ideas were going way beyond actual events. During his imprisonment in Spandau, Speer noted that Hitler had become obsessed with his building programme and the idea of *Lebensraum*. Both visions reflected Hitler's megalomania and his obsession with monumentality. It was during this period that Hitler ordered Speer to make an alteration to the roof of the Great Hall in Berlin, which was to have been crowned by a Reich eagle 290 metres high. 'This is to be changed', Hitler said, 'the eagle is no longer to stand upon the swastika, it is to dominate the globe. The crowning of this, the world's biggest building, must be the eagle on top of the globe.' Speer noted in his memoirs that this globe was not merely symbolic and represented one of Hitler's first claims to world dominion – long before he dared communicate it to his inner circle. However, by the time Speer was appointed Armaments Minister, he acknowledges that all the members of that elite group should have been fully aware that they were fighting a war for global dominance.[24]

On 12 March 1940 Sir David Kelly, the British envoy in Berne, gave the London Foreign Office information passed on to him by a Swiss industrialist. If these reports were true, then Hitler spent much of his time planning the redevelopment of Berlin: 'He is still as mad as ever about his building projects', wrote the diplomat, whose report also contained detailed information on those projects that had already passed the planning stages.[25] Officially however, building activity was still at a standstill during this period. It had been halted in September 1939 at the start of the Polish campaign, but as Sir David Kelly's report showed, not even the *Wehrmacht*'s imminent Operation Norway and the gruelling preparations for the forthcoming French campaign could keep Hitler from his favourite occupation. Time and again during the war he was drawn to the model rooms to be informed of the progress being made. Displaying considerable knowledge of the technical details Hitler would inspect these model buildings and quite calmly and decisively give instruction for any alterations he wanted.

Perhaps Hitler's visit to Paris in 1940 best illustrates his passion for architecture; he decided to make the visit three days after the armistice with France. Very early on the morning in question, Hitler decided to view the architectural sites of the city with a small entourage whom he then proceeded to amaze with his knowledge of the subject. Visiting the Grand Opera Hitler asked to see a small room which, he maintained was behind a certain wall. Despite repeated protestations from the French management that the room did not exist, Hitler insisted and the room was eventually discovered.

One of the immediate results of the victory over France was an order from Hitler that his building programme should be stepped up. The widespread euphoria which followed the French campaign and the ignominious British retreat from Dunkirk, increased even more when it looked as if 'Operation Barbarossa' would succeed in defeating the Soviet Union. Certainly from the summer of 1940 until September 1941, as new planning decisions are seen to come thick and fast in the wake of France's defeat, this mania appeared to assume a momentum of its own. It even gripped groups outside of Hitler's close circle, such as sceptical military leaders and experienced diplomats wanting suddenly to pursue *Weltmachtpolitik*. It spread beyond party organisations to city and town councils, who started petitioning Berlin to have their plans approved for state support. One could almost compare it with the mood of August 1914. Hitler's army adjutant, Engel, expressed something of this mood in a letter written at the end of 1940 to a friend.[26] Referring to the post-war role of the *Wehrmacht*, he stated that there was still a great deal to be done to protect the Greater German *Lebensraum*. Engel was referring to those areas in which German soldiers would have to be posted in future – Kirkenes, Lublin and Flanders, but most importantly to the new colonies, to which every German Division would have to be sent for a year at a time. 'So you can see from this', concluded the letter, 'that even after the war things will not be boring for us soldiers as we will be fully occupied carrying out the Führer's instructions.'

Looking at Hitler's plans for these years, one gets the clear impression of a Europe dominated by Nazi Germany. The most drastic measures were to be reserved for Eastern Europe, where whole cities like Warsaw and Leningrad would disappear. However, the plans would concentrate first and foremost on the infrastructure of the countries concerned, on new trunk roads, railway networks and harbours, and on landscape planning. Thus by 1940, under the direction of the Todt Organisation, work had started on a network of motorways which was to include continuous stretches from Calais to Warsaw and from Klagenfurt to Trondheim. Part of the scheme was to link the Danish islands with both the Jutland Peninsula and Skona, in southern Sweden, by means of bridges across the two Belts and the Helsingborg Sound. Hitler predicted that at the end of the Russian campaign the master race driving the new private vehicle of the future, the Volkswagen, would be able to ride on a further motorway stretching from Germany to the Crimea. In 1940, the regional railway authorities in Munich received a directive from Hitler instructing them to incorporate into existing plans for a giant main station a new main line four metres wide. Down this line, which was to terminate in Rostov-on-Don, double-decker trains travelling at 200 kilometres per hour and carrying 600 passengers per carriage would reach southern Russia in only a few hours.[27]

In Norway, Trondheim was to have been expanded into the most important naval port in Europe. The harbour's five basins would provide anchorage for the heaviest units of the projected 'Z-Plan fleet', which Hitler had ordered to be built in 1939 to be ready for action by the mid-1940s. These vessels would weigh 100,000 tons, measure 335 metres long and 50 metres wide and would have a gun calibre of up to 53 centimetres. The fleet itself would consist of 800 ships and being the largest in the world they would have made even the giant Japanese battleships of the Second World War look modest. The old Trondheim was to have been rebuilt, with terraced housing for 300,000 inhabitants and a naval dockyard and huge arsenal as well. All the North Sea and Baltic harbours were similarly to have been enlarged to serve as ports of call for the Strength-Through-Joy fleet, several of which were already at sea. Globe-trotting *Germanen* would have been able to enjoy a permanent Nuremberg Rally festive feeling. Of the many seaside resorts being enlarged, the plans for Rügen deserve special attention, for here work had already begun on the creation of the world's largest resort, with a projected 75 kilometres of beach and a main building 10 kilometres long. Its beaches and boats were designed to absorb 14 million German holiday makers each year. Its concrete framework can still be seen today.

Turning to the plans for new constructions in Eastern Europe, a distinction must be made between those which were to house German immigrants and those intended for Eastern Europeans. In his 'Table Talk' Hitler reveals that the new German towns were to have been modelled on the medieval towns of Regensburg, Augsburg, Weimar and Heidelberg. The German rural population would have been housed in model settlements, which would have ringed the new towns at a distance of some 30 to 40 kilometres. The surviving Eastern Europeans themselves would have no place in Hitler's future world, as is clear from his remarks in September 1941 on the subject of Russia's future; the remaining areas were to have formed

> another world, where we shall let the Russians live as they wish. Only we shall be their masters. If there is a revolution, all we shall

need is to drop a few bombs on their towns and that's that. Then, once a year, a troop of Kirghiz will be led through the Reich capital in order that they may fill their minds with the power and the grandeur of its stone monuments.[28]

Of the other large-scale projects, only a few can be listed here: for example, the national arenas (*Thingstätten*), opera houses, pyramidal burial mounds, war-memorials, spas, hotels, blocks of standardised city flats, village community buildings, schools, barracks, airports and mass transportation systems. What the Nazi's did build to defend Europe during the war is still to be seen all the way from the North Cape of Sicily, from France's Atlantic coast to the heart of middle Europe – bunkers, watch posts and gun turrets – architecture which did not prolong the Third Reich but outlived it, serving as a constant reminder of Hitler's megalomania.

Hitler's building programme, as even rough estimates reveal, could not have been financed by German or European sources alone. Neither could Europe produce enough hardstone to complete the projects. However, measures to overcome this problem had already been implemented before the outbreak of war. The SS set up a special enterprise, the 'German Earth and Stone Works' (DEST), to furnish material for the Führer's buildings. In 1938 the number of guards (Death's Head Unit) at the concentration camps was almost doubled, from 4,833 to 8,484 men.[29] New concentration camps appeared near outcrops of natural stone. The names are familiar: Natzweiler, Flossenbürg, Mauthausen, Gross-Rosen and Neuengamme. In other camps, such as Buchenwald, Sachsenhausen and Oranienburg, where there were no deposits or available facilities, works were set up in their stead. According to their own planning predictions, three million Eastern Europeans would be transported to the large-scale building sites in the Reich where they would work as forced labour for 20 years. This could be seen as another method of extermination, for the Nazis never intended to give these people adequate accommodation, care or payment. On the basis of the years 1937-8, the cost of the large-scale projects alone would almost certainly have exceeded one hundred billion Reichsmark. Significantly, Hitler forbade exact calculations and the example of Nuremberg illustrates just how unrealistic the financing of the project was, even in the early years. Speer estimated the overall cost of the *Parteitag* site at 125 million Reichsmark. But the hall alone, still standing in its near completed state, accounted for 208 million Reichsmark. The first cost estimate for the building was 2.2 million Reichsmark in 1934 and soon this had to be raised to 10 million Reichsmark.

Speaking at the height of his power in the summer of 1941, Hitler indicated that he was close to fulfilling his political ambitions: 'Those who enter the Reich Chancellory should feel that they stand before the lords of the world. From here, their passage through the Triumphal Arch along the wide streets past the Hall of Soldiers to the People's Square will leave them breathless'. He planned to have his own residence in a *Führerpalais* occupying an area of two million square metres near the Great Hall. The *'Diplomatenweg'* (Diplomats' Way), leading through the building complex, would stretch a further half a kilometre.[30] It was in 1941 that Hitler confirmed that Ancient Rome had been his inspiration for the building programme. Only the Roman Empire, in his estimation, deserved the name of world empire. Recognising that his successors would not necessarily possess his personality and tastes, Hitler stipulated that granite should be used on the construction projects, ensuring that the buildings would last 4,000, perhaps even 10,000 years. However, today, the crumbling state of the two remaining buildings on the Königsplatz in Munich and the façades of Nuremberg give the lie to these ambitions.

Hitler's renewed reference to the example of ancient Rome prompts the question as to what sort of function the towns would have and what type of economy was envisaged for the Greater Reich. The fact that not only old building forms but also past social and economic orders were to have been modified is a clear indication that they planned to break with patterns of the past. Appeals to antique architectural models, Breker's sculptures and the obscene realism of National Socialist painting: are these not harbingers of that insane obsession with a pure racial stock which inspired the *Lebensborn* institutions and the special homes and schools for the system's elite? Indeed, National Socialist urban construction with their standard town centres, reflect the desire for a return to pre-industrial and agrarian forms of existence. The towns have the air, not of modern cities, but of 'seats of court' from which those sections of the population formerly engaged in productive or service industries have been methodically transferred to the newly conquered 'living space' elsewhere. The plans testify equally to a general hostility to big cities and agrarian romantic ideas.

The exaggerated neo-classicism of the Leader's Buildings, partly permeated with Assyrian and Egyptian influences, was intended as nothing more or less than the physical setting for a grandiose attempt to turn back the clock by 1,000 years and, in so doing, to revolutionise the course of history by the breeding of an Aryan master-race. The attainment of this goal involved the extermination of world Jewry, since for Hitler there could be only one 'chosen people'. But the Social-Darwinist principles of organisation and domination would scarcely have spared other minorities. Indeed Hitler opined that the best thing would be to let Christianity fade out slowly, for the German people needed a war every 15 years so as not to lose their power instinct. The Propaganda Ministry even used the new buildings as publicity for their foreign propaganda. Lavishly illustrated magazines were put out in great numbers to show the regime's peaceful intentions. The bulk of one American issue was devoted to new church building, even though urban planning in the Third Reich almost entirely neglected ecclesiastical architecture and not one of the many glossy German brochures mentions a new church. In Munich, they even demolished a church which was in the way of Hitler's builders. In fact the SS occupied the cathedral of Quedlinburg and turned it into an SS shrine. Similar plans were outlined for Brunswick and Strasburg cathedrals. A note found with the plans for urban development in Hamburg states that the building works would be so radical 'that hardly an original stone would be left'.

Until the end of 1941 the Second World War had a more or less European dimension, but this changed with Pearl Harbor and Germany's declaration of war on USA. Whatever may have moved Hitler to take this step, one thing is certain; that those in power made their calculations without taking account of Britain and America. Hitler's belief that London would align itself to the new European overlord after the fall of France, had prevailed. The air battle for Britain ended in the autumn of 1940 with a painful German defeat, and after this the stream of foreign visitors to Berlin receded noticeable. People were waiting to see how things would develop. Among those waiting were the Spaniards and the Russians who of course had no inkling that plans for 'Operation Barbarossa' had already been laid down.

Hitler had speculated on the neutrality of American public opinion which he believed would prevent Roosevelt's administration from entering the European conflict. Even if the mood in America should change, Hitler hoped that the war would already have been decided in Germany's favour. To this end, four more operations using crack units were planned for the autumn of 1941, after the anticipated victory over the Soviet Union.[31] The first unit was to advance on the Afghan-Indian border, whose tribes had already been given weapons to use in uprisings against the British. A second unit was to march to the Persian Gulf and a third to the northern end of the Suez Canal. The fourth division would cross Spain in a surprise action should the Spanish refuse permission. Having then seized Gibraltar, the unit was to reach Morocco and by occupying strategic positions along the route to Dakar it was intended to gain a stronghold on the West African coast before the Americans could mobilise. From such a position, long-range bombing squadrons were to be stationed on the Azores and other groups of islands off the Dark Continent. From there they would undertake terror sorties on New York and Washington together with occasional attacks on armaments depots around the Great Lakes. According to Hitler, this would guarantee an American policy of neutrality.

Analysing Hitler's statements made in the period 1940 up to the spring of 1942, when both the Russian and North African campaigns appeared to be going favourably, it is clear that Hitler saw the deciding struggle with America over world domination as a form of 'annexation', a similar solution, in fact, to that which had been successfully carried out in Europe. His idea on racial ideology and the importance he attached to geo-politics, led him to trust this course of events. From 1940 onwards Hitler constantly proclaimed that with the annexed countries Germany represented a force that no combination of world powers could attack or conquer.

Like it or not, one cannot deny that National Socialism possessed certain revolutionary qualities. In 1933 it appeared more dynamic than either democratic republicanism or the Communist dictatorship – its two serious rivals. Even after Munich in 1938, Hitler still retained the support of the majority of Germans and, as Joachim Fest has rightly pointed out, had he left office then he would be honoured today as one of the greatest statesmen of all time by his countrymen. Disillusionment eventually set in when notices like 'Fallen for Führer and Fatherland' became standard news throughout Germany and added to this was a sense of leaden dejection following Hitler's death on 30 April 1945 with the final accompanying plea on 8 May: 'we had no idea'.

The military defeat of the Third Reich, whose moral and political repercussions are still felt today, really began years previously with the unlikely alliance between East and West. Without doubt this alliance was necessary to meet the global threat posed by National Socialism. But in the ruins of 1945 and the world's horror at the extent of the barbarity, neither the victors nor the vanquished gave serious thought to the very real danger of Hitler's transitory European Empire. Partly because its collapse was so total and also because its end came so quickly, only documents remained to bear witness to the regime's intentions, and of course these were used by the prosecution at the

Nuremberg trials. Historians are still using them today. However the buildings of the Third Reich and what remains of them tell us more about the scope of contemporary political expectations than the printed word. Not only do they show the reality of their time, but they also reveal the long-term objectives of the dictatorship in a far more relevant way than, for example, Hitler's casual remarks to his inner circle. The legacy of Hitler's unfinished building programme is proof of nothing less than his pretension to world domination which he had maintained since 1925.

Today, a visitor to Nuremberg, looking down from the fortress dominating the old town, can see in the south-east an unusual sight. It is an imposing structure that seems out of place in its surroundings. There are no directions leading to this building, so one must find one's own way there. On approaching it one feels apprehensive, for this stone monster lurks like some prehistoric creature. It is in fact the Assembly Hall of the former Reich Party Conference site. To all intents and purposes complete on the outside, it surpasses its model, the Roman Coliseum by 1.3 times in length and by 1.7 times in width. Part of the site now lies within the area of the American barracks and so is inaccessible to the public, but everywhere one discovers traces of the past that have escaped extensive post-war demolition. Indeed from the air the contours of Speer's buildings stand out even more – the wide parade, the Zeppelin Field and the Marchfield whose grandstands are still partially standing. An unreal atmosphere prevails in this part of Nuremberg, where those rummaging around the ruins of the Third Reich are involuntarily reminded of something Hitler remarked when laying the foundation stone of the hall in 1935. Should the movement at any time fall silent, he said, this building would still speak for them after a thousand years. Fortunately it is now silenced for ever – indeed, the stranger might be forgiven for thinking that in Nuremberg he is making an archaeological discovery – but in fact it is only 37 years old.[32]

Notes

1. H. Giesler, *Ein anderer Hitler* (Leoni, 1977), pp. 21, 96ff; J.C. Fest, *Hitler: Eine Biographie* (Frankfurt am Main, 1973), p. 44; cf. also n. 8 below.

2. A. Hitler, *Mein Kampf* (Munich, 1939), p. 782; see also pp. 234, 422, 437-40, 475, 740.

3. Ibid., p. 381, also pp. 288ff; See also J. Thies, *Architekt der Weltherrschaft. Die 'Endziele' Hitlers* (Düsseldorf, 1976, paperback, 1980), pp. 70ff.

4. Quoted in Fest, *Hitler*, p. 510; cf. also p. 1095, n. 201.

5. A. Schönberger, *Die neue Reichskanzlei von Albert Speer* (Berlin, 1981). more general information can be found in L.O. Larsson, *Die Neugestaltung der Reichshauptstadt* (Stockholm, Stuttgart, 1978).

6. Thilo Vogelsang, 'Neue Dokumente zur Geschichte der Reichswehr 1930-33', *Vierteljahreshefte für Zeitgeschichte (VfZ)* vol. 2, (1954), pp. 397-436; also K. Hildebrand, *Deutsche Aussenpolitik 1933-45* (Stuttgart, 1971), p. 38.

7. *Die Reden Hitlers am Parteitag der Freiheit 1935* (Munich, 1935), p. 32; *Die Reden Hitlers als Kanzler* (Munich, 1934), p. 18.

8. Thies, *Architekt der Weltherrschaft*, pp. 35ff, and p. 67.

9. Documents printed in J. Dülffer, J. Thies and J. Henke (eds.), *Hitlers Städte. Baupolitik im Dritten Reich* (Cologne, Vienna, 1978), pp. 90ff.

10. A. Speer, *Erinnerungen* (Frankfurt am Main, Berlin, 1969), pp. 88, 168ff.

11. A. Speer, *Spandauer Tagebücher* (Frankfurt am Main, Berlin, Vienna 1975), pp. 404, 634.

12. Archiv Institut für Zeitgeschichte (IfZ), Munich, Fa 88, Fasz. 52. Speech of 24 April 1936.

13. For information about the Nuremberg projects see, Dülffer, Thies and Henke, *Hitlers Städte*, pp. 209ff.

14. For the most recent work on Munich see H.P. Rasp, *Eine Stadt für tausend Jahre* (Munich, 1981); cf. also, Dülffer, Thies and Henke, *Hitlers Städte*, pp. 157ff.

15. Detailed information on Hamburg can be found in, Dülffer, Thies and Henke, *Hitlers Städte*, pp. 189ff; see also J. Thies, 'Hitler's European Building Programme', *Journal of Contemporary History*, vol. 13 (1978), pp. 413-31.

16. Hitler's speech of 10 February 1939 is printed in Dülffer, Thies and Henke, *Hitlers Städte*, pp. 283ff.

17. For a detail analysis of this extremely important speech see J. Thies, 'Adolf Hitler in Offenburg (8. November 1930); Eine Dokumentation', *Die Ortenau*, vol. 57 (1977) pp. 296-312.

18. The full text of Hitler's speech of 29 April 1937 can be found in H. von Kotze and H. Krausnick (eds.), *Es spricht der Führer* (Gütersloh, 1966), p. 174.

19. Bundesarchiv/Militärarchiv Freiburg RH 26/255 (WK XIII/823).

20. L.P. Lochner (ed.), *Goebbels Tagebücher aus den Jahren 1942-3* (Zurich, 1948), p. 327.

21. J. Dülffer, *Weimar, Hitler und die Marine* (Düsseldorf, 1973); see also K. Hildebrand, *Vom Reich zum Weltreich* (Munich, 1969).

22. The speech is analysed in Wilhelm Treue, 'Rede Hitlers vor der deutschen Presse 10 November 1938', *Vierteljahreshefte für Zeitgeschichte*, vol. 6, (1958), pp. 175-91.

23. M. Schmidt, *Albert Speer: Das Ende eines Mythos* (Berne, Munich, 1982), pp. 216f.

24. Speer, *Erinnerungen*, p. 175; cf. also pp. 83, 524ff.

25. Public Record Office, London, Foreign Office 371, 24380/C 3867/5/18.

26. Bundesarchiv/Militärarchiv Freiburg N 118/5, Engel's letter of 31 December 1940.

27. A. Joachimsthaler, *Die Breitspurbahn Hitlers* (Freiburg, 1981).

28. H. Picker, *Hitlers Tischgespräche im Führerhauptquartier 1941-42* (Stuttgart, 1963), pp. 143f, 190.

29. E. Georg, *Die wirtschaftlichen Unternehmungen der SS* (Stuttgart, 1963), pp. 42, 144.

30. A. Hitler, *Libres Propos sur la Guerre et la Paix, receuillis sur l'ordre de M. Bormann* (Paris, 1952), p. 81; Pictures of this project can be found in A. Speer, *Architektur. Arbeiten 1933-42* (Frankfurt am Main, Berlin, Vienna, 1978), pp. 64ff

31. A. Hillgruber, *Hitler Strategie* (Frankfurt am Main, 1965), pp. 377ff; cf. also A. Hillgruber, 'Der Faktor Amerika in Hitlers Strategie 1938-41', *Beilage zum Parlament*, vol. 19/66 (11 May 1966).

32. Hitler's speech of 11 September 1935 can be found in M. Domarus, *Hitler, Reden und Proklamationen 1932-45* (Würzburg, 1962/3), vol. II, p. 527. A documentary film, 'Baustelle Reichsparteitaggelände 1938/9', is deposited with the Institut für den Wissenschaftlichen Film, Göttingen.

5 EDUCATIONAL FILM PROPAGANDA AND THE NAZI YOUTH

David Welch

> This new Reich will give its youth to no one, but will itself take youth and give it its own education and its own up-bringing.
>
> — Adolf Hitler in a speech, 1 May 1937

One of the most striking features of the National Socialist movement was its youth. In *Mein Kampf* Hitler confidently predicted that the children and youth of Germany could be won for all time to the movement. This process was to take place mainly through education and involvement in the Hitler Youth organisations.[1] From the beginning its propaganda was directed towards this generation. The Hitler Youth leader Baldur von Schirach declared, 'The NSDAP is the party of youth.'[2]

Nazi propaganda offered youth a pioneering role: a National Socialist victory would mean the triumph of a rejuvenated Germany, liberated from the outdated fallacies of bourgeois liberalism or Marxist class war. By the way youth took up this call, Nazi propaganda once more demonstrated its extraordinarily effective manipulation of mass emotions.[3] Education therefore can show us the way in which the movement attracted and held the enthusiasm of German youth. The overriding tenet of the Nazi educational philosophy was the political indoctrination of the young. After all, it was to be this generation that would instil the Nazi *Weltanschauung* and create the New Order (*Neuordnung*) in Europe. Accordingly, the initial enthusiasm of youth was carefully directed and exploited through the concerted co-ordination of the mass-media – the press, radio, theatre and film. In particular, the Nazis chose to use the cinema to disseminate their political and cultural outlook: partly because they appreciated that the cinema was unexcelled in its ability to play upon the emotions, and also because it was the perfect medium for combining both entertainment and propaganda.[4] This article will examine different aspects of such indoctrination by analysing the role of film propaganda in schools and the Hitler Youth (*Hitlerjugend*) together with the film-making activities of the Hitler Youth.

Once they assumed power, the Nazis meticulously constructed an organisational network from which a child once caught had little possibility of escape. Three organisations served the new regime here: the Ministry for Popular Enlightenment and Propaganda (*Reichsministerium für Volksaufklärung und Propaganda* — RMVP), the Ministry of Education (*Erziehungsministerium*), and the Hitler Youth (HJ). The commercial film industry was not directly involved in the political indoctrination of Nazi youth. However both the *Filmwelt* and the RMVP were concerned that this potential audience should get into the habit of visiting the cinema more often than their parents. The Propaganda Ministry on the other hand also wished to shape this generation into an audience that would genuinely appreciate the aesthetic and revolutionary qualities of the National Socialist film and at the same time reject the degenerate and sensational blandishments associated with the Weimar cinema. In 1941 Joseph Goebbels informed a Hitler Youth audience:

> Our State has given the film a very important assignment; it is therefore one of the most valuable factors in the National Education ... Its success so far has led to a real breakthrough for German art and can be seen as an example for the peoples of Europe.[5]

The Organisation of Film Propaganda in the Schools

This however came later. At the beginning the Nazis had to establish a complex organisation for the use of these films in the school classrooms. The films shown were usually propaganda and culture films. Feature films were shown but as they tended to undercut the commercial exhibitor such screenings were restricted. Picture Centres for the regions and the towns (*Landesbildstellen* and Stadtb*ildstellen*) together with the use of film in schools had in fact been encouraged during the last years of the Weimar Republic. To some extent then, the aims and methods of such an exercise had already been proved and clearly formulated. Thus when the Nazis started with their reorganisation in 1933 they had the support of the teaching profession, who had for many years participated with considerable enthusiasm in the use of film as a visual aid to conventional teaching methods.[6]

On 16 June 1934 the Reich Centre for Educational Films (*Reichstelle für den Unterrichtsfilm*) was founded and took over from the Central

Institute for Education and Instruction (*Zentralinstitut für Erziehung und Unterricht*) which had been set up in 1919. The new organisation was to supervise the production and distribution of instructional films for the Picture Centres (*Bildstellen*) and the schools. The activities of these Centres were co-ordinated according to the demands of the new regime and by the end of the decade their range had been extended from school work to include film activities in high schools and universities.[7]

In 1940 the *Reichstelle*'s status was raised and its name changed to the Reich Institute for Film and Pictures in Science and Education (*Reichsanstalt für Film und Bild in Wissenschaft und Unterricht*, RWU). Although a limited company it was indirectly state-controlled (*staatsmittelbar*) and functioned virtually as a department within the Ministry of Education. The RWU specialised in films, slides and gramophones and attempted to co-ordinate all three as an integral part of teaching methods. By 1941 the *Reichsanstalt* owned nearly 42,000 16mm film projectors and over 300,000 film projectors. Thus as far as films in schools were concerned, the Nazis were able to construct a comprehensive network for the distribution of films and therefore for the dissemination of officially approved 'information'. Any resemblance to an amateurish civic institution had now been completely removed.

At the head of the RWU was a Governing Committee made up of representatives of various educational authorities under the Chairmanship of a permanent official of the Ministry of Education who, during the course of the Third Reich was Dr Kurt Zierold. There were also representatives from the Propaganda Ministry, the Party, and the Nazi Teachers' Association (*Nationalsozialistiche Lehrband*). The Committee seldom met, but there can be little doubt that Dr Zierold exercised a considerable influence over its general policy.[8]

Within the Committee there was also a President who had to be a member of the Nazi Party and whose job it was to work closely with the Ministry of Education. He was Dr Kurt Gauger, who was a member of the SA and the *Volkssturm*. Basically, the President's task was to formulate matters of general policy for the organisation as a whole. Each of the provincial centres (*Landesbildstellen*) were managed by a director appointed by the President with the approval of the Ministry of Education. These centres received films from the RWU and arranged for their distribution. Not only were they responsible for servicing the equipment, but they also arranged for the instruction of teachers and they provided library and working facilities. Occasionally, they produced films and slides on local subjects. It was at these centres that the teachers, who were to be the primary forces behind film education in the schools, received their instructions. The general principle was that every teacher should receive a thorough training in the effective use of visual aids and an understanding of their underlying psychology. Thus by 1939 193,000 teachers out of a total of 250,000 (ie 79 per cent) had undertaken some form of training in this field.[9] In conjunction with the production of films were the Teacher's Guides which were invariably put together by the subject specialists who had co-operated in the making of the film. Once the film and the Guide had been completed, preview copies were distributed to provincial and district centres which then ordered copies for their libraries. The work of the RWU had proved so successful that by 1943 37 provincial centres had been established advising over 1,200 local offices.

The financing of this national organisation was achieved in typical Nazi fashion. A levy (*Lernmittelbeitrag*), of 80 pfennig a year was imposed on every child, with certain exceptions, in all schools using visual aids. This amounted to a considerable sum paid annually into the account of the RWU. Students of the universities and trade schools also contributed by paying 1RM per semester. Ten per cent of the total money collected was paid back to provide the running costs of the *Landesbildstellen* and a further 50 per cent was refunded in the form of projection equipment and film material. This still left an adequate amount for the expenses of the RWU. Schools paying the levy were entitled to projection equipment free of charge according to the amount they had contributed. They were also allowed to borrow films, slides, and gramophone records from their local *Kreisbildstellen*. By such means, on 1 January 1943, all schools which were provided with electricity were equipped with projection apparatus. This amounted to over 45,000 projectors (approximately two projectors for every three schools), together with 590,000 copies of 16mm educational films that were available for screening. For the purpose of indoctrinating school children through film propaganda, this organisation was ideal.

It can be imagined how keen the Nazis were on using this organisation for propaganda purposes, but they were not entirely successful. From the above, it can be seen that appointments to the RWU were under the control of the Government by means of the Ministry of Education. Goebbels at the RMVP had a representative on the Governing Board of the RWU, but since this met infrequently his opinions did not always carry as much weight as they would have liked. Thus when the Nazis began using films for propaganda in earnest, they found it necessary to establish an entirely separate system of Regional and

District Party Film Centres (*Gaufilmstellen* and *Kreisfilmstellen*) parallel to that of the schools. Basically, Goebbels felt that the possibilities offered by film propaganda in schools were too numerous to be left solely in the hands of local educational authorities. Therefore the Party had to give a lead and provide an example. Goebbels decided that in future the Ministry of Education and the RWU should work more closely with the Propaganda Ministry. In particular the Party would place a clearly defined emphasis on the production and distribution of political films. Thus on 22 June 1934 Dr Bernard Rust, Minister of Education, ordered the showing of political propaganda films in all German schools. He explained his policy in a speech to a specially invited audience of teachers:

> The leadership of Germany increasingly believes that schools have to be open for the dissemination of our ideology. To carry out this task we know of no better means than the film. The film is particularly important for school children. Film education must not only clarify contemporary political problems but it must also provide children with a knowledge of Germany's heroic past and a profound understanding of the future development of the Third Reich.[10]

As a result of Rust's Edict, new areas of responsibility were laid down whereby the *Gaufilmstelle* would show political films and the *Landesbildstelle* would prepare and present instructional films for schools. It was the Propaganda Ministry's constant aim to combine the activities of the two centres, and in some areas they succeeded in superceding the Regional Film Centres with their own *Gaufilmstellen*. Indeed, it was quite common for the *Gaufilmstellen* to be in the same premises as the *Landesbildstellen*, and often they did work together — although this was not always the case.

While educational films could be presented on any theme during lessons as often as was required, political films could only be shown once a month, but had to be shown at least four times a year. For the screenings of overt political films, the regular lesson times had to be made available; the preparation and interpretation of political themes also had to take place during the lessons. Most of the educational films screened in schools, whether cultural or propaganda, were always silent and between ten and twenty minutes long.[11] They were shown in conjunction with a printed 40-minute lecture, referred to above as the Teacher's Guide. The lecture, which would highlight the salient points to be noted in the film, would always be presented before the screening.

After the lecture and the film the pupils took an examination on each topic in order to reinforce these themes. Teachers tended to resent sound films because the spoken commentary introduced another authority into their jealously guarded professional domain. By showing only silent films in conjunction with Teacher's Guides and written examinations, these new obligatory film courses were generally welcomed by the teachers and were therefore easily incorporated into the German school curriculum.

In 1944 the RWU decided to publish its own comprehensive film catalogue. This document reveals that they had extended their activities to include not only primary and secondary schools but also universities, trade and technical schools and colleges, and agricultural colleges. Indeed of the 905 films catalogued, 275 were intended for the primary and secondary schools and over 500 films were made to be distributed in the universities. In 1945 the Allies decided to analyse these films and came to some surprising conclusions. They discovered that Goebbels had not been altogether successful in using the RWU for his own propagandistic purposes – at least not in the way he would have hoped for.[12] The Committee of Allied Ministers reported that of the 175 films they had viewed only 19 could be classified as 'tendentious'. However, closer scrutiny of this report reveals that not only did they fail to view the films in conjunction with the supplementary information provided in the Teachers' Guides, but they also restricted their analysis to films intended for primary schools. Moreover because of the desperate shortage of educational material in post-war Germany, the report was quite prepared to overlook a 'tendentious' film if shots of Nazi flags, insignia, uniforms, etc could be edited at a later date. These findings were based on an earlier investigation carried out by Professor Christian Casselmann, who was Ministerial Secretary in the Ministry of Education and a former assistant to Dr Gauger in the RWU. Casselmann maintained that, out of the 271 films he viewed, only two dealt with themes strictly related to the Nazi Party, 'and of all the films produced only about 10 per cent are unfit for today's audience'.[13] The author conceded, however, that 'at first, before the War, a small section in the RWU were against the Party and a certain objectivity was discernable. But later, films had to be made not only for schools, but also for the morale of the *Wehrmacht*, so naturally they became more propagandist in tone.' Such films aimed at nothing less than an emotional and mental preparedness of the German youth for war. It is significant that the largest proportion of films made by the RWU were for the university age-group, the very section of the population who, during the war, would be called upon to display those attributes which the Nazis had instilled in their 'educational' films – self-sacrifice, discipline and comradeship. This is borne out by the exceedingly high number of films dealing with the War and *Wehrmacht* and general military themes, the so-called military educational films (*Wehrerziehungsfilme*).

Both before and during the War there were quite unmistakable tensions existing between Goebbels' Ministry and the RWU, and to a certain extent this explains the relative scarcity of Party political propaganda films in these special film courses. The Party was forever demanding more films about Hitler and Nazi leaders and 'heroes', but generally the RWU was able to resist these pressures. According to Casselmann they were particularly successful in thwarting the Party's demands for heavily slanted films for biology lessons dealing with such topics as hereditary disease, racial inferiority, and euthanasia: 'in the end the Party asked us to make a film on the subject, which we did – but managed to prevent it from being distributed'.[14] In this respect the RWU was fortunate in that being virtually a private organisation it was able to maintain some degree of independence. Furthermore, as the RWU continued to distribute silent films, it fell outside the immediate control of the RMVP and Goebbels, who were more concerned with consolidating their control over sound feature films and documentary newsreels.

In general the films produced for schools were, from the propagandist's point of view, rather disappointing. Surprisingly, given the high technical standard of German feature and documentary films, the overall impression of Nazi school film propaganda is one of poor technical quality. Compared with the length of educational film propaganda in other European countries, Nazi films were certainly long for this type of indoctrination.[15] The most tendentious propaganda films were in the fields of history and geography. The former were generally applied as a short cut to an understanding of rather complex political themes; the latter concentrated almost entirely on Germany and the need for colonial expansion.[16] By the beginning of 1940, the SD noted that colonial ideas in educational film propaganda 'created very positive and encouraging responses from German youth'.[17]

In conclusion, then, the possibilities for the dissemination of National Socialist film propaganda during school lessons were not as great as might be expected. However it must always be remembered that much of the propaganda value of these films depended on the *spoken* commentary given by the teacher. Indeed the teaching notes provided with the films are much more propagandist in tone than the films themselves. This was only to be expected as the teaching profession represented one of the most politically reliable sections of the population and from a very early stage was justly regarded by the Nazi Party as a vanguard for their propaganda.[18]

Film Propaganda and the Hitler Youth

While they were a valuable first step in the Nazis' declared aim to use film for propaganda purposes, the purely instructional films shown in the schools were, as we have seen, dependent for their effect on the accompanying Teachers' Notes. However schools were merely one part of the Party's scheme to manipulate youth. To this end the National Socialists were able to enter the schools through the Hitler Youth.[19] The assault on the individual so characteristic of the Nazi regime, was directed primarily at youth with the intention of enveloping the individual at every stage of development within a single organisation by subjecting him to a planned course of indoctrination. Consequently, education was not merely the concern of the schools. In *Mein Kampf* Hitler laid great emphasis on organisation and this included the organisation of leisure time as well.[20] The Hitler Youth was crucial here. A contemporary writer noted: 'The Hitler Youth seeks to embrace both the whole of youth and the whole sphere of life of the young German.'[21] Moreover membership in the Hitler Youth was all but compulsory and by 1936 it claimed a membership of approximately six million. This prompted Baldur von Schirach to declare: 'The battle for the unification of German youth is now over.'[22]

One explanation for this undoubted success was the Nazis' remarkable ability to stimulate the imagination of an alienated youth with promises of a romantic Utopia. This was due not only to compulsion and effective psychological pressure, but also to the considerable and spontaneous wave of nationalist enthusiasm by which the young were seized and carried away. For parents, however, more sinister forces were involved, particularly if their religious and political convictions did not coincide with those of the *Völkischer Staat*. They would simply have their children taken from them and removed to a local Youth Hostel (referred to as a 'politically reliable home'). These disturbing features were observed by an American correspondent in Berlin at this time:

with children more and more removed from parental and religious influence through the Hitler Youth, evacuations into the country, and exposed to Nazi propaganda through school, books, the press, radio, and motion pictures, it was to be expected that the young were succumbing to the Nazi wishes.[23]

As far as film was concerned, the most important weapon was the 'Film Hour for the Young' (*Jugendfilmstunde*) arranged by the Hitler Youth for its members. Within the training schedule of the Hitler Youth there were clearly defined and carefully controlled duties and attendance at the *Jugendfilmstunde* was extremely important. In co-operation, therefore, with the RMVP and the *Reichsjugendführung*, a Hitler Youth Film Headquarters was established and incorporated within the Propaganda Ministry's overall film administration. These *Jugendfilmstunden* were in addition to the compulsory film events in the schools; here special performances of selected current feature films were shown in ordinary commercial cinemas. The Hitler Youth screenings were financed in the same way as were the compulsory film exhibitions in the schools that were arranged by the *Landesbildstellen*. Hitler Youth members were required to pay 15 pfennig before they were admitted into the cinema where overt political films would invariably be shown. The rationale behind these 'Film Hours' was not only to disseminate ideas and a pattern of behaviour that was ideologic-ally acceptable, but also to encourage the young to visit the cinema more often than their elders. Thus the Party succeeded in providing an impressive system for the organisation and indoctrination of the Hitler Youth whilst imposing scarcely any extra cost on the State.

The first *Jugendfilmstunde* began in a casual manner on a monthly basis on 20 April 1934. However, with reports of their effectiveness the *Reichsjugendführung* decided that even more emphasis should be placed on film propaganda. Thus by 1936 the *Jugendfilmstunden* were being organised once a week on a Sunday and on a national basis by the joint efforts of the RMVP and the *Hitlerjugend*. These events were now widely advertised throughout the country not only to encourage attendance but also to demonstrate that they had been given an official seal of approval. A typical example of the enthusiasm which accom-panied the announcement of these Film Hours was the following state-ment from the Magdeburg region: 'Last Sunday the *Jugendfilmstunde* began for the whole Mittelelbe area. In collaboration with the Regional Party Film Centre of Magdeburg-Anhalt, a number of our biggest cine-mas were hired in order to show the film masterpieces created by our German directors and actors to the fortunate boys and girls of this area.'[24] The advertisement, quoted in *Der Film*, was headed: '50,000 attend Youth Film Hour'. The films shown were intended to represent the very best of the recent productions and were not entirely confined to political films although such films naturally formed the vast majority.[25] These events were important enough for Goebbels to intervene personally during the War when the *Wehrmacht* had taken over a number of club-houses used by Berlin's *Hitlerjugend*, thus depriving them of their facilities to show these films.

In these Film Hours the film was made the focal experience. The films were introduced by Party officials who outlined the relevant ideological and artistic points to be discussed following the screening. These lectures together with small political dramas that were often acted out by members of the *Hitlerjugend*, as well as community singing and flag hoisting, were intended to direct the young audience to the central propaganda themes and at the same time emphasise the importance and enjoyment of visiting the cinema regularly. It should also be noted that parents were strongly encouraged in the evening to continue these discussions within the family.

Even before the *Jugendfilmstunde* the cinema attendance of the young was already controlled by the youth protection clauses in the Reich Cinema Law (*Reichslichtspielgesetz*), which became law on 16 February 1934. According to Paragraph 11 of the 1934 Cinema Law:

> Films which are not licensed for showing to children or young people under the age of eighteen years, must not be performed in front of these persons . . . A licence to show a film to children or young people will also be refused if there is danger of the film having a harmful effect on the moral, intellectual or physical development of young people or on their political education and the cultivation of a Germanic consciousness, or the over-stimulation of their imagination.
>
> In special cases, the Censorship Office can restrict the licence of a film so that it may only be shown to young people over the age of fourteen years. Children under the age of six years may only be present at the showing of a film if the Reich Minister for Popular Enlightenment and Propaganda has given definite provision for this.[26]

Under Article 25 of this legislation, cinema owners were liable to one year's imprisonment and a fine if they 'willingly screened unlicensed films to children or young people'. From Goebbels' point of view, the specially arranged *Jugendfilmstunden*, restricted still further the possibility of uncontrolled attendance. The Propaganda Ministry also declared that these youth performances should be exempt from entertainment tax. The 1934 Cinema Law attempted to create a new 'positive' censorship by encouraging 'good' films instead of merely discouraging 'bad' ones. This was achieved by introducing a system of distinction marks (*Prädikate*), which were really a form of negative taxation. As films allegedly improved, the range of the *Prädikat* system was extended. The highest distinction mark ('politically and artistically especially valuable') meant that the entire programme would be exempt from entertainment tax while the lower *Prädikat* reduced the tax proportionate to their value.[27] In 1939 a special distinction mark 'Valuable for Youth' (*Jugendwert*) was specifically introduced for these occasions. The idea for this came from the famous actor Mathias Wiemann at the first Hitler Youth Film Congress held in Hamburg in 1937.[28] It was finally taken up by Goebbels after further suggestions by Youth Leaders at the same Congress held in Vienna in 1938. Although not strictly a *Prädikat*, in that it did not carry tax-relief, the award invariably boosted other *Prädikate* and greatly enhanced a film's status. Furthermore, it was decisive in the selection of films to be shown in schools and youth organisations.[29] The importance of the *Jugendwert* distinction mark was that it 'signified both the appreciation and recognition of German youth for works of art which reflect their own spirit'.[30]

The basic idea behind these *Prädikate* was to encourage film-makers to produce more films for the young and also to compel the cinema owners to exhibit more films designated *Jugendwert*, something they were loathe to do because of the extremely low admission price. The standard for this distinction mark was very high and only top quality films which could be shown to the young were ever given the award. Thus by 1945 only 30 feature films had been classified 'Valuable for Youth'. The majority were the so-called *Staatsauftragsfilme*, films commissioned by the State and generally given a disproportionate amount of time, financial assistance, and publicity. They included extremely prestigious films like *Heimkehr* (*Homecoming*, 1941), *Kampfgeschwader Lützow* (*Battle Squadron Lützow*, 1941), *Der grosse König* (*The Great King*, 1942) and *Die Entlassung* (*The Dismissal*, 1942).[31] These films were not always overtly political but were invariably classified at the time as *Tendenzfilme*. This was a term employed during the Third Reich to describe a certain type of film that exhibited 'strong National Socialist tendencies'.[32] In other words, without necessarily mentioning National Socialism, these films advocated various principles and themes identifiable with Nazism which the Propaganda Ministry wished to disseminate at intermittent periods.

Despite the all-embracing nature of the Hitler Youth organisation, there were a number of difficulties concerning the *Jugendfilmstunde*, particularly in the rural areas and small towns, although the Nazis made great efforts to overcome these difficulties. The recurring problem was that films requested by the Youth leadership were frequently not delivered on time. As a result, replacement films had to be shown which did not always correspond to what was originally asked for or expected. This caused considerable outrage in the areas concerned especially by the staunch Party guardians of public morality. One SD Report entitled, 'Misuse of the Youth Film Hours' revealed the following misunderstanding:

> It is now known that a number of abuses emerged at the *Jugendfilmstunden* which took place throughout the Reich on 5 November 1939. From Stuttgart we learn that the majority of cinemas were screening, during the Youth Film Hours, the current films on show. This meant that young people of 12-14 saw films like *Gern hab ich die Frauen geküsst* [*I Loved Kissing Women*] and *Andalusische Nächte* [*Andalusian Nights*]. The Youth Leader in question protested vociferously about the showing of such films, but the cinema owners made the excuse that they had received no other films from Berlin.[33]

Needless to recount, such episodes only served to increase the expectation of young cinema goers! The procedure for the delivery of films to the *Jugendfilmstunde* was that the individual Hitler Youth section applied for the film it wanted to the Regional Film Centre who then passed on the applications to the relevant Distribution and Hire Office. The film would then be sent directly to the cinema which was to be used for the performance. If the film asked for was not available, the Distribution Office chose an alternative film without consulting or even informing the Hitler Youth leadership. As a rule, there were only a limited number of films suitable for young people at these distribution centres (mostly with a political message as opposed to 'bawdy' comedies), and these were for distribution to cinema owners and regular performances as well as the Youth Film Hours. To overcome this difficulty it was frequently suggested that a centre stocking films solely for distribution to the *Jugendfilmstunden* be established on similar lines to that used by the *Wehrmacht*.[34] It would appear however, that this new system was never entirely successful in harmonising the contrasting interests of the film producers, the cinema owners and the Reich Youth Leadership.

Despite these occasional, and generally minor, problems the *Jugend-filmstunden* were extremely successful, especially when they were arranged on a regular basis. Goebbels was particularly pleased with them and in a speech delivered to a *Jugendfilmstunden* audience in 1941 he pledged that more films would be made available for these showings and that censorship restrictions on young people would be relaxed during the ordinary commercial screenings.[35] During the war the SD noted that they were much appreciated in the rural areas and small towns where they were often the only means of entertainment and information available. One Report mentioned that where these showings were on a regular basis, they tended to offset the influence of the Church and the revival in religious interest which had been observed in rural areas that did not have regular *Jugendfilmstunden.*[36]

Table 5.1, taken from a contemporary source, indicates the high attendance figures at the performances and also the rather obvious possibilities for propaganda. Such figures also explain why the Propaganda Ministry and the Reich Youth Leadership were eager to support these special performances. It should also be noted that from 1936 failure to attend a *Jugendfilmstunde* threatened some form of punishment, although there is little evidence that this was ever carried out.[37]

Table 5.1: Film Attendance and Performances of the Youth Film Hours, 1934-43

Year	Performances	Attendance
1934-5	—	300,000
1935-6	905	425,176
1936-7	1,725	897,839
1937-8	3,563	1,771,236
1938-9	4,886	2,561,489
1939-40	8,244	3,538,224
1940-1	12,560	4,800,000
1941-2	15,800	5,600,000
1942-3	over 45,290	11,215,000

Source: A.J. Sander, *Jugend und Film* (Berlin, 1944), p. 72.

It can be seen from these figures that both the number of performances and visits rose quite substantially in a very short period. This was due partly to the onset of war and the need for entertainment but it also reflected the Nazi regime's desire to use films as means of instilling a war-like mentality in the minds of the young.[38] Considerable attention was also paid to those areas without cinemas, as the following figures for the period 1942/43 show:

Areas with cinemas	—	24,100 performances with 8,355,000 cinema visits
Areas without cinemas	—	18,240 performances with 2,465,000 visits
Screenings shown in Hitler Youth Camps	—	2,950 performances with 395,000 visits

In order to ensure that as many rural areas as possible received a regular film service the Propaganda Ministry created a network of 1,500 mobile film units which travelled the country extensively. With these screenings German youth was not only assimilated into the Nazi *Weltanschauung*, but they were also used to encourage the young generation to enter the movement. The Youth Film Hours thus supplemented the initial work carried out in the schools and provided the second tier of a comprehensive system for the organisation and indoctrination of every individual. It was also hoped that these screenings would encourage the young to visit the commercial cinema more often than their parents. Indeed there is evidence to suggest that the regime was successful in its efforts to persuade German youth to attend the cinema on a regular basis. At the beginning of the war the average German over 15 years of age visited the cinema 10.5 times per year; by 1943 this had risen to 14.4 times per year.[39] A survey among 14- to 18-year-olds in 1933 revealed that 16.6 per cent visited the cinema on a weekly basis, 48.9 per cent on a monthly basis, and 34.5 per cent seldom went at all (nine times or less).[40]

In 1943 another questionnaire was circulated by the *Führerdienst der Reichsjugendführung* to 686 boys and 1,200 girls aged between 10 and 17. It discovered that 22.05 per cent visited the cinema at least once a week; 71.73 per cent went on a monthly basis, and only 6.22 per cent saw less than nine films a year.[41] Surprisingly, this questionnaire revealed that 26.82 per cent of the boys and 11.91 per cent of the girls visited the cinema on average once a week. This predilection for the cinema by boys was due mainly to the high number of films extolling the invincibility of German military might. Such militarist films set in a contemporary context came to be referred to as *Zeitfilme*.

During the war they included such titles as: *D 111 88* (1939), *Kampf-geschwader Lüdzow* (*Battle Squadron Lützow*, 1941), *Stukas* (1941), *Uber alles in der Welt* (*Above All in the World*, 1941), *Himmelhunde* (*Sky Hounds*, 1942) and *Junge Adler* (*Young Eagles*, 1944). Their central message was of the nobility of self-sacrifice, comradeship, and heroic death in battle. In the mythology of National Socialism, as J.P. Stern observed, war represented 'the consummation of all manly virtues . . . the true proving ground of men and nations'.[42] Together with the military educational films shown in schools, these *Zeitfilme* formed an integral part of the ideological chauvinism that pervaded all aspects of Nazi thought.

Although the Propaganda Ministry and the *Filmwelt* welcomed the increase in the number of times that the younger generation were visiting the cinemas, this did bring complications. During the war in particular, certain Party officials claimed that the rise in the rate of juvenile delinquency was directly linked to this trend, or they complained that children were taking cinema seats at the expense of munition workers and soldiers on leave. In the second year of the war police in some parts of the Reich actually banned children from the cinemas after 9 o'clock unless they were accompanied by adults.[43] However this practice proved impossible to implement and generally authorities turned a blind eye. The prevailing sentiments were summed up by a Hitler Youth leader in 1937 who stated that, because of the great efforts made by the Party, German youth was so enthusiastic and knowledgeable about the technical and intellectual aspects of film art that outdated 'bourgeois' habits like collecting cigarette cards of film stars were now simply 'unthinkable'.[44]

Film Making and the Hitler Youth

The Party hierarchy were particularly concerned that the commercial nature of the film industry should not work to the disadvantage of the young. One way to overcome this was to commission feature films for youth audiences. Although Nazi spokesmen continued to stress the importance of this link with the *Filmwelt*, it was a continual source of annoyance in certain Party circles that the industry had failed to back this plan. In fact only ten films were produced during the Third Reich specifically for the Hitler Youth.[45] They became known as *Uniform-filme* and highlighted the need for comradeship and discipline in the community as well as key Nazi icons like the flag, the eagle and the uniform – images that recur throughout the films of the Third Reich. But it was the reluctance of the commercial film industry to produce feature-length films for the *Hitlerjugend* together with the success of the Youth Film Hours which finally persuaded the Propaganda Ministry to encourage the Hitler Youth to make their own films.

The *Reichsjugendführung* had tentatively started to make their own films as early as 1932 when the *Reichsjugendtag* (Reich Youth Day) at Potsdam was filmed.[46] By 1936 film production was officially taken over by the *Hitlerjugend* with clearly defined responsibilities so as not to impinge upon the work of the commercial film producers. The film work of the Hitler Youth was encouraged for the simple fact that it was recognised by the Party as 'an important educational factor'. Film-making was thus taught within the movement as part of the educational curriculum.[47] It began initially in 16mm format but as they gained more experience they eventually started to learn to make films in 35mm. They rationalised the expense of such classes by claiming that the youth movement 'desired films borne and created by the young for the young'. Only from within their own ranks, it was argued, could their experiences, their struggle, and their present-day community be shaped: 'Artists will grow out of our movement who will give the German film the face of our young, who will make our experience and our community live.'[48] Accordingly, one of the first films celebrating the *Hitlerjugend* was a short documentary produced in December 1935 entitled, *Die Stadt der weissen Zelte* (*The Town of the White Tents*). This film gave an insight into the south-west Hitler Youth camp at Offenburg in Baden. It was also a film about the Hitler Youth which was the first television film shown at the Radio Exhibition in 1935.[49] On the whole, however, its subsequent endeavours in this field remained, with possibly a few exceptions, rather dull and uninspired. A random sample of the films made between 1939 and 1942 gives some idea of the type of productions and themes that were promoted: *Einsatz der Jugend* (*Youth's Mission*, 1939), *Der Marsch zum Führer* (*The March to the Führer*, 1940), *Die Erde ruft* (*The Earth Calls*, 1940), *Glaube und Schönheit* (*Faith and Beauty*, 1940), *Unsere Kinder – unsere Zukunft* (*Our Children – Our Future*, 1940), *Soldaten von morgen* (*Soldiers of Tomorrow*, 1941) and *Der Wille zum Fliegen* (*The Desire to Fly*, 1942).

In addition to the above-mentioned films, the *Reichsjugendführung* commissioned a series of eight documentary films which spanned the war years 1942-5. They were called *Junges Europa* (Young Europe) and attempted to give the German people a comforting insight into the work carried out by the *Hitlerjugend* during the war. Although purely propagandist in tone and content, they were well produced (indeed the first 'edition' won the European Film Competition held in Florence in 1942) and like all these films were destined not only for Hitler Youth camps, but would be shown in all cinemas together with the main feature film and the *Deutsche Wochenschau* (newsreel). It may be illustrative to summarise briefly the content of one of the films in the *Junges Europa* series and compare it with one of the more successful HJ productions – *Soldaten von morgen*.

Junges Europa, No. 7 (1944)

The film was released for general distribution on 24 April 1944. Although it outlines the various activities of fascist youth throughout Europe, it concentrates mainly on the *Hitlerjugend*. We are introduced to a well-organised parade of Spanish youth and see young Bulgarian girls picking roses and the boys assisting equestrian police patrols. Then a sequence of events which include: a group of young German youth from Hamburg being decorated for their service to the community in the Berlin Stadium, a *girl* glider test pilot, a boys' soap-box model car race in Stuttgart, members of the Marine sections of the HJ in Ulm collecting money for U-boat crews followed by shots of a U-boat returning from service in the Atlantic being greeted by Admiral Dönitz and the boys handing over their collection. The film ends by showing the extent of the Hitler Youth's contribution to the war effort: we see them working in the ammunition factories and carrying out an assortment of duties during Allied air raids.[50]

This film, together with the other seven in the series, was made specifically for domestic consumption. They were produced by the *Deutsche Filmherstellungs- und Verwertungsgesellschaft* (DFG) in conjunction with the *Reichsjugendführung*.[51] It must be remembered that they were made during the war years and their main objective was to portray the Hitler Youth and their activities in an extremely favourable light to the civilian population in Germany as a kind of mutual morale booster. One can in fact trace the decline in Germany's military fortunes through the series: the content reveals that from No. 2 (26 October 1942) onwards, the emphasis is no longer on youth's contribution to the home-front 'effort', but rather on their mobilisation for military action as a future strike force and a last line of defence at home. Indeed the last *Junges Europa* (10 January 1945), distinguished, as they all were by the *Prädikat* 'politically and artistically valuable', tried until the very end to subordinate reality by claiming, as the British and the Americans were crossing the Rhine, that the *Hitlerjugend* were trained and able to repulse the enemy. It was to be the last film produced by an NSDAP organisation in the Third Reich.

Soldaten von morgen (*Soldiers of Tomorrow*, 1941)

This is an altogether different film from the *Junges Europa* series and, from the point of view of propaganda as well as technical execution, is far superior.[52] Once again it is produced by the DFG but the *Reichsjugendführung* called in the assistance of a professional film director, Alfred Weidenmann, a specialist in children's films.[53] The film was released on 30 June 1941 and is a fair representation of the type of Nazi propaganda film made at this juncture of the war.

Soldaten von morgen takes the form of a Hitler Youth theatrical performance and is intended as a work of pure anti-British propaganda. We see a skit on the English public-school system and the resultant degeneracy, through this type of education, of Britain's youth. The film cites Winston Churchill, Lord Halifax and Anthony Eden as examples. The point is driven home with shots of London club- and night-life which are ridiculed quite savagely. This section of the film ends with pictures of dishevelled British troops captured at the beginning of the First World War who are compared with virile members of the Hitler Youth. In order to reinforce this, we are shown a sequence of *Hitlerjugend* activities: participating in a mountain obstacle race in the Alps, Sea Cadets in training for future naval action, fencing, gliding, parachute jumping, horse riding, 'mock' battles and a final parade. The film ends with shots of the German *Wehrmacht* as if to emphasise the fruition of such an educational and cultural process.

As opposed to *Junges Europa*, *Soldaten von morgen* was made at a precise stage in the war when German troops were experiencing unprecedented success. The film reflects the euphoric nature of Nazi propaganda in general during this period: it is brash, confident, one might almost say arrogant. There is also a clearly defined enemy to be identified, ridiculed and attacked. Unlike the 1944 edition of *Junges Europa*, which was really salvaging crumbs of comfort to boost morale during 'total war', *Soldaten von morgen* is essentially an optimistic production, illustrating the relentless, invincible resources of the Nazi military machine. It was intended not only for domestic consumption but for world-wide distribution (particularly to conquered countries); consequently, its intention is a contrived advertisement for Germany and its virile youth. Stylistically it is interesting to note the use made of captured archive film and the employment of amateur Hitler Youth actors for dramatic effect. A rapid editing technique enhances the comparisons made between British and Nazi youth which, although rather crude, successfully creates an identifiable image of the enemy. It was a favourite device in Nazi propaganda to use the leisure activities of an enemy as a source of ridicule. It was particularly common in anti-British feature films to present the decadence of the British in terms of their sordid 'night-life'.[54] However, the most important features to note in *Soldaten von morgen* are its overall compositional structure and the technical ability with which it is executed. These are important new departures in Hitler Youth film production, and although the *Reichs-jugendführung* would occasionally employ professional directors in the future in an attempt to emulate this film, they would never be totally successful in repeating its success.

Although the two films mentioned above are only analysed briefly, they reflect an appreciation of the enormous propaganda value of film on the part of the Youth leadership. After all, the very fact that the *Hitlerjugend* had their own film production unit is a clear indication of the importance the Nazi regime attached to the indoctrination of German youth through film propaganda. These facilities allowed the youth movement to express itself within carefully controlled boundaries. As a result of the elevated status the *Hitlerjugend* was given from the beginning of the Third Reich, it was the constant aim of Nazi propaganda to instruct youth in the spirit and ideals of National Socialism and to inculcate the teaching that all their pursuits were in the interest of the State and not for themselves. Therefore a recurrent theme in Nazi film propaganda in general was the need for discipline and absolute obedience. Linked to these general aims were the films produced by the Youth movement which were a specific attempt to capture the spirit of the *Hitlerjugend*, together with the equally important elements of comradeship and self-sacrifice. In doing so, films in this category served to highlight their virtues and appease the fears of many parents who foresaw in the *Hitlerjugend* the disintegration of the family. At the same time such films brought the young into line with the system and gained new recruits for the Youth movement in Germany and the occupied countries.

The importance of educational film propaganda together with the film-making activities of the *Hitlerjugend* should not be underestimated. One of the most important uses of the cinema in Nazi Germany was for the indoctrination of the young. Film propaganda in the schools and the accompanying spoken commentary given by the teacher carefully perpetuated the educational system and directed the young towards those ideological themes the Party wished to promote. To this end, a sustained film programme was meticulously formulated by the Ministry of Education which was very quickly backed up by similar film shows screened by Goebbels' Propaganda Ministry. Eventually these Ministries agreed to co-ordinate their work in an attempt to shape dedicated young National Socialists. Two main themes emerge from the films shown in schools: a distorted picture of German history and heavily slanted film lessons dealing with the purity of the Aryan race. The first emphasised German superiority and the need for colonial expansion, the second concentrated on Nazi racial theories and, for example, the dangers of miscegenation.

The National Socialists appreciated that the best way of achieving their objectives was to appeal to the emotions rather than to reason. Furthermore, they realised that the medium of film was unexcelled in its ability to play upon such emotions, for it could always be manipulated to combine entertainment with indoctrination. The emphasis in Nazi culture was primarily on the elaboration of a ritual which it was hoped would supersede that of both Church and State. The key icons in the creation of this imagery were the flag, the eagle and the uniform — images that recur throughout the feature films shown during the *Jugendfilmstunde*. Propaganda in a totalitarian police state must address large masses of people and attempt to move them to a uniformity of opinion and action. Since the aim is to get results, and not to promote or stimulate an understanding of the results, then the appeal must necessarily be emotional rather than rational. The constant repetition of these icons and the obsession with ritual ceremonies and military parades, which were an intrinsic part of the theatrical nature of the Youth Film Hours, were all part of the propaganda machine designed to increase the impact of strong words with strong deeds. By disguising its intent, such film propaganda was able to ensure complete interdependence between the propagandisers and the propagandised, so that consequently a uniformity of opinion and action developed with few opportunities for resistance. Moreover when the Second World War caused the *Hitlerjugend* to become more militarised in order to bolster the war effort, then the war-mongering sentiments of its leadership were once again reinforced by the aggressively militarist *Zeitfilme* that German youth were forced to see in the *Jugendfilmstunde*.

Finally, the *Hitlerjugend* film productions promoted in a positive light the manner in which German youth was being organised, by

stressing the numerous activities of the youth movement and the ideological commitment of its members. In this sense they also served to
give a lead to the rest of the nation. The aim of such films was to show
this 'new man' embodying the Nazi *Weltanschauung*, whose heroic
will would create and perpetuate the New Order in Europe. Belling and
Schütze, the official spokesmen of the *Hitlerjugend* summed up the
task of film propaganda in the schools and youth organisations as
follows: 'Thanks to the National Socialist film educational work, youth
is directed towards the heroic and is therefore psychologically prepared
and entirely capable of withstanding all pressures.'[55] It is a measure of
the success of the Nazis' ideological programme that even when all was
long lost in 1945, German youth in particular was still showing a tragic
loyalty and faith by fighting to the end for such out-worn notions as
Führer, *Volk*, and Fatherland.

Notes

1. A. Hitler, *Mein Kampf* (London, 1939), pp. 356-8. All references to *Mein Kampf* are taken from this edition.
2. B. von Schirach, *Die Hitlerjugend, Idee und Gestalt* (Berlin 1934), quoted in J. Fest, *The Face of the Third Reich* (London, 1972), p. 332.
3. For the most comprehensive account of the rise of the *Hitlerjugend* before the Nazis came to power see P.D. Stachura, *Nazi Youth in the Weimar Republic* (Santa Barbara, California, 1975). H.W. Koch, *The Hitler Youth: Origins and Development 1922-45* (London, 1975) takes their development up to the end of the Second World War.
4. Cf. J. Goebbels, 'Die lage des Kultur- und Lehrfilms in Deutschland', *Kinematograph*, no. 195 (9 October 1934). For a brief discussion on the import-ance of educational film propaganda in Nazi Germany see D. Welch, *Propaganda and the German Cinema, 1933-45* (Oxford, 1983), pp. 24-9.
5. J. Goebbels, 'Der Film als Erzieher. Rede zur Eröffnung der Filmarbeit der HJ' (Berlin, 12 October 1941) in *Das eherne Herz, Reden und Aufsätz aus den Jahren 1941-2* (Munich, 1943), pp. 37-46.
6. Information taken from Bundesarchiv Koblenz (hereafter BA), *Material zur Filmpolitik der Weimarer Zeit (Reichskunstwart), R 32/201-203, 322.*
7. Cf. 'Die Neue Reichstelle für den Unterrichtsfilm', *Deutsche Filmseitung* (25 November 1934). I would like to express my gratitude to Lutz Becker for drawing my attention to material I might otherwise have overlooked.
8. BA, *Reichsministerium für Wissenschaft, Erziehung und Volksbildung, R 21/710,* 'Unterlegen über die Reichsanstalt für Film und Bild in Wissenschaft und Unterricht, 1938-45'.
9. Figures taken from a report on RWU, *Sight and Sound*, vol. 14, no. 55 (October 1945), pp. 88-90. See also, G. Buckland-Smith, 'The Use of Visual Aids in German Schools', *Sight and Sound*, vol. 14, no. 56, (Winter 1945/6), pp. 109-11.
10. *Völkischer Beobachter* (23 June 1934). Also quoted in J. Altmann, 'Movies' Role in Hitler's Conquest of German Youth' in *Hollywood Quarterly*, vol. 111, no. 4 (n.d.), p. 381.
11. The division into cultural or propaganda film was always a purely Nazi

interpretation. The former dealt with geographical or scientific matters, the latter were considered more important for the political development of the child. Both were imbued with a typical Nazi *Weltanschauung.*

12. *Report on German Educational Films. Audio-Visual Aids Communication,* (British Film Institute, London, 1946).

13. BA, *R21/710.* The tone of this report is too self-congratulatory to be taken without critical reservations. I suspect the number of films in this category to be much higher. It is extremely difficult to assess, as most of the films have since been edited, and the objectional shots removed.

14. Ibid.

15. In Great Britain, for example, it was felt that to be effective the maximum length for this type of film should be ten minutes. Britain, however, did not possess the organisational structure of the Nazis — or their technical resources. See, *The Film in National Life* (London,. 1939), p. 20.

16. The Report on German Educational Films stated that these films were 'entirely tendentious — the lack of balance and the basis of selection of materials is clear, since only one frontier is dealt with and only one idea conveyed', p. 20. As regards the geography films, '73% were on German subjects, and the remaining were about German activities in Africa and Central America', p. 18.

17. BA, *Akten des Reichssicherheitshauptamtes, R 58/148, no. 51* (9 February 1940).

18. Fourteen per cent of teachers compared with 6 per cent of civil servants belonged to the Party's political leadership corps. As Richard Grunberger noted, 'This remarkable commitment to the regime was exemplified in the highest ranks of the Party hierarchy by seventy-eight District Leaders and seven Gauleiter who had graduated from the teaching profession.' R. Grunberger, *A Social History of the Third Reich* (London, 1974), p. 364.

19. The most comprehensive account of the use made of film propaganda directed at the Hitler Youth is still C. Belling and A. Schütze, *Der Film in der Hitlerjugend* (Berlin, 1937).

20. Hitler, *Mein Kampf,* p. 353. For an excellent account of how much of the student's after-school time was taken up by the Party and related ideological activity see, Ilse McKee, *Tomorrow the World* (London, 1960).

21. Hand Helmut Dietz, *Die Rechtsgestalt der Hitlerjugend* (Berlin, 1939), p. 63, quoted in Fest, *The Face of the Third Reich,* p. 345.

22. For the full speech see B. von Schirach, *Revolution der Erziehung. Reden aus den Jahren des Aufbaus* (Munich, 1938), pp. 22-3.

23. H.W. Flannery, *Assignment to Berlin* (London, 1942), p. 84.

24. *Der Film* (31 October 1936), quoted in J. Wulf (ed.), *Theater und Film im Dritten Reich. Eine Dokumentation* (Reinbek bei Hamburg, 1968), p. 359.

25. The complete list of films shown in the Jugendfilmstunden can be found in A.U. Sander, *Jugend und Film* (Berlin, 1944), pp. 145-6.

26. H. Tackmann, *Filmhandbuch als ergänzbare Sammlung herausgegeben von der Reichsfilmkammer* (Berlin, 1938).

27. For a detailed discussion of the Reich Cinema Law see Welch, *Propaganda and the German Cinema,* pp. 17-24.

28. The Hitler Youth Film Congress was established in 1937 and was authorised by the Nazi regime to discuss all questions of film propaganda for young people. This also included the making of films by the *Hitlerjugend.*

29. Tackmann, 'Dritte AO zur Anderung . . . der AO zur Sicherung angemessener Filmerträgnisse' (21 July 1938), paragraph 7. After 1938 owners could not refuse to show a film with a political Prädikat.

30. Sander, *Jugend und Film,* p. 79.

31. It is not the aim of this article to analyse the content of these feature

films. Detailed analyses can be found in Welch, *Propaganda and the German Cinema*.

32. An excellent account of *Tendenzfilme* can be found in G. Eckert, 'Filmintendenz und Tendenzfilm', *Wille und Macht, Führerorgan der Nationalsozialistischen Jugend*, Jahrgang 6, vol. 4 (15 November 1938), pp. 19-25.

33. BA, *R 58/145* (20 November 1939). Cf. also BA, *R 58/159* (3 April 1941).

34. The *Wehrmacht* had their own distribution centre which stocked films specifically for their own use. They were extremely 'film-conscious', particularly where their own image was concerned. Usually they employed a vigilant 'watch-dog' committee monitoring their affairs.

35. Goebbels, 'Der Film als Erzieher', p. 42.

36. BA, *R 58/159* (3 April 1941). Cf. also *R 58/155* (17 October 1940).

37. It would appear from all accounts that threat of punishment acted as a deterrent.

38. For a detailed discussion of this aspect of Nazi film propaganda see Welch, *Propaganda and the German Cinema*, pp. 186-237.

39. Ibid., p. 35.

40. A. Funk, *Film und Jugend* (2 vols., Munich, 1934), vol. II, pp. 47-9. These figures are based on a questionnaire sent to the parents of these age groups.

41. Sander, *Jugend und Film*, p. 54.

42. J.P. Stern, *Hitler. The Führer and the People* (London, 1975), p. 177.

43. BA, *Akten des Reichsministeriums für Volksaufklärung und Propaganda, R 55/343*, file on 'Ubermässiger Kinobesuch von Kindern, 1940'.

44. Belling and Schütze, *Der Film in der Hitlerjugend*, p. 65.

45. The complete list is cited in Sander, *Jugend und Film*, p. 30. The author cites twelve films, but two were produced before 1933 and subsequently passed by the Nazi Censor at a later date.

46. The film is mentioned in Koch, *The Hitler Youth*, p. 132. A fragment of the film can be found in the Film Archive of the Imperial War Museum.

47. Christel Reinhardt, *Der Jugendfunk* (Würzburg, 1938), p. 30, quoted in Wulf, *Theater und Film*, p. 358.

48. Belling und Schütze, *Der Film in der Hitlerjugend*, p. 69.

49. Reinhardt, *Der Jugendfunk*, p. 30.

50. A brief synopsis of this film can also be found in *Catalogue of Forbidden German Feature and Short Film Productions held in the Zonal Film Archives of the Film Section, Information Services Division, Control Commission for Germany (BE)* (Hamburg, 1951), p. 95.

51. BA, *Reichspropagandaleitung der NSDAP/Gruppe Filmwesen, NS 18/346* (13 December 1943).

52. A 16mm copy of the film is held by the Imperial War Museum and is available on loan to educational institutions.

53. Weidenmann was the most famous director of films for and about German youth. As well as numerous short documentaries he directed such feature films as *Jakko* (1941), *Hände Hoch!* (*Hands Up!*, 1942) and *Junge Adler* (*Young Eagles*, 1944).

54. The incorporation of captured enemy material and its manipulation in such a way that it testifies against the country of its origin is particularly striking in the two Nazi documentary films: *Feuertaufe* (*Baptism of Fire*, 1940), and *Sieg im Westen* (*Victory in the West*, 1941). The use of London 'club-life' can be seen in the anti-British film *Carl Peters* (1941).

55. Belling und Schütze, *Der Film in der Hitlerjugend*, p. 36.

6 STRUCTURES OF CONSENSUS AND COERCION: WORKERS' MORALE AND THE MAINTENANCE OF WORK DISCIPLINE, 1939-1945*

Stephen Salter

One of the main tenets of National Socialist propaganda after 1933 was that class conflict had been transcended, that a new order — the *Volksgemeinschaft* (People's Community) — had come into being in which the various social groups collaborated for the benefit of the community as a whole and to restore Germany's former greatness. The centrality of this concept to Hitler's plans for imperial expansion is now widely accepted. Hitler frequently claimed that he had entered politics in order to win the working class away from the Marxist social-democratic parties he had witnessed in Vienna before 1914, and he saw the successful integration of the German working class behind the Nazi regime as a prerequisite for imperial expansion — the threat of a repetition of the events of November 1918 must be eliminated.[1]

Yet the NSDAP never succeeded in undermining the allegiance of the bulk of the German working class to its traditional representatives — the Communist and Social-democratic parties — and its own embryonic trades union, the NSBO, made few inroads into the support of German workers for Communist, Social-democratic and Catholic trades unions.[2] The failure of Nazi attempts to win the support of the German working class before 1933 was spectacularly demonstrated in early May 1933 when the left-wing unions were forcibly suppressed.[3]

The collapse of the German labour movement during spring 1933 under the impact of the Nazi 'revolution from below' has been traced back to the financial and political damage sustained by the trades unions during the Depression. High unemployment, especially amongst workers who had traditionally made up the best-organised sections of the German working class, crippled the unions financially, ruled out the possibility of a political general strike at any point after 1930 and shattered the solidarity of the labour movement as a whole. Deprived of representative institutions which might have integrated daily experience at the workplace into a wider political consciousness, confronted by the threat of savage reprisals against any collective oppositional activity and subject to the most effective agent of work-discipline of all

– the threat of instant dismissal – German workers in the years immediately after 1933 were to become little more than the passive objects of the social and economic policies of the Nazi regime, with very little power to shape their working conditions and with none to express their political opinions.[4]

Yet after 1936, it has been argued, as a consequence of the full employment brought about by the rearmaments boom,

> alongside the resilient agitation and organisation of the illegal groups, economic class conflict re-emerged in Germany on a broad front . . . It manifested itself through spontaneous strikes, through the exercise of collective pressure on employers and Nazi organisations, through the most various acts of defiance against work-place rules and governmental decrees, through slow-downs in production, absenteeism, the taking of sick-leave, demonstrations of discontent etc.'[5]

Such economic class conflict constituted opposition to the regime since 'it posed a massive, but not fundamental, principled challenge to the regime'.[6]

There is little dispute about the re-emergence of class conflict in German industry after 1936. Workers were able to exploit the general labour shortage after 1937 to gain higher wages and concessions from employers in the form of improved working conditions. The removal of the threat of dismissal was accompanied by significant increases in sickness and absenteeism rates and there was widespread resistance by workers to the attempts of the regime to restrict labour mobility and to direct workers to priority projects. Rather, dispute centres around the political significance of such economically-based conflict. Such conflict, it has been argued, is characteristic of any economy enjoying full employment, is normally partial, and cannot be seen as opposition to a particular regime.[7] Rising absenteeism and sickness rates have also been explained in terms of the work-tempo characteristic of many industries by the later 1930s in combination with a deterioration in nutrition and the long-term effects of unemployment.[8]

Developments in workers' morale and work-discipline during the war years help to shed light on the political significance of economically-based conflict in industry and also demonstrate the increasing role of coercion in the 'containment' of the German working class. In this chapter, I shall first outline the main influences on workers' morale and sketch developments during the war years; I shall then trace develop-

ments in work-discipline after 1939; then try to give a picture of how
workers' morale and developments in work-discipline were perceived
by industrialists and state functionaries; and then examine the changing
patterns of coercion in the war economy. I shall conclude by
attempting to assess the political significance of developments in
workers' morale and work-discipline during the war.

Developments in Workers' Morale, 1939-45

Recent research on popular opinion in the Third Reich has confirmed
the subjective assessment of almost all contemporary observers that the
outbreak of war in September 1939 was greeted with no enthusiasm by
the civilian population. Hitler's foreign policy coups before 1939 had
been popular precisely because they had avoided bloodshed.[9]

German workers seem to have experienced disorientation on the
outbreak of war — the memories of the slaughter of the First World War
concentrated their attention on hopes that they would not be conscripted.[10] The entry of Britain and France into the war was greeted
by dismay. Yet the rapid victory of the *Wehrmacht* over the Polish
armed forces went some way to defusing popular anxiety, achieved
as it had been with light German casualties and accompanied as it was
by Hitler's 'offer of peace' to the western powers in his speech to the
Reichstag in early October 1939.[11] The dissipation of the hopes of the
population for an early peace and the experience of the first war winter
rapidly pushed the victory over Poland into the background as a factor
shaping popular opinion. Discontent with the working of the rationing
system and, above all, as a consequence of the coal-shortage, soon made
itself felt — especially amongst workers. Such working-class discontent
was reinforced by the closure of firms as a consequence of the coal
shortage and transport difficulties. The security services of the regime
noted an increase in Communist underground activity and commented
on the fact that discontent with material conditions was most pronounced in those factories where workers still remained loyal to their
pre-1933 political orientation.[12]

Nor did the mood of the population improve significantly in early
spring 1940. Despite the easy victory over Poland, the population
remained aware that the real test was still to be faced. The invasion of
Denmark and Norway in early April 1940 dominated popular discussion and silenced 'the miserable debate . . . about economic worries and
shortages';[13] but only temporarily, as the popular opinion reports

testify — Goebbels' propaganda ministry spoke of a sharp deterioration in the morale of the population.[14] The cautious mood of the bulk of the population at the beginning of the campaign against the Low Countries in early May 1940 rapidly turned to astonishment at the rapid victories of the *Wehrmacht*; an astonishment which reached its climax as the *Wehrmacht* advanced into France and entered Paris without a shot being fired. Hitler's personal standing amongst all sections of population reached its highest point ever with the conclusion of the armistice with France in mid-June 1940. The popular opinion agencies of the regime noted the massive integrative effect of the victories in the west. In late June 1940, the popular opinion agency of the secret service, the SD, reported that:

> Under the impact of the great political events and as a consequence of the military victories, an unprecedented solidarity has developed between the front and the domestic population, as well as an unprecedented solidarity amongst the whole population. The basis for any effective oppositional activity has been completely removed.[15]

In particular, the SD noted the effect of the victorious campaign on large sections of the working class:

> Within those groups formerly sympathetic to marxism or communism, it is no longer possible to speak of any organised oppositional activity. Here, the military successes have had a particularly crippling effect and nipped in the bud any potential support for organised oppositional activity.[16]

Perhaps only in the summer of 1940 was there ever any widespread enthusiasm for the war. Yet if one probes beneath the surface of the popular opinion reports, it becomes clear that the motives behind this outburst of enthusiasm for the victories of the *Wehrmacht* were to be found more in hopes for an early peace than in enthusiasm for military conquest as such.[17]

It is consequently less than surprising that as it gradually became clear in late summer and early autumn 1940 that the hoped-for invasion of Britain would take place only in 1941 (if at all), the prospect of a second war winter began to depress the morale of the civilian population. In particular, the discontent of German workers was to be traced back to the attempted wages freeze and to increases in the price of foodstuffs. Deterioration in the quality of foodstuffs also led to discontent – expressed by workers through higher absenteeism rates. Nevertheless, it would be premature to speak of a crisis of confidence in the regime amongst broad sections of the German working class: Hitler's promise in January 1941 that the year would see the 'completion of the greatest victory in our history' was interpreted by most Germans as meaning that 1941 would see the end of the war.[18]

Ian Kershaw has documented the development of the 'Hitler-Myth' and has stressed the quasi-religious faith in Hitler's ability demonstrated by large sections of the German population. It is clear that German workers were not immune to the power of this myth and that it was only with the defeat of the *Blitzkrieg* in the winter of 1941-2 that the 'Hitler-Myth' began to disintegrate. Despite the total unpreparedness of the civilian population for the attack on the Soviet Union in June 1941, the initial victories of the *Wehrmacht* served to still any open dissent. Nevertheless, leading circles of both party and state were aware of the extent to which the invasion of the Soviet Union had weakened the expectation of the German population that the war could rapidly be brought to a successful conclusion. In early October 1941, Hitler went so far as to claim publicly that the war against the Soviet Union was already as good as won.[19] Popular opinion reports noted the catastrophic effect on the morale of the civilian population of the call for the collection of winter clothing for the *Wehrmacht*, issued shortly before Christmas 1941. The defeat of the *Blitzkrieg* could not be concealed from the civilian population and combined with the entry of the United States into the war and the assumption by Hitler of personal command of the army to produce the first real crisis of confidence in the regime during the war.[20] The armaments inspectorates of the war-economics and armaments office of the high command (*WiRüAmt*) reported the effect of events on the eastern front on workers' morale: by February 1942, one armaments inspectorate was reporting that workers no longer spoke as frequently as before about the end of the war, adding the optimistic gloss that: 'at last the idea has got through that the length of the war is immaterial and that only final victory is important'.[21]

The defeat of the *Blitzkreig* strategy in December 1941 made clear to the civilian population that it might no longer expect a rapid conclusion of the war; the defeat at Stalingrad barely a year later, led broad sections of the population to conclude that the war was lost. Yet the intervening year saw both impressive German victories in the east and the first signs of a significant loss of confidence in the regime on the part of the civilian population.

That the set-back of December 1941 had shaken the confidence of the population in the leadership and – for the first time – in Hitler, was clear from the lukewarm response to Hitler's speeches of 30 January and 26 April 1942.[22] The slight improvement in the military situation on the eastern front in late winter 1941-2 was offset by the reduction in rations with effect from 6 April 1942. This reduction – according to the SD – led to 'great disappointment and, in working-class circles, to a not inconsiderable unrest'.[23] Many of the regional SD offices reported that the reduction in rations had had a greater effect on civilian morale than any other event during the war; in particular, workers in the larger cities and in industrial areas displayed little understanding for the reductions – their morale had reached a lower point than at any other time during the war.[24] As Ian Kershaw has argued, a subtle reading of the regime's secret popular opinion reports indicates that the 'Hitler-Myth' had already been badly shaken before the catastrophe of Stalingrad. Although the deteriorating military situation – and consequently the disappearance of any prospect of an end to the war – and ration cuts were the main factors shaping working-class morale, the beginnings of the allied air offensive in the west during 1942 also played a part. The full impact of allied air superiority was to be felt by the German civilian population only after the Casablanca conference, but the raids during 1942 on northern and western areas of Germany contributed to the deterioration of workers' morale, as the SD noted.[25]

Stalingrad represented a turning point not only in the military balance of the war, but also in the attitude of the civilian population towards the war and the regime. The contours of working-class morale after January 1943 were to be shaped by the increasing hopelessness of the military situation; by the allied air offensive in the west; by the drive for total mobilisation of all of Germany's human resources for the war effort; and finally by increasing burdens combined with inadequate supplies of food, clothing and housing.

The impact of Stalingrad on the morale of the German civilian population can scarcely be overestimated: as early as February 1943, the SD was speaking of 'the beginnings of a crisis of confidence' in the regime amongst broad sections of the population.[26] By May 1943, the SD had reached the conclusion that:

Many *Volksgenossen* no longer dare to think through the military/political situation, since they believe that this would merely result in them losing heart. In fact, in a not inconsiderable section of the population, despite external composure and blameless behaviour — especially in the field of work — a pessimistic groundswell is unmistakable.[27]

The defeat of the German offensives in the Soviet Union by July 1943 signalled the beginning of the end for the German war effort in the east: by the end of 1943, Soviet forces had recaptured two-thirds of the Soviet territory occupied by the *Wehrmacht*. By spring 1944, the SD concluded that the bulk of the population had given up any attempt to analyse the military situation and were easy prey to all kinds of rumours; some sections of the population were described as being resigned and fatalistic.[28] According to the SD, the bulk of the working population still hoped for some kind of decisive turn in the war and the prospect of peace:[29] such wishful thinking received further blows during the summer of 1944 with the allied landings in the west and the revelation of the long-promised 'revenge' (*Vergeltung*) — in the form of the V1 and V2 weapons — as an illusion.[30]

Although the *Reich*-level popular opinion surveys of the SD do not go beyond July 1944, regional and local material suggests that it was in a mood of increasing fatalism and disorientation that the working population regarded the collapse of the Third Reich during the succeeding nine months, concerned only to survive the inevitable collapse of the regime.[31] In early March 1945, one report on the morale of Hamburg dockworkers assessed the general mood as being simply one of hopelessness.[32]

Hitherto, it has been widely believed that the allied air offensive in the west was counter-productive and played little role in the demoralisation characteristic of the last two years of the war. The turning point in the air war came with the Casablanca conference in January 1943 and the evolution of the 'combined bombing operation'. Between 1942 and 1944, the tonnage of bombs dropped over Germany increased about 25-fold, and by the end of the war perhaps 20 per cent of the pre-war housing stock had been destroyed; in the worst-affected area — north-west Germany (Cologne to Hamburg) — the figure was nearer 40 per cent.[33] Recent research on popular opinion in Bavaria has demonstrated the massive loss of confidence in the regime after mid-1943 as allied bombers reached this part of the *Reich*. The overwhelming response of the civilian population was simply one of war-weariness, a picture which is confirmed by the SD material covering the *Reich* as a whole.[34] The response of German workers was, of course, by no means monolithic – war-weariness mingled with hopes that Goebbels' long-promised revenge would bring a halt to the bombing, and with increasing hostility towards the NSDAP.[35] The fundamental mistake made by allied strategic planners was not a psychological but rather a political one: area bombing *did* lead to a collapse in civilian morale but there was no way in which workers could affect the determination of the regime to carry on fighting to the bitter end.

Working-class hostility towards the NSDAP was fuelled by the transparent social injustice which accompanied the attempts of the regime to mobilise Germany's last reserves for 'total war'. In particular, the thorough mobilisation of the female population for war work in industry came to assume an almost symbolic importance.[36] The attempts – in many cases successful – of middle-class women to seek jobs in offices or with the Red Cross, and frequently the least arduous of such jobs, confirmed the suspicion of working-class men and women that such middle-class women would use their connections to avoid war work in industry and the rigours of 'total war'. By mid-December 1943, the worst fears of German workers seemed to have come true. The number of women who had been able to avoid industrial work remained very large; and it seemed to workers that this situation was hardly surprising granted the capacity of many Party functionaries to secure favourable treatment for their relatives.[37] Moreover, another component of the 'total war' programme – the closure of 'inessential' shops – seemed to have been carried out at the expense of 'the little man', whilst the middle and upper classes seemed to have been successful in avoiding the strictures of the total war economy.[38] The final, total mobilisation of German society from summer 1944 onwards and the creation of the *Volkssturm* – a kind of *levee-en-masse* – in September 1944, came too late: in the eyes of the working population, the Third Reich remained a class society to the very end.[39]

The final factor shaping workers' morale during the war years was the deterioration of the food supply to the civilian population from 1943 onwards. Whilst seasonal shortages of particular foodstuffs – in particular, of potatoes – and ration cuts during 1942 and 1943 had led to considerable discontent, the exploitation of occupied Europe had enabled the regime to secure a relatively high level of nutrition for the civilian population.[40] From 1944 at the latest, however, the deterioration in the adequacy of rations was considerable and gave rise to the expansion of the black market. Finally, in winter 1944-5, the average daily calorie intake of the population sank below the long-term nutritional survival minimum (1,800 calories/day).[41] As one authority noted in early April 1945, 'the morale of the population is determined essentially by the following factors: hunger, the air-terror and the military situation'.[42] The demoralisation of the German working class was complete.

Developments in Work-discipline, 1939-45

How far were developments in the morale of the workforce in German industry during the war reflected in the development of work-discipline? Were there any discernible patterns to be found in these developments? Such concerns are central to the political and social sense we make of developments in work-discipline during the war years. Was a deterioration in work-discipline to be attributed simply to individual action on the part of workers in response to exhaustion, for example, or are there any indicators which would suggest that such behaviour went beyond individual action and might be analysed in terms of class conflict?

Perhaps the first strand detectable in the development of work-discipline during the war years is that a widespread deterioration in work-discipline — rising absenteeism, lower productivity — normally accompanied and was a response to the initiation by the regime of policies which workers considered to be damaging to their interests, interests understood in the widest sense of the term. The classic case is the response of German workers to the War Economy Decree of 4 September 1939, which foresaw the abolition of overtime bonuses and bonuses for Sunday- and night-shift working, a depression of wages and the suspension of provisions regulating working hours and conditions.[43] Workers responded to the provisions of the decree by making use of one of the few weapons left to them — an informal withdrawal of labour, taking the form of increased absenteeism and sickness rates. The scale of this defensive campaign by the German working class rapidly assumed alarming proportions. By November 1939, for example, the armaments inspectorate in Münster was reporting that the Labour Trustee in Essen had over 1,000 cases of breach of work-discipline to deal with.[44] Reports from large industrial concerns confirmed the picture: the Krupp smelting firm in Rheinhausen faced increasing difficulties with workers guilty of absenteeism, as did a firm in Gelsenkirchen where 'a large proportion' of the workforce was guilty of absenteeism, despite the imposition of fines for such breaches of work-discipline.[45] A survey of large armaments plants in Berlin by the Berlin

armaments inspectorate in mid-November 1939 revealed that absenteeism and sickness rates were significantly higher on Saturdays than on
either Fridays or Mondays — a deterioration in the health of the workforce would have led to fairly uniform rates.[46] What was taking place
was a massive — if covert — campaign of passive resistance.

It is against this background that the easing of many of the provisions of the War Economy Decree is to be seen. The need to restore
an incentive to carry out overtime, night-shift and Sunday working, as
well as to halt the deterioration in work-discipline — acknowledged by
one state official to have all the characteristics of 'sabotage' — was one
of the main concerns of a *Reich*-level meeting in early November 1939
to discuss the question of bonus payments.[47] Indeed, the gradual withdrawal of the regime from the position it had adopted at the beginning
of the war bears all the hall-marks of a retreat in the face of massive
popular opposition. As the armaments inspectorates reported in
December 1939, the re-introduction of bonuses for Sunday- holiday-
and night-shift working seems to have gone some way to appeasing
workers and to have defused what had seemed to be potential mass
opposition to the policies of the regime in the social and economic
sphere.[48]

In this case, at any rate, developments in work-discipline must be
seen in the wider context of the policies of the regime towards the
working class. Such developments were also closely related to the
development of workers' morale. In the autumn and winter of 1941-2,
for example, all the authorities involved in the maintenance of work-
discipline and workers' productivity noted a sharp decline in work-
discipline. Thus, the Berlin armaments inspectorate reported a general
rise in absenteeism and sickness rates as early as September 1941; and
a meeting of insurance company doctors in the Berlin area concluded
that, in the light of recent sickness rates, perhaps only 20 per cent of
those registering sick were actually unfit for work — the rest were
guilty of absenteeism.[49] In some firms, the sickness rates had risen to
25 per cent of the workforce; and rising sickness rates were accompanied by a deterioration in work-discipline — the number of cases of
breach of labour-discipline reported to the labour authorities had risen
by up to 50 per cent.[50] The situation was little different in the Ruhr or
Saxony.[51] In this instance, the authorities had no hesitation in tracing
the deterioration in work-discipline back to the prospect of a third war
winter and the disappearance of any hope of a rapid conclusion to the
war.[52]

In other words, during the period of the *Blitzkrieg*, crises in work-discipline tended to coincide with the initiation by the regime of policies which workers perceived as damaging to their interests: in the first instance, an offensive against working-class living standards; in the second, a prolongation of a war with which the German working class had little sympathy. After 1942, the war affected German workers more immediately — the Allied air offensive in the west, evacuation, ration cuts and the disappearance of any prospect of an end to the war. The growth of war weariness during and after 1942 documented above, combined with material deprivation, disorientation and the extension o of terror and coercion into every aspect of daily life to produce a disintegration of the collective consciousness and solidarity of the German working class. Adult male German workers gradually came to constitute an elite within the workforce and this combined with a basic defensive patriotism to preclude widespread campaigns of passive opposition.

The relationship between the policies of the regime, the interests of workers and the development of work-discipline is nevertheless clear throughout the war in the behaviour of three groups of workers singled-out by all authorities concerned with labour mobilisation and allocation as being characterised by particularly poor work-discipline: female workers, young male workers and civil conscripts (*Dienstverpflichtete*).

Everywhere, armaments firms employing mainly female workers reported lower productivity and higher sickness and absenteeism rates than those employing mainly male workers. The Münster armaments inspectorate, for example, reported in February 1940 that one Westphalian firm employing 400 women had become accustomed to expect 75 workers to absent themselves on any one day.[53] Another, *Luftwaffe*-supervised, firm reported in late 1940/early 1941 that of its 845 female workers, 22 per cent were absent on any one day; starting from a working week of 54 hours, the firm calculated that as a consequence up to 10,000 working hours were being lost each week.[54] Nor was this exceptional — in January 1941, the armaments commando in Nuremberg reported absenteeism and sickness rates amongst the female workforce of up to 25 per cent.[55] That the poor work-discipline of female workers was a response to their general situation as well as to specific policy initiatives on the part of the regime, is demonstrated by the continuity of poor work-discipline throughout the war.[56]

The roots of the problem were to be found in the profound unattractiveness of industrial work to women — an unattractiveness which was compounded by the social policies of the regime. Less than 5 per cent of the female workforce in industrial employment in 1936 had been skilled and despite retraining schemes both before and during the war, this figure probably rose only slightly.[57] Large wage differentials between male and female workers, and the concentration of women in the more poorly-paid sections of industry, gave women little incentive to remain in industrial employment once they married.[58] The social policies pursued by the regime after the outbreak of war gave many women the option of abandoning industrial employment: the wives of conscripts into the *Wehrmacht* received a 'family support allowance' of up to 85 per cent of their husbands' former earnings – a measure designed to avoid a repetition of the demoralisation of soldiers at the front which had occurred during the 1914-18 war when such allowances had been set at such a level as to force the wives of soldiers onto the labour market.[59]

Many female industrial workers were able to exploit the contradiction between the two distinct policy objectives of the regime – to gain female workers for industry on the one hand and to prevent widespread demoralisation of serving members of the *Wehrmacht* on the other – to their advantage. Between June 1939 and March 1940 alone, 540,000 women left insured employment.[60] Those women who remained trapped in industrial employment after September 1939, whether as a consequence of lack of economic choice or of the refusal of the local labour office to agree to their abandonment of industrial work, gave vent to their discontent through consistently poor work-discipline. The failure of the regime to mobilise the whole of the adult female population for the war effort merely strengthened the conviction of those women who were trapped in industrial employment that they constituted a social group which was being consistently discriminated against[61] If anything, the problems which such women experienced – the double burden of trying to run a household under difficult war-time conditions combined with exhausting industrial work – grew steadily worse as the war went on.

Civil conscripts constituted another group singled-out by the labour authorities as being characterised by particularly poor work-discipline. Civil conscription (*Dienstverpflichtung*) pre-dated the war and was intended as a mechanism whereby workers could be directed to priority projects by the labour authorities. Thus, over 800,000 workers had received civil conscription orders before September 1939 – over half of them being drafted to work on the West Wall fortifications.[62] In the first twelve days of the war, a further 500,000 workers received such orders – despite poor experiences with the productivity and work-discipline of civil conscripts.[63] The armaments inspectorates singled-out civil conscripts as a particularly troublesome group and in mid-

November 1939, Hitler himself intervened in the matter ordering a reduction in the use of civil conscription orders.[64] The programme reached its high point in January 1940, when there were 1.4 million civil conscripts.[65] The gradual reduction in the use of civil conscription after this point was less a consequence of a more total mobilisation of labour for the war effort than of a calculated attempt by the regime to restrict what was clearly a very unpopular measure to a minimum. By mid-April 1942, there remained only 640,000 civil conscripts, of whom 210,000 were women.[66]

The origins of the poor work-discipline which characterised civil conscripts are not difficult to trace. Leaving aside separation from their families, the main cause of discontent amongst civil conscripts was the loss of earnings many of them experienced in their new jobs, and the standard and cost of the accommodation made available to them. The civil conscription system was clearly open to much abuse: the Stuttgart armaments inspectorate reported the complaints of skilled workers who had been conscripted to supposedly priority projects in north Germany only to be set to work on semi-skilled work – in one particularly crass case, a skilled fitter had been given unskilled conveyor-belt work.[67] In another area, the armaments inspectorate described the work-discipline of civil conscripts as being characterised by open 'resistance'.[68] Tactless handling of such workers by the labour authorities merely reinforced their sense of anger: one authority concluded that 'civilians are not soldiers who can simply be given orders. The impression created in those affected is of unnecessary hardship and lack of planning.'[69] The same authority reported a fortnight later that one firm had called in the Gestapo to break up a demonstration by civil conscripts at the local railway station, at which they had demanded the right to return to their old factories.[70]

Everywhere, workers who had been drafted to other firms were seen as disruptive of the work-morale and work-discipline of the permanent workforce. In October 1939, the armaments inspectorate in Saxony reported that civil conscripts were largely responsible for the doubling of sickness and absenteeism rates in a whole range of firms; they constituted 'a permanent source of awkwardness and poor work-discipline'.[71] It is against this background that the gradual reduction in the use of civil conscription orders after autumn 1939 must be seen.

Young workers made up the third group of workers singled-out by the labour authorities as being characterised by poor work-discipline throughout the war. It is important to note that this group overlapped heavily with the female workforce – the age-range 18-25 was very heavily represented amongst the female workforce as a whole. The authorities attributed the poor work-discipline of young male workers to the frustration experienced by such workers at their continued employment in industry, when they might have been serving with the *Wehrmacht*; and from summer 1940 onwards, the loss experienced by industry as many apprentices volunteered for service in the *Wehrmacht* was to be considerable.[72] The authorities also noted the absence of paternal authority as a consequence of conscription. Perhaps the partial success of the regime's youth policies in dissolving the ties of traditional socialisation agencies, in particular of the family, also played a role – a suggestion which finds some confirmation in the general increase in juvenile crime during the early stages of the war.[73] Nevertheless, it is significant that young male workers were able to exploit the contradictions between the various policies of the regime to their advantage – thus, young miners or apprentices in the ship-building industry volunteered in large numbers for the motorised sections of the *Wehrmacht*, and especially for the navy and airforce, in an attempt to find a way out of monotonous and often ill-paid employment often with an eye to gaining a skill which would enable them to seek better-paid work once the war was over.[74]

What emerges from the sketch above of some of the developments in work-discipline during the war, is that absenteeism, reporting sick more frequently and other phenomena grouped by the officials of the regime under the general heading of 'poor work-discipline' were not isolated examples of individual awkwardness and uncooperativeness. These informal protests characterised *particular sections* of the workforce in German industry *throughout* the war, and the *whole* of the workforce at *particular times*. The coincidence of such informal protest with offensives against working-class living standards, or the initiation by the regime of policies which the workers directly affected perceived as running contrary to their interests, demands that we analyse informal protest in terms of class behaviour, often motivated by a common awareness of common interests.

The Regime's Perception of Working-class Informal Protest

The very ideology of the *Volksgemeinschaft* militated against any open acknowledgement by the regime that working-class informal protest reflected the continuation of class struggle into the war period. In the first instance, the regime fell back on a crude version of the labour reserve army theory: poor work-discipline was simply a consequence of the labour shortage — 'asocial' workers, workers who would never otherwise have found employment, were now being drawn into industry.[75] Yet, parallel to this, the authorities were also concerned to investigate all strikes, or other forms of collective protest, apparently relating only to material concerns, to try to find traces of Communist or social-democratic inspiration.[76] In other words, the authorities were reluctant to admit openly that collective informal protest might be initiated by large groups of workers themselves.

Occasionally, however, the language of class slips through the ideological and political net. Significantly, a more realistic appraisal of the true causes of working-class informal protest came most frequently from those sections of the state bureaucracy most immediately concerned with the problems caused by such protests and from the firms themselves. The armaments inspectorates were unanimous in attributing the crisis of work-discipline which occurred in autumn 1939 to the offensive launched by the regime at the beginning of the war against working-class living standards. Similarly, the inspectorates accurately located the origins of the deterioration in work-discipline which occurred during the autumn and winter of 1941-2 in the frustration of working-class hopes for an early end to the war, as a consequence of the invasion of the Soviet Union.[77] During the autumn 1939 crisis, one firm had spoken out against any further 'depression of wages or deterioration in the income of the working *class*'.[78] Another had described the behaviour of its workforce as amounting to a kind of 'concealed strike'.[79] If both the armaments inspectorates and employers were amongst the strongest advocates of the increased use of terror to halt the collapse of work-discipline, this was less because they believed that isolated acts of terror against 'asocial' workers would solve the problem than because they hoped that if an example were made of a small number of workers the rest would learn the prudential lesson; and in many cases, the exemplary intervention of the Gestapo *did* produce a *general* improvement in work-discipline.[80]

In many cases, problems with work-discipline were interpreted at the highest levels as essentially collective protest. Thus, in November 1942, the head of the Economic Group Air Industry felt obliged to draw attention to the problem of rising sickness and absenteeism rates in the aircraft industry. Noting sickness rates amongst the workforce of 10.1 per cent in June 1942, rising to 13 per cent in September 1942, he commented that, even allowing for the deterioration in food supply and the increasing burdens being placed on the workforce, such sickness rates must be interpreted as 'a kind of strike [pursued by] other means and in different ways'.[81] Speer, an advocate of the most brutal measures to maintain work-discipline, was also concerned with the effect of exemplary terror on the workforce as a whole. In October 1942, he suggested that: 'the SS and police could intervene sharply and transfer those workers notorious as absentees to concentration camp factories . . . There's no other way. It need only happen a few times; the news would soon spread.'[82] Occasionally, the language of the *Volksgemeinschaft* itself could be eloquent. In October 1942, concluding a survey of problem with work-discipline, the SD commented: 'the concrete achievement of the *right* to work has not been accompanied by any conversion of the working population to the National Socialist concept of the *obligation* to work.'[83] The rhetoric of the *Volksgemeinschaft* could, in any case, be a double-edged weapon. Thus, the women who remained in industrial employment after September 1939 were able to use the language of the *Volksgemeinschaft* to demand greater social justice in labour mobilisation policies – as the reports of the SD on the subject eloquently testify. In other words, the SD reports reflected the awareness of such women of themselves as a group which was being consistently discriminated against by the regime, and the reports interpreted the poor work-discipline of such female workers as being, to at least some extent, a form of class-based behaviour.[84]

The Response of the Regime to Working-class Informal Protest: Terror and Coercion, 1939-45

If the conflict between the ideology of the *Volksgemeinschaft* and economic and social reality conspired to produce a certain ambiguity in the construction placed on workers' informal protest by the regime, the response of the regime to such protest was less ambiguous.

The basic criminalisation of labour law pre-dated the war; and if the regime was prepared to make concessions (as in late autumn 1939) when confronted by mass working-class opposition, it is signiciant that the importance of those institutions formally charged with the task of integrating the German working class into the *Volksgemeinschaft* declined from 1939 onwards. In particular, the importance of the German Labour Front (DAF), declined during the war years. On the one hand, workers had little confidence in the effectiveness of the DAF as a representative of their interests – one regional SD post reported in

March 1941 that the workforce had little trust in the 'councils of trust' (established after 1933 in most firms to regulate relations between workers and management) and saw in the DAF simply an organisation which took money out of their pay-packets, but otherwise represented only the interests of the employers.[85] On the other hand, employers had a low opinion of the DAF's capacity to maintain work-discipline – employers in the Hamburg area complained in 1941 that the DAF contented itself simply with pep-talks to the workforce, and called for an extension of the powers available to employers to punish workers guilty of absenteeism.[86]

By 1941, in any case, in most areas employers had already resorted to coercion as a means of maintaining work-discipline. In reporting combined sickness and absenteeism rates of up to 35 per cent in some sections of one large firm in late September 1939, the Berlin armaments inspectorate stressed the urgent need for both 'educative' and punitive measures – in that order: barely six weeks later, in November 1939, the same inspectorate merely noted that the firm had already consulted the Gestapo and was calling for the exemplary punishment of some workers.[87] In December 1939, the regional authorities of the Labour Ministry responsible for regulating wages, working conditions and work-discipline, the Labour Trustees, had received the right to bring cases against workers before the criminal courts; and in February 1940, a so-called 'accelerated procedure' was introduced to facilitate proceedings against workers – the courts had found themselves unable to cope with the numbers of cases of breach of contract brought before them.[88]

Behind the structure of fines by employers, warnings from the labour authorities and court cases against workers, stood the Gestapo. Employers frequently turned to the Gestapo with the request that individual workers to be taken into 'protective custody' (*Schutzhaft*), and the length of time for which a worker might be detained by the Gestapo had been increased from ten days to three weeks in early October 1939, as such a procedure became a more commonly-used or 'preventive' or 'educative' action.[89] The chaos produced by the attempts of employers to bypass the Labour Trustee and involve the Gestapo directly in their attempts to maintain work-discipline, led to Himmler's decision to order the Gestapo to withdraw from all cases involving work-discipline offences in spring 1940.[90] The extent to which the Gestapo actually did withdraw from this role seems to have depended largely on the attitude of the regional Labour Trustee. Thus, in Bavaria the withdrawal of the Gestapo was – to the considerable annoyance of both employers and the armaments inspectorates –

apparently complete; in the Ruhr, on the other hand, the Gestapo seems to have remained deeply involved in the maintenance of work-discipline – between January and August 1940, no fewer than 767 workers were taken into protective custody by the Gestapo.[91]

The confusion of the attempts of the various authorities to maintain work-discipline was revealed in a survey by Heydrich in June 1940 of the methods used to combat poor work-discipline and breach of contract during the first six months of 1940. Heydrich noted that involvement of the Labour Trustees or their deputies occurred in only a small proportion of the cases: in a large proportion of cases, the DAF, the NSDAP, local police and even the factory inspectorate were brought in by employers – Heydrich's concern being that such authorities were, he believed, unable to assess poor work-discipline from the security angle. Under an agreement reached between Heydrich and the Ministry of Labour in mid-June 1940, all cases of persistent absenteeism or breach of contract reported to the Gestapo were henceforth to be passed on in writing to the appropriate Labour Trustee or his deputies. The Labour Trustee was then to decide whether such cases could be dealt with within the firm concerned or whether he need intervene to warn or fine the worker involved. If the trustee decided that the intervention of the Gestapo was necessary, the latter should decide whether a warning would suffice or whether the offending worker should be taken into protective custody for a short spell or even transferred to a concentration camp. If large-scale disturbances of 'industrial peace' were to occur, the Gestapo might intervene immediately. The Labour Trustees were ordered to build up card-index systems to record information about workers brought to their attention; such information might then be passed on to other trustees should the worker concerned change jobs, but might also serve to guarantee some uniformity of sentencing policy.[92]

Far from decreasing the involvement of the Gestapo in the maintenance of work-discipline, the June 1940 agreement seems to have paved the way for a greater involvement. Thus, the number of workers sentenced to a short spell in protective custody by the Labour Trustee in Essen rose from 171 in June 1940 to 499 in August, and remained at a monthly level of between 260 and 320 for the remaining four months of 1940.[93] Similarly, the armaments inspectorate in Nuremberg reported in August 1940 that the recent improvement in work-discipline in the area was to be attributed to the new powers of the Labour Trustee to sentence workers to three weeks detention in protective custody adding that, as a consequence, the Gestapo was over-worked.[94]

The coercive activity of the state in the sphere of labour-discipline was to expand yet further during 1941. Perhaps the most significant innovation during 1941 was the formal recognition and regularisation of the 'labour education camp' (*Arbeitserziehungslager*, AEL) system by Himmler in May 1941. The arrest and detention of 'asocial' elements in special camps had preceded the war; though the first AELs proper were established in 1939-40, initially in connection with the Westwall fortification building programme.[95] Such camps soon sprang up all over Germany. Himmler's regularisation of the AEL system provided that the camps were to be used exclusively to punish workers guilty of labour-discipline offences: they were intended to hold 'work-shy' elements whose behaviour threatened work-morale and was so to be equated with sabotage. In every case, the prior permission of Himmler was essential for the construction of such camps, and the camps were placed clearly under the jurisdiction of the regional SS and police chiefs. The maximum period of detention was to be 56 days and the regime was to be harsh: inmates were to work a minimum of ten and a maximum of twelve hours a day. That the AELs were not simply regional concentration camps is indicated by Himmler's order that inmates were not to be 'annihilated through work'; rather, their detention was for a limited period, they were to receive payment for their work (RM 0.50 per day) and were to sign a contract to this effect. Inmates were 'to be forced to carry out arduous work in order to make them aware of the damage caused to the community by their behaviour, and to educate them to work.'[96] Apart from the obvious attempt to instil work-discipline in inmates, the AELs were clearly intended to intimidate other workers.

Alongside the formal recognition and regularisation of the AEL system, 1941 was also to see the widespread use of a measure designed to combat breaches of work-discipline amongst juvenile workers, the *Jugendarrest*. The scale of the problem is clear from the report of one firm in Frankfurt/Oder: of its 180 juvenile workers, no fewer than 36 had been given verbal or written warnings from the labour authorities between August 1941 and March 1942 — and this figure did not include those young workers against whom the firm had requested the labour authorities to take harsher steps.[97] Under the *Jugendarrest* system, young workers might be detained and set to arduous work for up to a month, or for four successive weekends.[98] Although the procedure had been introduced only in October 1940, by March 1941 the state prosecutor in Nuremberg could report that: 'Generally, widespread use is made of the *Jugendarrest*. Some detention centres are permanently full.'[99] In 1941, the Labour Trustee for Westphalia-Lower Rhine issued 544 requests for the imposition of *Jugendarrest* – a figure which rose to 1,352 for 1942 and to 856 for the first six months of 1943.[100]

Alongside these established procedures, new measures were introduced in autumn 1941 which were intended to accelerate existing procedures designed to punish breaches of work-discipline and to provide them with greater deterrent effect. As early as August 1941, Göring had ordered that the DAF and employers combat every case of absenteeism. Significantly, the procedure which he set out failed to mention the labour trustees and placed the burden of the maintenance of work-discipline on the employer: if workers were found guilty of breaches of work-discipline, they might simply be brought together in penal work battalions.[101] Göring's abrupt intervention succeeded in making the point that employers did not consider the existing powers and procedures of the labour trustees adequate to cope with a crisis in work-discipline. Possibly as a response, a directive from the Labour Ministry in November 1941 stressed the importance of an acceleration of existing procedures: the labour trustees and their deputies were urged to impose severe punishments where they were convinced of the guilt of the worker charged – any objections on the part of the worker concerned were to be left to a complaints procedure. They were also empowered to levy substantial fines – of up to RM 100 – where this seemed appropriate, and employers were urged to make the name, alleged offence and punishment of the worker concerned known as a deterrent to the rest of the workforce.[102]

By late 1941, the structure of state coercion of the workforce was essentially complete. From 1942 onwards, the attention of the state authorities – especially of the Gestapo – was to turn mainly to foreign workers and prisoners-of-war employed in German industry. German workers suspected of labour-discipline offences were increasingly dealt with through the courts, whilst the labour education camps were to become the preserve of foreign workers. Table 6.1 indicates the increasing reliance of the authorities on the courts and the decreasing reliance on the Gestapo in the maintenance of the work-discipline of German workers.

In this area, requests that German workers to be taken into protective custody by the Gestapo had fallen to 24 per cent of their 1940 level by 1942.

This picture is confirmed by Table 6.2, based on the monthly arrest statistics of the regional Gestapo authorities (*Staatspolizeileitstellen*).

Table 6.1: Disciplinary Measures Taken Against German Workers by the Labour Trustee for Westphalia-Lower Rhine, 1940-3

	1940	1941	1942	1943[a]
Warnings	17,960	24,057	19,611	8,726
Requests for protective custody	2,452	1,771	584	228
Requests for transfer to an AEL	608	1,693	1,361	417
Requests for transfer to a concentration camp	29	50	64	48
Requests for prosecution through the courts	562	1,485	1,733	1,268

Note: a. To June only.
Source: Material in STAM Oberpräsidium/5065 and 5210.

Table 6.2: Arrests by the Gestapo for Labour-discipline Offences, 1941-4

	1 All arrests for 'avoidance of work' (monthly averages)	2 Germans arrested (monthly averages)	3 2 as a % of 1
January to December 1941	6,083	1,416	23,3
May to August 1942	21,521	1,566	7,3
January to September 1943	31,042	2,108	6,8
January to June 1944	34,324	2,154	6,3

Source: Deutschland im 2. Weltkrieg vol. 4 (Berlin 1981), p. 306

The main outlines of the shift of the burden of coercion onto foreign workers are clear. Whilst the total number of arrests for labour discipline offences rose by 464 per cent between 1941 and 1944, the number of foreigners arrested rose by 589 per cent. During the same period the number of foreign workers and prisoners-of-war in the economy rose by only 136 per cent (from 3 million to 7.1 million).[103] During the period 1941-4, the number of German workers arrested for labour-discipline offences rose by 52 per cent; yet the proportion of those arrested for labour-discipline offences made up by German workers fell dramatically.

From 1942 onwards, innovations in the range of procedures designed to maintain the work-discipline of the German workforce were to take place largely within the firms themselves. The first of these was the provision for the removal of bonus ration cards for those engaged in heavy industrial work from such workers as were considered guilty of absenteeism. Although the threatened removal of such ration cards seems to have been practised in some industries before hand, the use of this disciplinary procedure throughout industry as a whole began only in autumn 1943. Nevertheless, the difficulies involved in such a procedure may well have robbed it of much of its effect. Ley, the head of the DAF, had opposed this measure from the outset; and employers were unanimous that any reduction of *normal* civilian rations was out of the question. The alternative – the removal of tobacco ration stamps and of the bonuses awarded to those living in areas badly affected by bombing – was soon deemed to be too complicated, leaving aside the possible effects on civilian morale.[104]

The expansion of the medical supervisory system within industry (*Vertrauensärztesystem*) formed the second prong of the employers' offensive against what they considered to be excessively high sickness rates. By autumn 1944, there were perhaps 8,000 doctors and a further 90,000 trained personnel involved in the scheme. That the emphasis of the system came increasingly to rest on controlling absenteeism is clear from its being seen as an adjunct to the introduction of control books for each worker; and from the emphasis placed on it by the Plenipotentiary for Labour Mobilisation, *Gauleiter* Sauckel. In at least one case, workers believed that the system resulted in doctors refusing to recognise genuine cases of illness.[105]

The Political Significance of Developments in Workers' Morale and Work-discipline, 1939-45

In my outline above of some of the more salient structures in the development of workers' morale and work-discipline during the war years, I have argued that the phenomena which the authorities grouped under the general heading of 'poor work-discipline' should not be seen simply as an aggregation of individual unco-operativeness or awkwardness. Rather, such informal protest by particular sections of the German workforce throughout the war, and by the whole of the workforce at particular times, should be seen as grass-roots protest by workers against policies they conceived to be contrary to their interests – interests understood in the widest sense of the term. Further, that such widespread informal protest was characterised by a common perception of common interests on the part of the workers involved, and that we should consequently analyse such behaviour in terms of *class*.

Critics of the attempt to use the categories of class to analyse
workers' attempts to defend their interests during the pre-war period,
have consistently argued that the weapons used by workers — especially
going absent and reporting sick more frequently — are characteristic of
any society enjoying full employment and that such *individual* forms of
protest cannot be seen as resistance to any particular regime.[106] In
other words, such behaviour is essentially devoid of any political content. Leaving aside any methodological defects in such an approach —
that it tacitly assumes as the norm a sociology of integration and
stability rather than one of conflict, an assumption which is nowhere
made explicit or justified — such criticism seems to be both ahistorical
and to advance too narrow a concept of what constitutes political
behaviour. It ignores the circumstances under which workers were
forced to attempt to protect their common interests — the impossi-
bility of an open statement of their objectives. Clearly, such circumstances are crucial to the construction we place on workers' informal
protest — absenteeism and informal strikes in the Third Reich, with
the constant threat of immediate and savage reprisals, have a political
significance different to that of similar phenomena in the British war
economy, let alone in post-war Western liberal-democratic societies.
The historically-specific politicisation from above by the regime of
such phenomena should make us wary of broad ahistorical comparisons.

This is not to argue that informal protest by German workers during
the war years was political protest in the narrower sense of the term.
The most recent studies of the political activity of the KPD after 1933
suggest that the sacrifices made by tens of thousands of Communists in
the attempt to politicise workers' discontent to the stage where this
would threaten to topple the Nazi regime, were out of all proportion to
their results.[107] The SPD had a clearer and more realistic view of the
limits to such activity: from the mid-1930s at the latest, former
members of the SPD concentrated on the one political aim they might
realistically hope to achieve — the maintenance of the political awareness of sympathetic workers through informal meetings in pubs and
clubs, whilst they waited for the toppling of the regime from outside.[108]

All the evidence suggests that the bulk of the German working class
stood closer to the position adopted by the SPD than that adopted by
the KPD. The majority even of those workers who were former members of the KPD did not follow the instructions of their leadership
underground or in exile to carry out illegal work. Similarly, recent
studies of the working class in Augsburg and of the Bavarian mining

community of Penzberg reveal few acts of sabotage inspired by the KPD.[109] The bulk of German workers drew on their class experience and common sense in shaping their industrial behaviour after 1933; and the pragmatic sobriety which characterised their attempts to protect their material interests left little room for spectacular and dangerous acts of defiance. Workers started from their immediate material situation – principally, the state of the labour market and the possibilities of collective action within their places of work – in their attempt to defend their interests. After all, even after 1942 workers possessed *some* scope for collective action. The very logic of the labour mobilisation process itself gave them some room for manoeuvre – the labour authorities stressed that, in the light of the labour shortage, removal of workers from the labour process as a punishment for persistently poor work-discipline was to be a last resort. In 1944, one authority reported that employers were reluctant to bring charges against young workers guilty of absenteeism and so risk the loss of the worker concerned.[110] Workers were occasionally able to turn the language and laws of the *Volksgemeinschaft* itself to their advantage. In February 1944, a group of workers in a tank factory in Dortmund launched a one-hour strike against the announcement by the management of a lengthening of the working day by one hour. In this case, the strike was successful – the workers were able to exploit a legal technicality in the issuing of the notice, the proposed extension of the working day was cancelled and, aside from small fines, the strikers remained unpunished.[111]

Martin Broszat has recently suggested the need for a broadening of our concept of resistance to the Nazi regime. He argues that the regime had effectively monopolised public political life by the summer of 1933, and that, as a consequence, any effective resistance could only be rooted in a stable *social* base outside the public sphere; and advocates the notion of 'structural resistance' as the most useful tool to analyse the relationship between the regime and the population during the Third Reich. On this reading, any blocking of the aspiration of the regime to total control of society constituted a form of resistance.[112]

Clearly, the developments in workers' work-discipline sketched above are a prime candidate for classification as such a form of resistance. Whether *intention* on the part of the workers involved can be demonstrated or not, workers' informal protest and attempts to defend their interests objectively *functioned* to restrict rearmament before 1939, the shift to a total war economy before 1942, and the working at full capacity of the war economy after 1942. Nazi functionaries and

German industrialists were aware of this, and their response – massive coercion of the German working class – is indicative of the significance they attached to such protest. That the transition from informal defence of economic and social interests to the public formulation of clearly political demands is not an impossible one has been demonstrated by the recent history of the Polish working class. That such a transition never occurred in Germany between 1933 and 1945 is to be traced back principally to the – perhaps typical – combination of brutal coercion and the attempt to create a consensus through strategic concessions which characterised the policies of the Nazi regime towards the German working class.

Notes

* The research on which this article is based was made possible by the generous financial support I received from the Freiherr-vom-Stein Stiftung, Hamburg. I am also grateful to Tim Mason and Jeremy Noakes who read an earlier draft of this article and who, from their different positions made many helpful comments. I have benefited greatly from my conversations with Ian Kershaw, Peter Lambert and Wolfgang Werner about the issues discussed in the article. Wolfgang Werner's doctoral thesis "Bleib Ubrig! Deutsche Arbeiter in der nationalsozialistischen Kriegswirtschaft'. Bochum 1981) discusses many of these issues, though from a different perspective.

1. T.W. Mason, *Sozialpolitik im Dritten Reich. Arbeiterklasse und Volksgemeinschaft* (Opladen, 1977), pp. 15-41.
2. Ibid., Ch. 2. Jeremy Noakes, *The Nazi Party in Lower Saxony 1921-1933* (London, 1971), esp. pp. 174-82. and Wilfried Böhnke, *Die NSDAP im Ruhrgebiet 1920-1933* (Bonn Bad Godesberg, 1974), also make this point.
3. See the discussion in Mason, *Sozialpolitik*, Ch. 3; Martin Broszat, *Der Staat Hitlers* (Munich, 1969), pp. 180-4.
4. The material situation of the German working class between 1933 and 1936 is summarised in Mason, *Sozialpolitik*, pp. 124-73.
5. Tim Mason, 'The Workers' Opposition in Nazi Germany', *History Workshop Journal*, no. 11 (spring 1981), pp. 120-37, here p. 120.
6. Ibid.
7. The most trenchant critique along these lines is Ludolf Herbst, 'Die Krise des nationalsozialistischen Regimes am Vorabend des Zweiten Weltkrieges und die forcierte Aufrüstung', *Vierteljahrshefte für Zeitgeschichte* no. 26 (1978), pp. 347-92.
8. This was the position adopted by the SPD in exile (Sopade) in its reports on the working-class in Germany. See *Deutschland-Berichte der Sozialdemokratischer Partei Deutschlands* (Sopade) (7 vols., Frankfurt am Main, 1980). See esp. Jg. 6, 12 July 1939 A77-96, pp. 757-78.
9. Ian Kershaw, *Der Hitler-Mythos: Volksmeinung und Propaganda im Dritten Reich* (Stuttgart, 1980), esp. pp. 113-23; also Marlis Steinert, *Hitlers Krieg und die Deutschen. Stimmung und Haltung der deutschen Bevölkerung im Zweiten Weltkrieg* (Düsseldorf, 1970), p. 91f.
10. *Deutschland-Berichte*, Jg. 6, 2 December 1939 A16-25, pp. 1034-43 g. 'es

a good impression of this general disorientation.
   11. Steinert, *Hitlers Krieg*, pp. 92, 108f. Kershaw, *Hitler-Mythos*, pp. 125-8.
   12. Steinert, *Hitlers Krieg*, pp. 113f, 119-22; Kershaw, *Hitler-Mythos*, p. 129;
Heinz Boberach (ed.), *Meldungen aus dem Reich. Auswahl aus den geheimen
Lageberichten des Sicherheitsdienstes der SS 1939-44* (Neuwied and Berlin
1965), pp. 13f, 31f, 34-6.
   13. Boberach, *Meldungen*, p. 59.
   14. Ibid., pp. 61f; Steinert, *Hitlers Krieg*, p. 124.
   15. Boberach, *Meldungen*, p. 77; Kershaw, *Hitler-Mythos*, pp. 136-8;
Steinert, *Hitlers Krieg*, pp. 131-6.
   16. Boberach, *Meldungen*, p. 78; Steinert, *Hitlers Krieg*, pp. 136f.
   17. Kershaw, *Hitler Mythos*, p. 138.
   18. Ibid.
   19. Ibid., pp. 139f, 150-2.
   20. Steinert, *Hitlers Krieg*, pp. 263-73; Boberach, *Meldungen*, pp. 202-6;
Kershaw, *Hitler Mythos* pp. 152f.
   21. MA RW20-11/28, 13 February 1942.
   22. Kershaw, *Hitler Mythos*, pp. 157-9; Steinert, *Hitlers Krieg*, pp. 283f.
   23. Boberach, *Meldungen*, pp. 242.
   24. Ibid., pp. 242f.
   25. Kershaw, *Hitler Mythos*, pp. 176f.
   26. Boberach, *Meldungen*, p. 358.
   27. Ibid., p. 387.
   28. Ibid., p. 503.
   29. Ibid., p. 509.
   30. Ibid., pp. 529f.
   31. Kershaw, *Hitler Mythos*, pp. 186-94; Steinert, *Hitlers Krieg*, section IV,
pp. 455-586.
   32. Steinert, *Hitlers Kireg*, p. 564.
   33. R.J. Overy, *The Air War 1939-1945* (London, 1980), p. 120; Marie-Luise
Recker, 'Wohnen und Bombardierung im Zweiten Weltkrieg' in Lutz Niethammer
(ed.), *Wohnen im Wandel. Beiträge zur Geschichte des Alltags in der bürgerlichen
Gesellschaft* (Wuppertal, 1979), pp. 408-28, here p. 410.
   34. Kershaw, *Hitler Mythos*, pp. 177-80.
   35. Gerald Kirwin, 'Waiting for Retaliation – a Study in Nazi Propaganda
Behaviour and German Civilian Morale', *Journal of Contemporary History* vol.
16/3 (July 1981), pp. 565-83.
   36. Dörte Winkler, *Frauenarbeit im Dritten Reich* (Hamburg, 1977) is the
most thorough treatment of the subject. See especially Ch. 7, pp. 134-53. See
also Leila J. Rupp, *Mobilising Women for War: German and American Propaganda
1939-45* (Princeton, 1978) and 'Klassenzugehörigkeit und Arbeitseinsatz der
Frauen im Dritten Reich', *Soziale Welt* vols. 31/2 (1980), pp. 191-205.
   37. Winkler, *Frauenarbeit*, pp. 135-8. Boberach, *Meldungen*, p. 373.
   38. Boberach, *Meldungen*, pp. 470f.
   39. On the impact of the formation of the *Volkssturm* on popular opinion,
see Steinert, *Hitlers Krieg*, pp. 501f, 506-9.
   40. Lothar Burchardt, 'Die Auswirkungen der Kriegswirtschaft auf die deutsche
Zivilbevölkerung im Ersten und im Zweiten Weltkrieg': *Militärgeschichtliche
Mitteilungen*, vol. 1/74, pp. 65-97, here pp. 78-82.
   41. Ibid., pp. 75f.
   42. Steinert, *Hitlers Krieg*, p. 570.
   43. T.W. Mason, *Arbeiterklasse und Volksgemeinschaft. Dokumente und
Materialien zur deutschen Arbeiterpolitik 1936-9* (Opladen, 1975), pp. 1074-83.
Mason, *Sozialpolitik*, pp. 295f.

44. MA RW20-16/17, Lagebericht 22 November 1939.

45. Ibid.

46. MA WilF.5.1222, Rüstungsinspektion des Wehrkreises III to WiRüAmt, OKW 9 December 1939 Anlage 1.

47. Mason, *Arbeiterklasse*, doc. 224 pp. 1183-7.

48. MA RW20-6/17, Lagebericht 20 December 1939; MA RW20-10/26, Lagebericht 6 December 1939; MA RW20-13/10, Lagebericht 20 December 1939.

49. MA RW20-3/16, 16 September 1941.

50. MA RW21-16/6, p. 124 Monatsbericht, 5 August 1941; MA RW21-16/8, Monatsbericht 6 December 1941; ibid., 15 November 1941; ibid., 15 December 1941.

51. See the material in files MA RW20-6/22 and MA RW20-4/13.

52. Ibid.

53. MA RW20-6/17, 21 February 1940.

54. MA RW20-13/11, 13 January 1940.

55. Martin Broszat, Elke Fröhlich and Falk Wiesemann (eds.), *Bayern in der NS-Zeit. Soziale Lage und politisches Verhalten der Bevölkerung im Spiegel vertraulicher Berichte* (Munich and Vienna, 1977), p. 295.

56. See Winkler, *Frauenarbeit*, pp. 92-101, 110-14.

57. T.W. Mason, 'Women in Nazi Germany 2', *History Workshop Journal* vol. 2 (autumn 1976), pp. 5-32, here pp. 8f.

58. In 1939, the weekly wages of a skilled or semi-skilled man in German industry were more than double those of a skilled female industrial worker; those of an unskilled male worker 50 per cent higher than those of an unskilled female industrial worker. Ibid., p. 9.

59. Winkler, *Frauenarbeit*, pp. 102f; Mason, 'Women 2', pp. 18f.

60. Mason, 'Women 2', pp. 21f.

61. See Rupp, 'Klassenzugehörigkeit' pp. 202f.

62. Mason, *Arbeiterklasse*, p. 667f.

63. Ibid., p. 737.

64. Ibid., pp. 157f, 1220ff (document 240). Berenice A. Carroll, *Design for Total War. Arms and Economics in the Third Reich* (The Hague, 1968), p. 204.

65. D. Petzina, 'Soziale Lage der deutschen Arbeiter und Probleme des Arbeitseinsatzes während des Zweiten Weltkrieges' in W. Dlugoborski (ed.), *Zweiter Weltkrieg und sozialer Wandel* (Göttingen, 1981), pp. 65-86, here p. 71.

66. BA R26 I/18, p. 54. 'Ergebnisse der Vierjahresplan-Arbeit. Ein Kurzbericht nach dem Stande von Frühjahr 1942 (Arbeitseinsatz).'

67. MA RW20-5/6, 23 January 1940.

68. MA RW20-4/12, 6 March 1940.

69. MA RW20-5/6, 21 November 1939.

70. Ibid. 5 December 1939.

71. MA RW20-4/11, 25 November 1939.

72. E.g. MA RW20-4/13, 14 January 1941. One medium-sized Hamburg shipyard reported in spring 1941 that, whilst 11.5 per cent of the apprentices who had begun their training in 1939 had been conscripted, 38.5 per cent had volunteered for the *Wehrmacht*. BA R11/1234. 'Industrie u. Handelskammer Hamburg to Reichswirtschaftskammer 16 May 1941 betr: Abwanderung der Lahrlinge aus den Betrieben.'

73. BA R22/1160. 'Die Entwicklung der Kriminalität im Deutschen Reich vom Kriegsbeginn bis Mitt 1943 (Statistisches Reichsamt, Berlin 1944).'

74. This was especially the case in coal-mining. The number of apprentices volunteering for the *Wehrmacht* from shipyards in the Hamburg area seems to have varied greatly, being lower in larger firms which might have been able to offer better working conditions. See n. 72.

75. Mason, 'Workers' Opposition', p. 128.

76. Ibid., pp. 124f.

77. MA RW20-4/13, 13 September 1941; MA RW20-4/14, 14 January 1942; MA RW20-13/13, 13 January 1942.

78. MA WiIF.5. 1222. 'Rüstingsinspektion des Wehrkreises III to *WiRüAmt*, OKW' 9 December 1939 Anlage 6. My emphasis.

79. Mason, *Arbeiterklasse*, p. 169.

80. E.g. MA RW20-10/26, 6 December 1939.

81. BA R41/228, pp. 27f. 'Der Leiter der Wirtschaftsgruppe Luftfahrtindustrie to Staatssekretär der Luftfahrt und Generalinspekteur, Milch', 20 November 1942.

82. BA R3/1697, p. 17. Zentrale Planung: Stenographischer Bericht der 21. Besprechung betr: Arbeitseinsatz, 30 October 1942.

83. BA R58. 'SD Meldungen aus dem Reich Nr. 324' (8 October 1942).

84. Rupp, 'Klassenzugehörigkeit' pp. 199f.

85. Broszat (ed.), *Bayern I*, p. 617.

86. MA RW20-10/27, 15 May 1941; ibid., 13 September 1941.

87. MA RW20-3/12, 28 September 1939; ibid., 9 November 1939.

88. Mason, *Sozialpolitik*, p. 320; *Arbeiterklasse*, doc. 244, pp. 1231f. BA R22/3373, p. 11. 'Oberlandesgericht Kiel to Reichsjustizministerium', 30 March 1940.

89. BA R58/1027. Heydrich to Geheime Staatspolizeiamt, 4 October 1939.

90. Winkler, *Frauenarbeit*, p. 226 fn 90.

91. HSTAD R37/HSSPF Karton 2: 'Reichstreuhänder der Arbeit für das Wirtschaftsgebiet Westfalen-Niederrhein to Höhere SS- und Polizeiführer West', 16 August 1940.

92. BA NS6/456 RSHA. IVB (Heydrich) to Staatspolizeileitstellen 14 June 1940 betr: Massnahmen gegen Arbeitsuntreue; ibid., Reichsarbeitsminister to Reichstreuhänder der Arbeit, 15 June 1940 betr: Bekämpfung der Arbeitsvertragsbruchs.

93. STAM Oberpräsidium/5210. 'RTA Westfalen-Niederrhein 2 January 1941. Zusammenstellung über die Massnahmen zur Bekämpfung von Diziplinlosigkeiten in den 12 Monaten des Jahres 1940.'

94. MA RW20-13/11, 13 August 1940.

95. H. Auerbach, 'Arbeitserziehungslager 1940-1944', *Gutachten des Instituts für Zeitgeschichte*, vol. 2 (Stuttgart, 1966), pp. 196-201, here p. 196.

96. BA R58/1027. 'Der Chef der deutschen Polizei im RMdI to Befehlshaber und Inspekteure der Sicherheitspolizei und des SD, 28 May 1941 betr: Errichtung von Arbeitserziehungslagern.' On the AELs see further: Wolfgang Franz Werner, 'Die Arbeitserziehungslager als Mittel nationalsozialistischer "Sozialpolitik" gegen deutsche Arbeiter' in W. Dlugoborski (ed.), *Zweiter Weltkrieg und Sozialer Wandel* (Göttingen, 1981), pp. 138-47; Detlev Peukert, 'Arbeitslager und Jugend-KZ: die "Behandlung Gemeinschaftsfremder" im Dritten Reich' in Detlev Peukert and Jürgen Reulecke (eds.), *Die Reihen fast geschlossen* (Wuppertal, 1981), pp. 413-34.

97. BA/R58. 'SD Meldungen aus dem Reich Nr. 342' (10 December 1942).

98. Arno Klönne, 'Jugendprotest und Jugendopposition. Von der HJ-Erziehung zum Cliquenwesen der Kriegszeit' in Martin Broszat *et al.* (eds.), *Bayern in der NS-Zeit IV. Herrschaft und Gesellschaft im Konflikt Teil C* (Munich, 1981), pp. 527-620, here pp. 594f.

99. Ibid., p. 596.

100. Material on disciplinary measures against workers by Reichstreuhänder Hahn (Essen) in STAM Oberpräsidium/5065 and 5210.

101. BA R13 I/653. 'Göring Anordnung', 22 August 1941.

102. BA R3/2780. 'Mansfeld to Reichstreuhänder der Arbeit, 22 November 1941 betr: Bekämpfung der Diziplinlosigkeiten in den Betrieben.'

103. D. Petzina, W. Abelshauser and A. Faust (eds.), *Sozialgeschichtliches Arbeitsbuch III. Materialien zur Statistik des Deutschen Reiches 1914-1945* (Munich, 1978), p. 85, Table 17a, 'Mobilisierung der Arbeitskräfte 1939-44'.

104. Reichsminister für Ernährung und Landwirtschaft Erlass 17 April 1942 in BBA 13/1333, 'Bezirksgruppe Ruhr to Mitglieder' 29 August 1942. BA R3/1813, pp. 88-92, 'Erste Betriebsführerstimmen zur Auswirkung der Anordnung des REM vom 20 October 1943 über die Einbehaltung von Zulage- und Zusatzkarten bei Arbeitsbummelei und pflichtwidrigen Zurückhaltung mit der Arbeitsleistung.'

105. Newspaper cutting in BA R12 I/255 Völkischer Beobachter 19 October 1944 'Die Vorteile der betriebsärztlichen Betreuung'; BA R58/193. SD Meldungen aus dem Reich 2 March 1944 'Klagen der Ruhrbergarbeiter über die Behandlungsweise der Vertrauensärzte', pp. 86-8.

106. See n. 7 above.

107. See especially Detlev Peukert, *Die KPD im Widerstand. Verfolgung und Untergrundarbeit an Rhein und Ruhr 1933 bis 1945* (Wuppertal, 1980).

108. Detlev Peukert, 'Zur Rolle des Arbeiterwiderstandes im "Dritten Reich" ' in Christoph Klessmann and Falk Pingel (eds.), *Gegner des Nationalsozialismus* (Frankfurt am Main 1980), pp. 73-90; Günter Plum 'Die Arbeiterbewegung während der nationalsozialistischen Herrschaft' in Jürgen Reulecke (ed.), *Arbeiterbewegung an Rhein und Ruhr* (Wuppertal, 1974), pp. 353-83, esp. pp. 379-82.

109. Gerhard Hetzer, 'Die Industriestadt Augsburg: Eine Sozialgeschichte der Arbeiteropposition' in Martin Broszat *et al.* (eds.), *Bayern in der NS-Zeit III. Herrschaft und Gesellschaft im Konflikt Teil B* (Munich and Vienna, 1981), pp. 1-233; Klaus Tenfelde, 'Proletarische Provinz: Radikalisierung und Widerstand in Penzberg/Oberbayern 1900-1945' in Broszat *et al.* (eds.) *Bayern IV*, pp. 1-382.

110. BA R22/3361, pp. 158f. 'Präsident des Oberlandesgerichts Darmstadt to Reichsjustizminister', 1 December 1943; BA R22/3374, p. 143f. 'Generalstaatsanwalt Köln to Reichsjustizminister', 1 August 1944.

111. Peukert, *KPD*, p. 387.

112. Martin Broszat, 'Resistenz und Widerstand. Eine Zwischenbilanz des Forschungsprojekts' in Broszat *et al.* (eds.), *Bayern IV*, pp. 691-709.

7 PROPAGANDA, AUTARKY AND THE GERMAN HOUSEWIFE

Jill Stephenson

In order to pursue its aim of autarky – of liberating the German economy from dependence on foreign imports – Hitler's regime endeavoured from the start to achieve a high measure of 'direction of consumption' (*Verbrauchslenkung*) among the population at large. The options open to it were indeed narrow: as Petzina points out, firm control, in the form either of rationing food and other consumer goods or of allowing prices of scarce goods to rise beyond most people's reach, was neither socially nor politically desirable. The sole remaining choice up to the outbreak of war in 1939, he says, was 'indirect control of consumption, that is influencing the consumer through propaganda, to make demand match supply'.[1] Certainly, a massive barrage of propaganda issued forth from party and state agencies in order to promote autarky, with increasing force after the announcement of the Four Year Plan in September 1936. It was, however, neither aimed indiscriminately at all sections of the population nor abandoned when the exigencies of war made rationing, on an ever-larger scale, justifiable. Rather, at least during the first half of the war, propaganda activity to direct and restrain consumption assumed even greater proportions than in peacetime, until paper rationing in summer 1942 began to restrict its scope.[2] Both the extent and the nature of the propaganda utilised to try to promote autarky owed much to the relationship between the National Socialist regime and the society which it governed, to the regime's leadership's conception of the nature and purpose of propaganda, and to the audience at which the bulk of propaganda about everyday consumption was aimed. These three factors also imposed strict limitations on the potential for success which a policy of consumer restraint, with propaganda as its main accessory, could enjoy.

It was the extent to which Hitler's regime depended on the consent and co-operation of the 'Aryan', 'politically reliable' population of Germany which rendered it peculiarly reliant on the power of propaganda.[3] It was one thing to terrorise political opponents and racial 'enemies of the people', but the mass of Germans in the 'master race' had to be won round to the National Socialist point of view on every issue of national importance. Given the totalitarian aspirations of the NSDAP's leadership, with the aim of winning over 'the whole man' to their ideological standpoint,[4] this in effect meant every issue of even the most mundane kind in everyday life. It is true that the palpable threat of terror, through the Gestapo or the concentration camp, was ever-present, although its effect was chiefly negative, discouraging open criticism or overt opposition. But Hitler's regime wished to elicit far more than mere passive compliance from the governed: enthusiasm for the regime's policies and the subordination of self-interest in order to permit their realisation would not be achieved by threats of brutality and confinement. The stick was to be a last resort, used in exemplary fashion against individual dissidents. The carrot, however, was a luxury which the regime would not allow itself, with the drive towards autarky. Yet active commitment to his objectives by the mass of the people was what Hitler desired, so that the only remaining tactic available to him lay in the highly labour-intensive activity of persuasion. The result was to turn every office of party and state into a propaganda agency devoting at least some of its energy to the uphill task of trying to persuade people to adjust their habits to meet the regime's requirements. Virtually every public statement or project became an act of propaganda.

This was freely admitted by a regime to whose leaders 'propaganda' was not a pejorative term; neither did they regard as offensive the deliberate saturation of human minds with one-sided, heavily censored information and exhortation geared towards radically altering attitudes and behaviour. National Socialists used 'education', 'enlightenment', 'training' and other less loaded terms to describe the process to which Germans were to be subjected to make them comply with the regime's requirements, but they did not shrink from using the word 'propaganda' to describe their contribution to the 'educative' process. It seems to have been regarded as at worst a neutral term, but often enough as a term with favourable connotations, signifying the activity necessary to apprise unenlightened fellow-citizens of the true way forward and, as important, of their role in pursuing it. Thus 'propaganda against department stores and Jewish businesses, to support and promote the middle class'[5] was justifiable as a tactic to achieve a desirable and beneficial aim. Similarly, 'attracting women through propaganda'[6] simply meant winning over women to National Socialism by making them aware of the extent to which its ideas and policies would benefit them. Propaganda could be used to defame and distort, it was readily admitted, not least by critics of National Socialism who were responsible for 'all the hateful lies in the hostile foreign press'.[7] But this was not that benevolent, informative, persuasive propaganda used by Nazis to convey their inescapable truth; rather it was 'atrocity propaganda' (*Greuelpropaganda*),[8] itself a distortion of a legitimate and helpful means of imparting information.

Given the extensive and unashamed effort expended by Hitler's regime on propaganda to convince the population of the necessity and desirability of its policies, the return was not impressive. With alternative sources of information closed down or censored, the Nazis had a virtual monopoly, yet the task was in many respects more complex after 1933 than before, when largely negative slogans had sufficed to attract substantial electoral support. From 1933, however, there was not only the desire to generate positive support but also the necessity of trying to sell policies which reflected the power-political ambitions of the leadership clique, while demanding self-restraint and sacrifice from the population at large in the pursuit of autarky. The individual was to be persuaded by propaganda to sink his/her identity in the collective entity of the *Volksgemeinschaft* (community of the people), to subordinate personal aspirations – now designated axiomatically 'selfish' – to the notional interests of the community, and to reorientate his/her habits to accord with the regime's demands of the moment. Hardly surprisingly, this was not a popular approach in a formerly prosperous nation which, in recent memory, had suffered much through war and economic crisis. The success of Nazi propaganda was at its most apparent when the message being purveyed was a popular one. When thrift and stringency were its repetitive themes, its reception was at best cool and often enough frosty.

Nazi propaganda efforts met particular resistance among German women, especially in three areas regarded as important: the pro-natalist campaign to raise the birth rate dramatically; the intensive propaganda aimed at bringing women into war-work; and the attempt to recruit to the women's organisations associated with the Nazi Party in more than penny numbers.[9] Yet it was to be at women that a barrage of propaganda to promote autarky was to be directed. This owed much both to the precise nature of self-sufficiency envisaged by the government and to the NSDAP leadership's male chauvinist mentality. As 'wives, mothers and homemakers', women had a preordained place in Nazi society and Nazi relationships which made them overwhelmingly responsible for 'the smaller world of the home',[10] while men concerned themselves with the larger issues of the outside world. Yet, while women were not to participate in public life, they were increasingly expected to take an interest in matters of national importance, to become 'politically aware' — which meant to understand, accept and implement the demands made of them, as private individuals, by the ruling elite.[11] Gregor Strasser, more acute than most of his colleagues, had pointed out before 1933 the vital part played in the national economy by the housewife, 'through whose hands, when she is shopping, passes the largest part of the German national income'.[12] The housewife as consumer had to be persuaded and trained to direct her patterns of purchase and household provision in ways that would best accord with the aim of self-sufficiency. With complete unself-consciousness, Nazi propagandists — women and men alike — addressed themselves to 'the German housewife and mother', with the implication that only married women were housekeepers and that consumption by men, single women and children was overwhelmingly directed by the choices of a wife or mother. Contesting or upholding the validity of this assumption is not the purpose here; its importance for this essay lies in the extent to which German housewives became the target of intensive and unremitting propaganda about the need to adopt 'responsible' (i.e. restrained, thrifty) patterns of consumption.

The obsessiveness with which the message was repeated derived from the crucial role of autarky in the regime's military preparations for territorial expansion virtually from the start of the Third Reich. Germany was not alone in turning in on herself economically in the inter-war years: the political, economic and financial effects of the First World War, heavily compounded by the cataclysm of the Great Depression, gravely disrupted international trade and drove most European countries, among others, to seek salvation through protectionism and self-sufficiency. But in Germany's case there were, too, factors which combined to make autarky a positively attractive policy. The memory of the 'Hunger Blockade' imposed on the Central Powers by the Allies during the war was a bitter one: on political as well as humanitarian grounds, a recurrence of that experience was to be avoided at all costs, by making Germany as nearly 100 per cent as possible self-sufficient in foodstuffs, fuel and other essential raw materials. To many Nazis, too, autarky was ideologically desirable, with a virtue made out of 'buy German' exhortations by claiming that German goods were essentially superior to others.[13] Further, even before 1933 the Nazis had their own 'Immediate Programme' for alleviating the appalling misery of the Depression — a plan which owed much to Gregor Strasser — which bore a strong resemblance to Schacht's 'New Plan' of September 1934 with its heavy bias towards domestic raw materials production, including food, and strict controls on foreign trade.[14] This policy had notable success in the years 1933 to 1936, but by summer 1936 it was recognised that in terms of boosting home production of food supply and raw materials Germany had reached the limits of 'natural' achievement. In accepting that production in agriculture and certain raw materials could be raised little further, Hitler did not abandon his aim of autarky. Rather, he affirmed that he was determined to allow the importation only of those goods which could be obtained by no other means – including the use of substitutes. The Four Year Plan, announced in September 1936, was intended to 'find out what we cannot do. We must now show what we can do.'[15] From autumn 1936 through into the Second World War, the task of Reich Ministries, the Four Year Plan Office and party agencies, particularly the *Reichsnährstand* (Reich Food Authority), was on the one hand to find ways of circumventing the need for imports, above all through resort to new inventions and substitutes, and on the other hand to exude insistent propaganda to exhort the consuming public to make as few demands on German industry and resources as possible, by using frugally materials which were readily available, by choosing substitute foods where necessary, and by saving on everything else from paper to energy.

Cast in the role of major consumer, the housewife was subjected to a constant barrage of propaganda and advice about ways of promoting autarky. In a society in which every member was assigned, willy-nilly, to the supervision of a group affiliated to the NSDAP, above all to effect ideological indoctrination, responsibility for transmitting the will of state and party authorities to the mass of German housewives fell to the Nazi women's organisations. These were the leadership group of nominally enthusiastic activists[16] in the *NS-Frauenschaft* (NSF – Nazi Women's Group) and the notional mass of 'followers' in the *Deutsches Frauenwerk* (DFW – German Women's Enterprise). But the regime's task was at once rendered particularly difficult by the passive refusal of more than a tiny minority of eligible 'Aryan', 'politically reliable' women to join the DFW, and therefore make themselves readily accessible to the propaganda disseminated to DFW members by 'tireless' NSF workers.[17] Nevertheless, the central office for 'the women's work of the nation', the *Reichsfrauenführung* (RFFg – National Women's Leadership) in Berlin, set about the massive task of trying to persuade German women to bend themselves to the will of the regime's leadership, and to do it gladly. In autumn 1934, a new section of the RFFg's work was created whose primary purpose was the promotion of the objectives of autarky as they were intended to involve German housewives. Its name, *Volkswirtschaft/Hauswirtschaft* (Vw/Hw — National Economy/Domestic Economy), reflected Strasser's view that 'national economic training for the German housewife' must be a top priority in the work of the NSF, whose founder he was.[18] The name also neatly encapsulated the relationship that was expected to develop between the needs of the German economy, defined by the ruling elite, and the performance of the housewife in her domestic sphere — in that order of priorities.

From its founding, under the leadership of Dr Else Vorwerck and her deputy, Dr Aenne Sprengel, the Vw/Hw's 'most responsible and necessary task . . . [was] the direction of consumption for the future'.[19] To this end, it engaged in a variety of propaganda activities, disseminating information and advice through obvious means like leaflets, brochures, posters and personal contact and also utilising the facilities of modern technology, including radio, films and slides, as well as the mass-circulation press. There were also demonstrations, exhibitions, courses and advice bureaux. This battery of equipment was used for a variety of related purposes: to communicate measures taken and requirements made by ministries — especially the Ministry of Food — and other major agencies like the *Reichsnährstand*; to provide guidance about goods that were scarce and items to be saved for recycling; to give a wide range of homecraft advice; to outline ways of making do with what was available; to give recipes and advise about substitutes; to combat adverse foreign propaganda; to publicise books and leaflets on the theme of autarky; and to discourage anti-social practices, for example the bartering of goods. The section also took an interest in the Homecraft Year for school-leavers and, allied to it, matters concerning domestic servants. Its experimentation unit tested new recipes, new cooking techniques and new household equipment. With some justification, it claimed to have a role to play as representative of the consumer. Apart from issuing vast amounts of propaganda, its largest public operation was the running of homecraft courses, at different levels to meet different needs. To mount these courses, the section had a substantial staff of full-time and part-time teachers, many of whom themselves received training through the Vw/Hw. And all its officers, whether administrators or teachers, were strongly encouraged to attend not only practical but also ideological training courses, since only those with 'a faultless attitude'[20] were regarded as trustworthy enough to give, for example, cookery instruction from the correct point of view.

Through its various functions, the Vw/Hw encountered many other organisations and agencies, and much energy was spent on sending delegates to sit on their committees to try to achieve co-ordination across an increasingly complex bureaucratic structure. First, the Vw/Hw had to work within the guidelines set by the state and party agencies chiefly involved in promoting autarky. But its representatives were primarily officials of the women's organisation and had to work within its framework, under its leader, Gertrud Scholtz-Klink, and alongside the other sections into which the RFFg's work was divided. The *Reichs-mütterdienst* (National Mothers' Service) was the most senior element of the 'women's work', and was regarded as the most important. Breaking the Vw/Hw's monopoly, it was permitted to run cooking and sewing courses, although its main concerns lay in child care and 'racial hygiene'.[21] The Press and Propaganda section of the RFFg was respon-sible for providing propaganda materials and for preparing items produced by other sections for the press.[22] But this caused problems when its editors altered beyond recognition recipes prepared for publi-cation by Vw/Hw cookery experts whose command of the written word was limited.[23] If there was occasional friction between the sec-tions of the RFFg, it was as nothing to the demarcation disputes which ran on between the RFFg and other organisations, notably the *Bund deutscher Mädel* (BdM – League of German Girls) and the Women's Office of the German Labour Front. Not until December 1941 did the RFFg win a partial victory over the Reich Youth Leader by being unequivocally permitted to be the sole provider of homecraft instruc-tion, through the Vw/Hw, for the oldest BdM girls.[24] And in July 1936 Gertrud Scholtz-Klink had to obtain a ban on the Labour Front's recruitment of housewives and recommend that to avoid friction local committees of Labour Front and Vw/Hw members meet to discuss matters of mutual interest affecting housewives.[25]

It was, of course, the regime's toleration of 'institutional Darwin-ism'[26] which permitted the development of a plethora of organisations and agencies, often with overlapping functions and scope for jurisdic-tional conflict. In economic policy, it was also true that there was 'no organisational concept, but . . . for twelve whole years Hitler's regime experimented unsystematically and senselessly . . .' What the Four Year Plan lacked above all, as Wolfram Fischer points out, was a plan.[27] If this made much of the Vw/Hw's activity *ad hoc* in nature, it also ensured that the Vw/Hw's leaders were allowed some scope for initia-tive within a hierarchical system in which the women's organisation was at a very low position in the pecking order. Its central office had no say whatsoever in policy-making, and much of the time its function was simply to pass on decisions from above to its section leaders in the

Gaus and further down the line. The message was predetermined; propagating it most effectively was the Vw/Hw's task. Unless firm propaganda guidelines came from another agency, like the *Reichsnähr-stand*, which expected the Vw/Hw to assist in its periodic campaigns to promote the collection of windfall fruit and nuts[28] or the best exploita-tion of a particularly good apple crop in 1937,[29] the Vw/Hw could devise its own approach to the problem of conveying the message to as wide an audience as possible. This degree of discretion was permissible because of the strictly hierarchical structure of the Vw/Hw itself, with local section workers receiving from district or Gau section leaders detailed instructions which left little or nothing to their imagination. Such room for manoeuvre as there was lay at central office in Berlin, where the leadership of Else Vorwerck was utterly 'politically reliable'. She seems, indeed, to have been the Vw/Hw's *political* chief, with Aenne Sprengel, her deputy, in direct charge of the practical business of the office.[30]

The Vw/Hw's propaganda effort had to be directed on three different levels. First, there were its own committed workers, from the most senior category of Gau Vw/Hw section leader down to local branch section workers and the professional instructors who ran a variety of courses. No less than the uncommitted, these women had to be encouraged, to maintain their enthusiasm. Next came those who formed the larger minority of women who participated in the section's activities. It is too much to say that half the battle was over once they had been persuaded to attend film or slide shows illustrating the autarkic message, to visit exhibitions or demonstrations, or to take courses mounted by the Vw/Hw, but at least in their case the first battle for access had been won. There remained the large mass of German, 'Aryan', 'politically reliable' women who had not come for-ward to participate in the section's activities: in this, the Vw/Hw's experience was consistent with that of the women's organisations as a whole. Yet, according with the totalitarian aspirations of the regime's leadership, they had to be involved somehow and, above all, they had to be reached with propaganda promoting autarky. For once the Vw/Hw's claims can be believed: it was indeed the case that all its endeavours would be to no avail unless it could depend on 'the loyal co-operation of each individual housewife in town and country . . . Only this common effort can produce the energetic teamwork for the great goal set for us.'[31] It was into the task of gaining access to individual housewives who remained aloof from the women's organisa-tions, to propagate the aims and methods of autarky, that the Vw/Hw poured most of its human and material resources.

Nevertheless, propaganda activity was particularly necessary among the small minority of the committed in the women's organisations because so many of them – '99%', boasted Gertrud Scholtz-Klink[32] – worked as unpaid volunteers. The Gau Vw/Hw section leaders and the majority of their immediate subordinates, the subsection leaders and the 'subject experts', were full-time, paid employees, as were some of their multifarious 'assistants'. These were the administrators who supervised the Vw/Hw's work in the 32 Gaus into which Germany was divided (40 in the Greater German Reich of 1939). In the districts (*Kreise*), barely 12 per cent of NSF/DFW employees, including all the section leaders, were paid, full-time workers and in the local branches all staff were volunteers. But the Vw/Hw's vocational workers were generally salaried: in 1938, only 14 of the 93 homecraft instructors and 27 of the 68 staff in homecraft advice centres were not employed on a full-time, paid basis.[33] Nevertheless, most of the enthusiasts who were in touch with the mass of women at local level were unpaid, so that there was a constant need to issue instructions from the centre in morale-boosting fashion, even before the war made jollying propaganda as necessary inside the organisations as among the population at large. Unashamed self-congratulation and continual inflation of the extent of their alleged 'successes' were the rather transparent tactics employed to maintain the morale of volunteer workers in the districts and local branches.[34] Constantly reinforcing the commitment of enthusiasts through flattery and encouragement was essential to motivate these women to continue to give 'tirelessly' of their time and effort in a cause which benefited them little beyond enhancing their sense of self-importance and, as the stringencies of war increased, which uncomfortably associated them with the unpopular side of the regime's policies. It was also necessary, though, because of the belief – long an article of faith among Nazi women[35] – that there was no substitute for personal contact and the opportunities for convincing others face-to-face that it provided.

This merely enhanced the preoccupation already constantly present at the RFFg about maintaining reliability and conformity among those who were running courses and giving advice. Apart from the obvious concern that anyone who served in an official capacity, however humble, should be 'politically reliable', it was also deemed essential that she should be thoroughly disciplined. Failure to manifest 'the correct attitude' guaranteed dispensability, as Frau Ervens, an aspiring Vw/Hw local section leader in Kochem, found to her cost.[36] There was also concern that, further, all advisers and instructors should have a ready practical command of their subject. These two elements, practical proficiency and ideological conformity, were fused in the desire to transmit accurate and useful information which would enable the housewife, as recipient, to serve the aim of autarky. To this end, the Vw/Hw, like other sections of the women's work, kept strict control over its accredited spokeswomen. In October 1937, Else Vorwerck circulated to her Gau section leaders and to Gau NSF leaders a list bearing the names of women who were 'on no account' to be allowed to speak in public.[37] Seven weeks later, her deputy was seeking names for a list of women who would be suitable to speak on behalf of the section's 'subject area: nutrition'. She asked her Gau representatives three questions as a guide to assess suitability. First, did the nominee have the necessary practical and personal qualities? Secondly, was she able to deliver a lecture plausibly? And finally, even if she did not completely meet the first two requirements, was her attitude to the DFW's work nevertheless sufficient guarantee of her reliability?[38]

Vetting of spokeswomen and other representatives was not merely an initial, one-off process, however. Those who were deemed generally suitable had to be kept under surveillance and both their 'attitude' and practical skills reviewed and updated, most of all because of the changing demands made by Ministries and other agencies. The method used was that of the purpose-built course. In 1937, for example, as the campaign to prevent waste and promote thrift in the purchase and use of food gathered pace, the Vw/Hw's leaders called their officials to five- or six-day courses to instruct them intensively in both the propaganda and the practical techniques which its office had devised, following guidelines laid down by the Ministry of Food. The Gau section leaders met at Coburg in May 1937, for preliminary exposure to the new strategy,[39] and in August they were each invited to nominate an 'expert' to attend a course on nutritional questions in Berlin in September 1937. Prominent among the topics for lecture or discussion were 'direction of the consumption of food', 'giving recipes over the radio and in the press' and 'supervision of courses and cookery demonstrations'. At the course, demonstrations were given of the use to which unfamiliar substitutes, like dried skimmed milk, curds, soya and dried vegetables, could be put in everyday cooking, and different methods of applying heat to food were also shown. Time was devoted to discussing the special problems which women in rural areas, especially the wives of new settlers, and working wives would face in meeting the new demands. While much of the work of this course was of a practical nature, Else Vorwerck emphasised its inescapable orientation in her address about the structure of the women's organisations in the Third Reich which, she said, was so designed that 'through the gathering together of [sectional] workers under the political leadership of the *Frauenschaft* an ideologically good alignment of the *Frauenwerk* is guaranteed'.[40]

Far from running down its activities during the Second World War, the Vw/Hw actually increased them, the rationale being that the more shortages there were, the more administration and training were required to enable the section's officials to instruct the mass of women to cope with them. The number of courses multiplied accordingly. There were 'ideological and practical' courses for leaders of the Vw/Hw's advisory bureaux in both September and November 1941,[41] and in the depths of December 1941, when Germany seemed on the threshold of victory in Russia, intricate plans were laid for the first really intensive course to train 'suitable' section workers, with three to four weeks in a 'selection camp' followed by three to four months of specialist training in groups.[42] As the war dragged on, the courses had to function on a more modest level, although it was regarded as important that homecraft advisers should continue to receive regular instruction, especially with the 'changes' (the euphemism for reductions) in rations being introduced with increasing frequency.[43] While practical considerations were, perforce, the major preoccupation, the matter of 'attitude' remained of paramount importance. The courses were seen as particularly vital for reinforcing and maintaining the morale and commitment of section workers, in the face of both adversity and temptation. Although it was widely suspected – sometimes with justification – that party officials enjoyed special perks in wartime,[44] the Vw/Hw's central office, at least, was determined that attempts by some of its workers to acquire extra rations must be stamped out because of the 'shattering effect' that this had on the morale of the population at large.[45] Thus the frequent meetings held to keep Gau section leaders, especially, in touch with each other and to bring them under the periodic scrutiny of central office leaders, were intended to have an inspiring as well as an informative function. With rationing becoming more severe, these conferences were a major operation. It was one thing to take ration card tokens from one side of Germany to another, but the number of other items to be carried by participants steadily increased and included not only foodstuffs, with butter, marmalade and so on specified down to the last gram, but also towels, bed linen, blankets and shoe-cleaning materials.[46] Participants in the homecraft advisers' course in September 1941 were also instructed to take soiled clothes and clothes requiring mending for the washing and sewing lessons given at the course.[47] With so many burdens to bear – quite literally – Vw/Hw workers needed the boost to morale that the section leadership provided through praise and encouragement at courses and in publications.[48] Further, the preoccupation among section workers with bureaucratic arrangements and hierarchical order[49] becomes more comprehensible, since these were the only perk they were allowed – status did not cost money or waste rations.

Once the small circle of committed Vw/Hw workers had been instructed and encouraged, their task was to guide in a uniform manner the larger minority of women who participated in the section's various activities. Briefed through their courses and conferences, section workers at Gau and district level, particularly, were entrusted with mounting exhibitions, demonstrations and courses, above all in cookery but also in other household skills, including laundry. They could also hire, borrow or buy film strips and slides to provide visual aid for lectures on autarkic themes. In June 1937, Aenne Sprengel announced that both a film 335 metres long, costing RM 209, and a series of 75 slides, costing RM 3.50, were available on 'Preserving fruit and vegetables', showing how to preserve in glass jars, how to extract juice, and how to make jellies and sauerkraut. The film and slides were accompanied by an introduction and a commentary, respectively, to ensure that the same message was being purveyed wherever these visual materials were shown.[50] In December 1937, Else Vorwerck informed her Gau section leaders that the film 'Scrap material – Raw material' was ready and that each of them would receive one copy for each of their districts as well as some slides, with commentary, free of charge. The film, demonstrating the collection and recycling of old clothes, was to be shown 'intensively' in all districts and local branches to alert as many women as possible to the importance of not throwing anything away and of contributing where they could to the periodic collections of scrap materials of all kinds.[51] Visual aids for propaganda continued to be prepared in wartime, although on a less lavish scale. The film strip 'Dressing well for home and outside', publicised in October 1941, was part of a continuing campaign to try to alert women to what was fashionable, German and possible under restricted circumstances.[52] In the same context, the transparency showing a woman sewing, with the legend 'Take advice', was intended to persuade women to seek guidance about appropriate dressmaking. This assumed a grim aspect with the decision in March 1942 to restrict the distribution of clothing coupons for mourning dress and to encourage women, especially, simply to add black crepe to clothes which they already possessed.[53] Visual aids were also used to exhort women to help with the war effort: the transparency 'Free time should be spent helping with the harvest' was distributed free, with extra copies available for Gaus where the recruitment of volunteers in 1942 was required to be particularly strenuous.[54] No area of consumption was immune: a film was available, free of charge, to instruct women on how to make (rather than buy) Christmas presents.[55]

Confidence in the efficacy of visual instruction led the Vw/Hw's leaders to encourage Gau representatives and their subordinates to mount a variety of exhibitions and demonstrations, with the theme of directing consumption. They strongly recommended a ready-made exhibition on the use of bones as a source of raw material, which could be obtained from a private firm at a cost of RM 27.[56] The motive was to persuade housewives not to throw away bones but to save them for collection and recycling. The Gaus were also encouraged to borrow stalls which could be easily packed, sent and set up as part of a textiles exhibition, to demonstrate the development of new synthetic materials, like rayon, from their raw state into ready-to-wear clothes,[57] to persuade women to accept synthetics as a substitute for the natural fabrics to which they were accustomed. Small-scale exhibits featuring synthetic fibres were recommended for use in advice centres and courses, and could be ordered from an approved private firm and paid for out of Vw/Hw funds.[58] Another much-favoured visual effect was the cookery demonstration (*Schaukoche*), which was used both by central office to enlighten section officials at their conferences[59] and also by section workers in the localities to show women the most approved methods of cooking. Efficient cooking methods would save energy and economise on the use of fats. Demonstrations were also used to introduce women to a variety of ways of cooking more plentiful foods, to avoid monotony, and unfamiliar substitutes, both of which were being propagated to replace commodities which Germany could not herself provide in large enough quantities to meet demand. Instead of meat, fish was especially favoured, and '25 x Fisch' and 'Salzhering einmal anders' ('25 ways with fish', 'salt herring done differently')[60] were ideas which lent themselves to the art of demonstration.

While demonstrations were an approved form of passive learning, greater participation was generally favoured. The means of achieving this was, once again, the course. Courses ranged widely in nature, scope and duration, from full-time instruction to an occasional evening class, catering for everyone from absolute beginners to experienced house-wives. Above all, there was the two-year homecraft course for school-leavers, to attract girls into domestic service and at the same time to prepare them for running a home of their own. In 1937 the Vw/Hw launched a massive 'recruiting offensive' (*Werbefeldzug*) for these courses,[61] and the numbers enrolled rose from 2,400 in 1937 to 3,400 in 1938. This was not as expensive of Vw/Hw resources as might appear, since the girls were trained in the household of a 'capable housewife', whose reward was very cheap labour indeed to help with her chores. At the other end of the scale were courses to turn house-wives with at least five years' experience into 'Master Housewives', through a two-year part-time theoretical and practical course. There were 1,070 housewives in training in 1937.[62] The intention was to train unpaid volunteers in the manner approved by the section so that they would become the new generation of section leaders and workers at local level.[63] Most of the Vw/Hw courses were, however, much shorter, on part of one day a week for several weeks. They were conducted in either the 15 homecraft colleges or the 218 'instruction kitchens' which had been opened across Germany by the end of 1938,[64] mostly by paid professional instructors who geared their teach-ing towards *Verbrauchslenkung* in the approved manner. Again, there was a strong emphasis on fish cookery, with special courses devoted to it, as well as courses dealing with potato and curds cookery, instruction in baking, as a method using less fat, and in preserving, to make the most of a good crop at the season when there was a glut.[65]

On a more informal basis, the Vw/Hw's advice centres answered queries about all aspects of household and consumer affairs and pro-vided leaflets and recipes, some free and some at a charge of a few Pfennigs. By August 1938, 110 advice centres had been established in the Gaus and districts, the number rising to 148 by the end of the year. Some had their own kitchen which could be used for *ad hoc*, small-scale practical advice.[66] The advice centres had to be in towns to be acces-sible to any significant number of women, yet there was special anxiety about reaching women living in rural areas, above all the wives of new settlers on the land who, it was felt, would face particular problems in adjusting to a new life-style at the very time when the regime wanted to control their consumption patterns. Accordingly, full-time settlers' wives' advisers had been appointed by the end of 1937 in 27 Gaus, with a further 26 in selected districts, while nine advice centres special-ising in settlers' wives' problems had been opened. As usual, the inten-tion was to depend overwhelmingly on part-time voluntary workers for staff.[67] By the end of 1938, there were three training schools for the advisers, 33 Gau advisers and 485 district settlers' wives' advisers, of whom 440 worked as volunteers.[68] While settlers' wives were expected, like everyone else, to require instruction in food consumption, the advisers were also to help them with tasks which urban wives would not encounter, in large-scale gardening and work with small animals,[69] tasks traditionally performed by farmers' wives. The settlers' wives' advisers had their own training courses, run by the Vw/Hw; one, for example, in June 1941, dealt with making unfermented wine from the fruit yield, in keeping with the strongly anti-alcohol stand adopted by the Nazi women's organisations, which led them to campaign for greater consumption of fresh fruit when it was in season and consumption of fruit juice preserved by an approved method.[70]

All the exhibitions, demonstrations, courses and advice centres were backed up by what was admitted, in July 1937, to be a 'flood' of publications designed to further the aims of the 1936 Four Year Plan. Authors seeking recognition had greatly added to the workload of party and state officials, importuning them with requests for patronage, trying to play off one office against another, or claiming official support which had not been given.[71] Yet the Vw/Hw had no desire to discourage people from writing on autarkic themes, since its leadership was constantly on the lookout for new ideas about how to propagate what was essentially the same message over and over again, with new variations on the theme most welcome.[72] A list of titles offered for purchase by Gau sections clearly indicates the main preoccupations: 'Preserving fruit and vegetables', 'Cook well – budget well', 'Mend well –darn well' were among those to be sold to Gau sections at 15 Pfennigs each, with the price to individual purchasers set at 20 Pfennigs to allow Gau sections a small profit to meet running costs. No doubt Else Vorwerck received a royalty for her predictable contribution, 'The German Housewife in the National Economy'. Some of the Gau sections produced their own booklets which were, if approved, recommended for general sale. Gau Hessen-Nassau's 'Our Little Herb Garden' and Schleswig-Holstein's 'Cook cheaply, thriftily, responsibly and healthily' were two such.[73] Particularly recommended was Gau Kurhessen's 16-page leaflet giving 'excellent recipes' for utilising curds and milk.[74]

Through their various activities, Vw/Hw officials and workers at both central and local level undoubtedly made a herculean effort to acquaint German housewives with detailed methods of housekeeping which would help to serve the aim of autarky. But how widely and how

deeply did their message penetrate? It was one thing to issue instructions about the mounting of exhibitions, demonstrations and courses,
to run advice centres and to produce a vast array of publications, but
the effect of all these devices was only as great as the number of women
attracted to them. It is clear that substantial numbers did attend events
and buy leaflets, although there is no way of knowing whether there
was genuinely widespread support or whether a small number of
enthusiasts visited an exhibition or saw a film several times: numbers
were always reported as 'attendances', and generally on a national
scale. In any case, impressive-looking figures, running to thousands or
hundreds of thousands, were perhaps less prepossessing when considered as a proportion of the 30 million women in the population of
the Greater German Reich. The DFW's yearbook for 1939 reported
that in 1937 the Vw/Hw section had mounted 27,885 courses which
attracted 613,300 participants to learn about cooking with substitutes
and economical methods of cooking and preserving. In addition, there
had been 114 exhibitions at Gau level and 1,551 in the districts.[75] In
1938, in the Greater German Reich, the number of courses and participants rose to 85,985 and 1,822,732, respectively,[76] which reflects the
undoubted popularity of the cookery courses, especially by comparison with some of the women's organisations' other instruction, notably
in 'political education'.[77] The cookery courses continued in wartime,
with the Minister of Food still prepared to allocate provisions – albeit
increasingly exiguously – for them even when rationing was becoming
stringent in summer 1942.[78] This was partly to maintain courses in the
'old Reich', but also because it was regarded as essential that 'desirable'
women in the occupied territories, too, be similarly instructed.

The results from the new Strasbourg district, in Gau Baden, may not
be a reliable indication of women's response to Vw/Hw activities, since
there was, at least in 1940 to 1942, not only an active women's organisation but also an unusually high degree of support for it from the
volksdeutsch (ethnic German) women of Alsace.[79] Yet even here, it is
clear, the events which attracted most support were those where
women were spectators rather than participants. It is true that cookery
courses were well-attended, as they were also in the new eastern
Warthegau.[80] In Strasbourg in the year ending October 1942, the new
advice centre held 45 cookery courses which attracted 605 participants,
and in the new settlement area within the district, at Schiltigheim, the
corresponding figures were 18 and 240. At the same time, though, 14
cookery demonstrations attracted 4,800 spectators. In May 1941 alone,
four demonstrations had been held at the usual venue, the municipal

gasworks, and 950 women had attended. This compared with eight 'training lectures' in the same month which had attracted 550 of an audience, and a staggering 44 lectures on 'appropriate washing', to conserve clothing, whose attendance is not recorded.[81] Other than the demonstrations, the advice centres seem to have proved most popular. The new Strasbourg centre had 2,960 visits in its first year, including 600 people in August 1942 alone who came to seek advice about food-stuffs, mostly about preserving. The centre seems to have been able to give recipes free to enquirers, with 5,700 handed over in the year ending October 1942. Courses did attract quite good attendances, with 36 needlework, mending and dressmaking courses – held in mornings, afternoons and evenings to accommodate working as well as non-employed women – attracting around 300 participants. In addition, 77 slipper-making courses had an attendance of 1,050. There can be no doubt that with strenuous cloth-rationing in force many women were anxious to seek advice about how best to use their quota. But visits to demonstrations, which implied less involvement in the work of the women's organisations, remained more popular. Further, women were obviously more prepared to purchase instruction books to help with cooking and sewing at home than to attend courses: over 10,000 copies of booklets with various homecraft tips were bought in 1941-2 from the Vw/Hw's advice bureaux in Strasbourg district.[82]

Without comparably detailed data from other areas of Germany and German-occupied territory, it is impossible to gauge the number of women who attended Vw/Hw events and advice centres and who bought or acquired free the huge number of publications which poured out. Up to August 1938, the Vw/Hw distributed 4.7 million copies of leaflets about fish cookery and an additional 4 million copies of a recipe for herring and buckling, as well as 29.5 million copies of other recipes for marmalade, potatoes, curds and preserving, especially.[83] Yet by contrast the Vw/Hw's own magazine, devoted to propagating the 'new homecraft suggestions',[84] had a circulation of a mere 140,000 in 1938.[85] This perhaps helps to set in perspective the implicit claims of widespread support contained in figures quoted in millions. In their undoubtedly energetic exertions to promote the message of autarky among as wide a circle of German women as possible, Vw/Hw workers remained aware that the success of their efforts depended on women coming to them, taking the initiative to attend a course or demonstra-tion or to call at an advice centre for information or leaflets. Those who joined the DFW were relatively easy to reach even if they were active in another section, because there was at least a line of contact with them

— although the disturbingly high incidence of 'inactive members' meant that far from all of the 'around four million' members claimed for the DFW at the end of 1938[86] were actually readily accessible. In addition, there remained the large majority of German women who were unorganised, for whom most of the Vw/Hw's efforts were intended but who remained aloof from its activities and therefore largely — often deliberately — ignorant of the message which its workers were trying to impart.

Yet the unorganised had to be reached, for otherwise, as section workers acknowledged, all their efforts would have little effect in realising their aim of changing the entire nation's consumption patterns. Here the spread of the radio network, to some 70 per cent of homes by 1939,[87] was vitally important since those most resistant to other forms of propaganda might well listen while they worked and thus absorb at least some of the message about autarky, through programmes like 'The housewife at the centre of the national economy', 'German vegetables' and 'Cheap, but good — the menu of the week'.[88] Yet radio propaganda had its disadvantages. The time allocated for dictating recipes was found to be too brief for women unused to writing (*schreibunge-wohnt*).[89] In Strasbourg, competition for air time was such that the Vw/Hw's programmes were transmitted at what was admitted to be an 'unfavourable broadcasting time for housewives'. Nevertheless, reports about the section's activities, including collections of waste material and cookery demonstrations, continued to be given over the air.[90] Further, although it was possible to introduce some regional variations, during the war, when paper rationing made the Vw/Hw more dependent on radio, it was found necessary to omit detailed reference to the differing availability of foods, since uneven supply could give rise to discontent among the less well-provided for, if it were revealed.[91] Radio was, additionally, a two-edged weapon, with enemy 'Black Radio' spreading despondency during the war with rumours about plans for more stringent rationing.[92]

Nevertheless, radio remained a highly convenient medium for bringing the regime's message quite literally home to large numbers of housewives, and it was used especially to publicise major campaigns and projects launched to promote autarky, for example 'the campaign against waste' (*Kampf den Verderb*).[93] In November 1937, the intensification of waste-paper collection, with exhortation to save paper on packaging, was introduced by a special appeal from Else Vorwerck on radio.[94] The press, too, was heavily involved in publicising autarky-directed activities, for example the 'offensive' to be waged in winter 1937-8 to win recruits for homecraft courses,[95] and advice to housewives about how best to use the large surplus of cooking apples available in autumn 1937.[96] In spite of some reports of difficulties, many Gau section leaders found it very helpful to give approved recipes over the air or in the press.[97] The only other relatively easy way of reaching the mass of women was to display posters. For 'the campaign against waste', one of the many tactics used was the distribution of posters which bore, as the symbol of the campaign, a slice of dried-out bread. These were to be displayed in all shops, advice bureaux, schools and other appropriate public places. This major project, running from harvest time in 1937 until the end of February 1938, was directed by the *Reichsnährstand*, with the Vw/Hw heavily involved in promoting its campaign to encourage the thrifty use of grain and bread.[98]

While it was hoped that the Vw/Hw's propagandists would gain at least some access to the mass of unorganised women through advice and information given over the radio, in the press or on posters, there remained anxiety that these relatively impersonal means would make only the most limited impact among those who had chosen to remain aloof from the section's activities. The Party Leaders' faith in the power of 'personal contact with fellow-citizens' extended especially to attempts to win over women, as Robert Ley showed: 'in many cases the NSF leader can entrust her Block leaders with many tasks. The wife and mother can approach her female fellow-citizens much more easily than a man can, since she understands women's needs . . .'[99] This, then, was the most labour-intensive and the most intimate means of propaganda. Persuasion by one convinced woman of another who was not aware of her new responsibilities was encouraged in a variety of contexts. Women who employed domestic servants under the Homecraft Year scheme were often reluctant to pay insurance for them; the local Vw/Hw worker's duty was to visit them to explain the necessity of insurance.[100] A survey of a very small sample of family consumption patterns showed that there was a need to give advice about more 'responsible' budgeting; again, personal persuasion was preferred.[101] Mothers with reservations about the Compulsory Year of Service introduced for teenage girls in 1938 would benefit, it was felt, from a chat with a local Vw/Hw worker.[102] As the war continued, women had to be persistently reminded about the need to contribute what they had to old clothes' collections, for recycling. In a particularly energetic campaign in spring 1941, housewives were to be visited twice, with a fortnight's interval between visits, to impress on them the importance of co-operation.[103] Group meetings, too, were arranged, with a Vw/Hw

worker spending an afternoon discussing current problems and requirements with the housewives in her local branch, 'so that no housewife
goes without advice and has to fend for herself in difficult times'.[104]

The implied altruism of this statement was not entirely misplaced.
It is true that the motive was chiefly to direct housewives' purchasing
and housekeeping and to maintain morale when goods were in short
supply. Yet there was also a wholly genuine concern that changes in
diet patterns should in no way damage the nation's health. The painstaking efforts of both the Nazi Welfare Organisation (NSV) and the
RFFg's own *Reichsmütterdienst* section to raise the standard of health
of 'Aryan' Germans, especially mothers and children,[105] were not to be
vitiated by removing familiar nutritious foods from the diet and diver-
ting consumption towards less healthy items. The Vw/Hw took great
care to investigate the properties of unusual new foods, to ascertain,
for example, their protein content. The section's own research bureau
carried out tests and devised palatable recipes using new substitutes, to
replace items which were becoming unobtainable in some areas. It was
reported that in August 1937 – 'as in the previous month' – there were
marked shortages of butter, eggs and pork. Lard and pork were
'scarcely to be had' in Gau Düsseldorf, where flour was much dearer
than a month earlier. It was even worse in Hessen-Nassau, with butter,
margarine, fat, oil, eggs, pork and in some places also beef, sausages,
beans, cabbage and some fruits very scarce indeed. By contrast,
Schleswig-Holstein reported 'a very good state of the market'.[106] In
October 1937 it was reported that the best supplies of meat and fats
were, not surprisingly, in more agricultural areas, but also in Berlin and
Hamburg; worst-served was the southern-central area around Würzburg
and Nuremberg.[107] The Vw/Hw claimed – as part of its own 'success'
– that in 1937 the consumption of fish, potatoes and cheese was
markedly higher than in 1936, but it seems improbable that a 6 per
cent increase in fish consumption, along with 9 per cent for potatoes
and 13 per cent for cheese,[108] would suffice to meet the shortfall in
supplies of meat and fats, at a time when demand as a whole was
rising.[109] The search for substitutes was pursued with ever greater
vigour, and dried fruit and vegetables, 'German pudding meal' and
'German teas' were the result.[110] In the new 'type 502' flour, a 7 per
cent maize content eked out more accustomed grain, while flour was
also obtained from soya. Dried skimmed milk and dried curd were
tried and found adequate for certain recipes. But substitution was not
to involve extra expense – quite the reverse – so that short-cuts like
soup cubes and custard powder were not to be recommended by the

Vw/Hw, since they would only add to household expenditure.[111]

The task which the Vw/Hw set itself − or had set for it by more powerful agencies − was thus trebly complicated. It would have been enough to try to divert housewives' consumption from accustomed foodstuffs and familiar materials to substitute foods rich in protein and synthetic fabrics. Yet over and above this was the aim of throttling back demand altogether and reducing consumer expenditure of all kinds, at a time when most Germans were better off than they had been for years. Much was said, in Vw/Hw propaganda, about how an 'extremely economical and especially skilful housewife can feed even a large family adequately on a small income'.[112] It was, alleged Else Vorwerck, simply a matter of using available income more rationally,[113] and the Vw/Hw assumed responsibility for trying to educate women to this end. But even with higher taxes and a relatively high level of personal savings in the later 1930s,[114] the middle class and some sections of the industrial working class, with a rising real income, had more money to spend, and most Germans were no worse off than they had been before the Wall Street Crash and the Depression.[115] In these circumstances, exhortations to restrain demand in the national interest were bound to be not only unpopular but also ineffective. Yet since the government would not act to reduce dramatically the availability of goods − including imported luxury goods[116] − either through rationing or through the running down of consumer goods production, its agents were restricted to exhortation as the only means of trying to depress demand.

In the Vw/Hw's case, the appeal to housewives consisted not only of propaganda about thrifty ways with food, but also of pleas to abjure 'unnecessary' luxury, in the form, for example, of gadgets 'which are not required for the improvement of housekeeping . . . since they unnecessarily increase the costs of the household'.[117] Much time was spent investigating methods of washing, and in 1937 the Vw/Hw issued three pages of detailed instructions to try to ensure that housewives prolonged the life of clothing to the utmost.[118] Also in 1937, women were urged to take bags or baskets for shopping, to reduce the need for packaging goods and thus save paper.[119] Propaganda of this kind made sense in wartime, and was greatly intensified then, with advice about dyeing clothes, combating moths, repairing household goods and conserving energy.[120] But in pre-war years, without rationing in force and with imported goods still available on a substantial scale,[121] it was doomed to remain in large measure a pious hope. The uninhibited discontent manifested about shortages in wartime[122] suggest that Hitler's regime was prudent to refrain from trying to impose controls of a more than superficial kind on peacetime consumption.

Yet the consequence of this, dependence on the power of propaganda, demonstrated once again the limits to totalitarian control in the Third Reich, prevented the possibility of the achievement of autarky, and revealed rather the powerlessness of propaganda when its message was unpalatable. The mammoth effort made by the activists of the Vw/Hw to persuade women to adjust their habits and to instruct them on how to economise perhaps had some effect among those whose meagre income necessitated economy. A special effort was certainly made by Vw/Hw workers to help housewives in needy families to obtain the maximum nutritional benefit from a minimal income.[123] But those who could afford to eat meat regularly and were able to obtain it were unlikely to be fobbed off with exhortations about eating fish or cheese or more potatoes instead if that was not what they wished. Those who could afford new clothes – following fashions advertised in the DFW's own magazine[124] – would not be willing to mend, darn and dye in order to look dowdy and shabby. A domestic servant, allocated, perhaps, through the Homecraft Year scheme, might obviate the need for household labour-saving devices, but the over-whelming majority of households did not have such help. With more women going out to work in 1939 than ever before,[125] and with added pressures in wartime, the time available for preserving fruit, making Christmas presents and attending courses was actually decreasing. It is not impossible to persuade people to exert self-restraint and make sacrifices in the cause of a compelling ideology: the Christian Churches, especially, have succeeded in this. Nevertheless, the task which National Socialists set themselves, of convincing Germans to make sacrifices which seemed unnecessary – without the sanction of hellfire – was formidable. Propaganda clearly failed to make the German housewife identify herself with a cause which was manifestly not in her interests. That is a comment both on the wickedness of the cause and on the natural limits which there inevitably are to the power of propaganda.

Notes

1. Dieter Petzina, *Autarkiepolitik im Dritten Reich* (Stuttgart, 1968), p. 175.

2. NSDAP Hauptarchiv (Bundesarchiv Koblenz), reel 13, folder 253 (HA/13/253), 'Rundschreiben' ('R') 'Nr. 141/42', 8 June 1942.

3. See Timothy W. Mason, *Sozialpolitik im Dritten Reich* (Opladen, 1977), Ch. 1, pp. 15-41.

4. Judge Freisler, quoted in Ger van Roon, *German Resistance to Hitler. Count von Moltke and the Kreisau Circle* (London, 1971), p. 279.

5. HA/13/254, Hildegard Passow, 'Zur Chronik der N.S. Frauenschaft', 1 July 1934, p. 6.

6. HA/13/254, Hildegard Passow, 'Propagandistisch Erfassung der Frau', autumn 1931; Gertrud Scholtz-Klink, *Die Frau im Dritten Reich* (Tübingen, 1978), pp. 82-90.

7. Berlin Document Center, *Sammlung Schumacher* (*Slg.Sch.*), 230, n.d. (?1940), p. 7.

8. Scholtz-Klink, *Die Frau*, 'H. Hauptabteilung Grenz- und Auslandsarbeit', p. 255.

9. Jill Stephenson, *The Nazi Organisation of Women* (London, 1980), pp. 130-43, 180-5; Jill Stephenson, ' "Reichsbund der Kinderreichen": the League of Large Families in the Population Policy of Nazi Germany', *European Studies Review* (July 1979), pp. 350-75; Leila J. Rupp, *Mobilizing Women for War: German and American Propaganda 1939-1945* (Princeton, 1978), pp. 115-36, 167-75.

10. Max Domarus, *Hitler. Reden und Proklamationen 1932-45* (Munich, 1965), vol. I, p. 450.

11. Stephenson, *Nazi Organisation*, pp. 145-6.

12. Bundesarchiv (BA), *Slg.Sch.*, 230, 'Die Organisation der nationalsozialistischen Frauen in der Nationalsozialistischen Frauenschaft', 1 November 1931.

13. Wolfram Fischer, *Deutsche Wirtschaftspolitik 1918-1945* (Opladen, 1968), pp. 71-5; Mason, *Sozialpolitik*, p. 35; Petzina, *Autarkiepolitik*, pp. 18-20.

14. Fischer, *Wirtschaftspolitik*, pp. 59-60.

15. Fischer, *Wirtschaftspolitik*, pp. 75-6.

16. Stephenson, *Nazi Organisation*, pp. 148-9, 155.

17. Stephenson, *Nazi Organisation*, pp. 139, 141-3, 169-72.

18. BA, *Slg.Sch.*, 230, 1 November 1931.

19. Reichsfrauenführung (ed.), *NS-Frauenschaft* (Berlin, 1937), p. 25.

20. HA/13/253, 'R Nr. F.W. 90/37', 5 October 1937.

21. Stephenson, *Nazi Organisation*, pp. 157-8, 163-5.

22. BA, NS22/vorl. 318, 'Reichsfrauenführung', Nr. PP1.

23. HA/13/253, 'R FW Nr. 97/37', 21 October 1937.

24. Stephenson, *Nazi Organisation*, p. 91.

25. Berlin Document Center, *Slg.Sch.*, 230, 'NS-Frauenschaft, Juli 1936, Betrifft: Zugehörigkeit der Hausfrauen zum DFW bzw. zur DAF'.

26. David Schoenbaum, *Hitler's Social Revolution* (London, 1967), p. 206, coined this term.

27. Fischer, *Wirtschaftspolitik*, pp. 77, 82.

28. HA/13/253, 'R FW Nr. 71/37', 4 August 1937.

29. HA/13/253, 'R FW Nr. 98/37', 23 October 1937.

30. HA/13/253, 'R FW Nr. 97/37', 21 October 1937.

31. 'Hauptabteilung Volkswirtschaft-Hauswirtschaft', *Deutsches Frauenschaffen im Kriege* (1941), p. 50.

32. Institut für Zeitgeschichte Archiv (IfZ), MA 130, frame 86493, 'Pgn. Scholtz-Klink: Die NS-Frauenschaft', 17 April 1939.

33. BA, *Slg.Sch.*, 230, *Reichsfrauenführung Jahresbericht 1938*, pp. I-II, 8.

34. E.g. *Deutsches Frauenschaffen* (1941), pp. 36-50; *Nationalsozialistische Frauenschaft*.

35. See e.g. HA/13/254, Gau History Halle-Merseburg, pp. 4-6.

36. Stephenson, *Nazi Organisation*, p. 187.

37. HA/13/253, 'R FW Nr. 89/37', 6 October 1937.

38. HA/13/253, 'R FW Nr. 110/37', 24 November 1937.

39. HA/13/253, 'R Nr. FW 64/37', 3 July 1937; 'R FW Nr. 77/37', 20 August 1937.

40. HA/13/253: 'R FW Nr. 73/37', 9 August 1937; 'R FW Nr. 97/37', 21 October 1937.

41. HA/13/253, 'R Nr. FW 92/41', 13 August 1941.

42. HA/13/253, 'R FW 149/41', 19 December 1941.

43. HA/13/253: 'R Nr. 60/42', 19 March 1942; 'R Nr. 113/42', 7 May 1942; 'R Nr. 126/42', 20 May, 1942.

44. Dietrich Orlow, *History of the Nazi Party 1933-1945* (Newton Abbot, 1973), pp. 415, 425-6, 456; Heinz Boberach (ed.), *Meldungen aus dem Reich* (Munich, 1968), pp. 346, 405, 411.

45. HA/13/253, 'R Nr. 182/42', 24 July 1942.

46. HA/13/253, 'R Nr. FW 93/41', 14 August 1941; Stephenson, *Nazi Organisation*, p. 186.

47. HA/13/253, 'R Nr. FW 92/41', 13 August 1941.

48. HA/13/253, 'R FW Nr. 97/37', 21 October 1937; *Deutsches Frauen-schaffen* (1941), pp. 36-50.

49. HA/13/253, 'R Nr. F 137/41', 19 November 1941; Stephenson, *Nazi Organisation*, pp. 187-9.

50. HA/13/253, 'R Nr. F.W. 54/37', 9 June 1937.

51. HA/13/253, 'R FW Nr. 120/37', 20 December 1937.

52. HA/13/253, 'R FW. 123/41', 22 October 1941.

53. HA/13/253, 'R Nr. 56/42', 11 March 1942.

54. HA/13/253, 'R Nr. 182/42', 24 July 1942.

55. HA/13/253, 'R FW Nr. 107/37', 6 November 1937.

56. HA/13/253, 'R FW Nr. 88/37', 6 October 1937.

57. HA/13/253, 'R FW Nr. 99/37', 25 October 1937.

58. HA/13/253, 'R FW Nr. 74/37', 11 August 1937.

59. HA/13/253, 'R FW Nr. 73/37', 9 August 1937.

60. HA/13/253, 'R FW Nr. 120/37', 20 December 1937; Dr Else Vorwerck, 'Hauptabteilung Volkswirtschaft-Hauswirtschaft', *Deutsches Frauenschaffen* (1939), p. 35.

61. HA/13/253, 'R Nr. FW 108/37', 11 November 1937.

62. Vorwerck, 'Hauptabteilung', pp. 41-2.

63. *Nationalsozialistische Frauenschaft*, p. 27.

64. BA, *Slg.Sch.*, 230, *Jahresbericht 1938*, p. III.

65. Vorwerck, 'Hauptabteilung', p. 35; HA/13/253, 'R Nr. FW 98/37', 23 October 1937.

66. Vorwerck, 'Hauptabteilung', p. 43; BA, *Slg.Sch.*, 230, *Jahresbericht 1938*, p. III.

67. Vorwerck, 'Hauptabteilung', p. 44.

68. BA, *Slg.Sch.*, 230, *Jahresbericht 1938*, p. IV.

69. HA/13/253, 'R FW Nr. 97/37', 21 October 1937.

70. HA/13/253: 'R FW Nr. 70/41', 25 June 1941; 'R FW Nr. 97/37', 21 October 1937.

71. HA/13/253, 'R FW Nr. 69/37', 30 July 1937.

72. HA/13/253: 'R FW 62/37', 4 July 1937; 'R FW Nr. 73/37', 9 August 1937; 'R FW Nr. 34/37', 11 August 1937.

73. HA/13/253, 'R Nr. FW 61/37', 26 June 1937.

74. HA/13/253, 'R Nr. FW 65/37', 3 July 1937.

75. Vorwerck, 'Hauptabteilung', pp. 35-6.

76. BA, *Slg.Sch.*, 230, *Jahresbericht 1938*, p. III.

77. Stephenson, *Nazi Organisation*, pp. 152-5, 160-1.

78. HA/13/253, 'R Nr. 166/42', 17 July 1942.

79. Stephenson, *Nazi Organisation*, pp. 194-5.

80. IfZ, MA 225, frame 2-408,812, 'Aus der Arbeit der NS-Frauenschaft im Wartheland', 29 April 1942.

81. IfZ, MA 130, frames 86403, 86411-2, 'Jahresbericht der Arbeit der Kreisfrauenschaftsleitung Strassburg vom 1.10.41 bis 1.10.42'.

82. IfZ, MA 130, frames 86411-2, 'Jahresbericht . . . bis 1.10.42'.

83. Vorwerck, 'Hauptabteilung', p. 35.

84. Scholtz-Klink, *Die Frau*, 'G. Hauptabteilung Volkswirtschaft-Hauswirtschaft', p. 234.

85. BA, *Slg.Sch.*, 230, *Jahresbericht 1938*, p. 28.

86. BA, *Slg.Sch.*, 230, *Jahresbericht 1938*, p. I.

87. Z.A.B. Zeman, *Nazi Propaganda* (London, 1964), pp. 51-2, 116; Richard Grunberger, *A Social History of the Third Reich* (London, 1974), pp. 506-7.

88. HA/13/253, 'Der Frauenfunk der Woche 21.3 – 27.3.37'.

89. HA/13/253, 'R FW Nr. 97/37', 21 October 1937.

90. IfZ, MA 130, frame 86402, 'Jahresbericht . . . bis 1.10.42'.

91. HA/13/253, 'R Nr. 125/42', 26 May 1942.

92. HA/13/253, 'R Nr. 96/42', 30 April 1942.

93. HA/13/253,'R FW Nr. 87/37', 6 October 1937.

94. HA/13/253, 'R FW Nr. 104/37', 1 November 1937.

95. HA/13/253, 'R Nr. FW 108/37', 11 November 1937.

96. HA/13/253, 'R FW Nr. 98/37', 23 October 1937.

97. HA/13/253, 'R FW Nr. 97/37', 21 October 1937.

98. HA/13/253, 'R FW Nr. 87/37', 6 October 1937.

99. Peter Diehl-Thiele, *Partei und Staat im Dritten Reich* (Munich, 1971), p. 168; BA, NS22/vorl.110, 'Aufgabe des Blockleiters sowie des Blockwalters' (n.d.), pp. 3, 5.

100. HA/13/253, 'R Nr. FW 93/37', 13 October 1937.

101. HA/13/253, 'R FW Nr. 96/37', 20 October 1937.

102. *Deutsches Frauenschaffen* (1941), p. 48.

103. BA, NS22/vorl. 110, Winfried Thomsen, 'Aufklärungs- und Informations-Material zur Reichs-Spinnstoff-Sammlung 1941' (6 March 1941).

104. BA, NS22/vorl. 396, 'Die Partei im Kriege (IV)', *Völkischer Beobachter*, 12 July 1940.

105. I am grateful to Mrs Cecilia Smith, Edinburgh University, for information about the NSV's concern about the national health; Stephenson, *Nazi Organisation*, pp. 163-5.

106. HA/13/253, 'R Nr. FW 81/37', 30 September 1937.

107. HA/13/253, 'R FW Nr. 96/37', 20 October 1937.

108. Vorwerck, Hauptabteilung', p. 36.

109. Mason, *Sozialpolitik*, pp. 232-3.

110. Vorwerck, 'Hauptabteilung', p. 37.

111. HA/13/253, 'R FW Nr. 97/37', 21 October 1937.

112. HA/13/253, 'R FW Nr. 97/37', 21 October 1937.

113. Vorwerck, 'Hauptabteilung', p. 39.

114. René Erbe, *Die nationalsozialistische Wirtschaftspolitik 1933-1939 im Lichte der modernen Theorie* (Zürich, 1958), pp. 147-60, warns against overestimating the extent and importance of higher personal savings in the years 1933-8.

115. Mason, *Sozialpolitik*, p. 231.

116. Mason, *Sozialpolitik*, pp. 233-4.

117. HA/13/253, 'R FW Nr. 97/37', 21 October 1937.

118. HA/13/253, 'R FW Nr. 60/37', 28 June 1937.

119. HA/13/253, 'R FW Nr. 104/37', 1 November 1937.

120. HA/13/253: 'R Nr. 74/42', 9 April 1942; 'R Nr. FW 140/41', 10 December 1941; 'R Nr. 24/42', 2 February 1942; 'R Nr. 96/42', 30 April, 1942; 'R Nr. 175/42', 17 July 1942; 'R Nr. 199/42', 27 August 1942.

121. Mason, *Sozialpolitik*, pp. 233-4; Petzina, *Autarkiepolitik*, pp. 111-14; but c.f. Marlis G. Steinert, *Hitlers Krieg und die Deutschen* (Düsseldorf, 1970), pp. 62-3, for reports on complaints made about shortages before the war.

122. BA, NS22/vorl. 110, 'Wo steht die innere Front?' (n.d.); Boberach, *Meldungen*, pp. 80, 210-12, 277-8, 361-3, 366-8, Steinert, *Hitlers Krieg*, pp. 164-5, 179-83, 197-8, 213-15, 283-6, 389

123. HA/13/253, 'R FW Nr. 96/37', 20 October 1937; Vorwerck, 'Hauptabteilung', pp. 37-40.

124. *Frauenkultur im Deutschen Frauenwerk* regularly carried both features and advertisements about smart ladies' clothes in the 1930s; Jill Stephenson, *Women in Nazi Society* (London, 1975), pp. 190-1.

125. Dörte Winkler, *Frauenarbeit im 'Dritten Reich'* (Hamburg, 1977), pp. 194-5; Stephenson, *Women in Nazi Society*, pp. 100-1.

8 NAZI PROPAGANDA IN OCCUPIED WESTERN EUROPE: THE CASE OF THE NETHERLANDS

Gerhard Hirschfeld

On 10 May 1940 German troops attacked and invaded the neighbouring Netherlands without a formal declaration of war. It was the carefully prepared start of the Western Offensive which was to culminate in the surrender of France six weeks later on 22 June. After a short and brave fight the Dutch armies conceded defeat. In view of the high number of casualties, particularly amongst the civilian population, General Winkelman, the Dutch Commander-in-Chief, signed the capitulation document on 15 May in Rijsoord, a small village near Rotterdam.

While the German military were still concerned to establish a straightforward military administration, 'strictly observing the Hague Land Warfare Convention', and without appearing to have any intention of annexing the country, Hitler, on 17 May, issued an order that the 'unpolitical German military administration' should be replaced by a civilian administration and that the 'highest executive authority' should be transferred to a political *Reichskommissar* (Reich Commissioner), as was already the case in occupied Norway.[1] Before taking office the newly-appointed *Reichskommissar für die besetzten niederländischen Gebiete*, Arthur Seyss-Inquart, had two audiences with Hitler (19 and 25 May), during which he was put in the picture regarding the Führer's ideas for a 'New Order' in the *Reichskommissariat Niederlande* and the basic principles of the policy to be pursued. In his First Report, presented to Hitler on 23 July 1940,[2] Seyss-Inquart formulated his instructions again, pointing out that they consisted of 'securing public order and public life for the protection of the Reich's interests'. Then he specified the political mission bound up with these instructions of 'economically linking the Netherlands as closely as possible to the Reich, but at the same time preserving their formal independence in order to maintain control over the Dutch-Indian areas' (i.e. the Dutch colonies in the Far East). This could most easily be achieved 'if we succeed in formulating a series of political objectives which make an economic link with the Reich seem to be the will of the Dutch people'.

The *Reichskommissar* was well aware of the difficulties and contradictions which were, of necessity, fundamental to such an under-taking. The interests of the occupation force demanded, on the one hand, 'the complete suppression of all possible forms of public activity'; on the other hand, it was desirable 'in order to awaken and manoeuvre the political objectives, to allow such freedoms as will make the end result a decision which the Dutch have made themselves'. By his own definition, the task would have to be considered accomplished when the adhesion of the Netherlands to National Socialism and the German Reich was accepted as an autonomous and unforced act on the part of the populace. The cautious tactics of the occupation authorities in the first months were thus determined by the desire to create a broad basis as quickly as possible from which to assist the breakthrough of the concept of 'self-nazification'.[3]

However, this tactical variant of a cautious policy did not prevent the Nazi leadership from further elaborating their vision of a post-war European order. Ideas that had been formulated in connection with the so-called *Lebensraum* doctrine in the East were, in accordance with the 'racially' based assessment of the European peoples, also applied to the Western nations. Indeed even in his first address to the people of the Netherlands (on 25 May) *Reichskommissar* Seyss-Inquart referred frequently to the 'blood-ties' between the German and Dutch peoples, which were the precondition for a common life and fate ('*Schicksals-gemeinschaft*').[4] The *Reichsführer-SS* and head of the German Police, Heinrich Himmler, went one step further. In a New Year's greeting to Seyss-Inquart he characterised the latter's 'historically so important task' as to

> bring back, with a firm but gentle hand, nine million Germanic-Dutch people who for centuries had been estranged from all that is German and to re-introduce them to the German-Germanic comm-unity (*Deutsch-Germanische Gemeinschaft*). We are both absolutely certain that this task of creating a community of 110 million people is just the base for a real Greater Germanic Reich.[5]

Hitler also shared the vision of a Greater Germanic Reich in which the Netherlands, as a Germanic brother-nation, would to some extent take a privileged place. Undoubtedly as far as Hitler was concerned direct annexation would have been the simplest and 'cleanest' solution, but at the time political considerations made this impossible – the Führer was still hoping for a possible arrangement with England. At the same time he made no secret of his intention of making the Netherlands directly dependent upon Nazi Germany ideologically and politically, regardless of their constitutional status. To this end Hitler was initially even prepared to offer the hitherto insignificant Dutch Fascist movement a chance to co-operate, possibly even by forming a National Socialist government. The establishment of a government run by the Dutch did not, however, mean that the essential idea of annexing the Netherlands had been abandoned; in fact it was to represent an important step in this direction. Naturally they would have to be 'very cautious towards the Dutch and the Norwegians in discussing these issues', Hitler informed his dinner guests on 5 April 1942:

> In 1938 he had not told the Austrians that he wanted to absorb them into Germany: rather he had suggested that he wanted to unite them with Germany into the Greater Germanic Reich. Thus the Germanic peoples of the North-west and North must always be reminded that this is a question of the Germanic Reich . . . which happens to have its strongest source of ideological and military strength in Germany.[6]

The message was clear enough: the concept of a 'Greater Germanic Reich' had, according to its foremost prophet and Führer, no other function than to prepare the ground by means of propaganda and psychological persuasion for the *Anschluss* of the 'Germanic' peoples to the Reich, just like the Austrian solution of 1938. The National Socialist 'revolution' they were looking for was still – as Goebbels stressed in a confidential talk with leading German journalists in April 1940 – the 'same revolution' they had carried out on a smaller scale in Germany after 1933. This time it would be executed on the basis of the same 'principles, experiences and methods', but in greater 'dimensions'.[7] In analogy to the social and political *Gleichschaltung* (enforced 'co-ordination') after the seizure of power, this process was now to be repeated outside the borders of the old Reich 'in rapid succession' (Goebbels).

The *Reichskommissar*'s attitude during the first phase of the German occupation reflected this recommendation to an amazingly high degree. This applies to Seyss-Inquart's attempt to win over the minds of the Dutch people in favour of adhesion to Nazi Germany and to induce them, as it were, to 'self-nazification' with the aid of collaborating institutions and well-tested propaganda devices. It also applies, however, to the ideological and organisational *Gleichschaltung* of Dutch public life, promoted above all by *Generalkommissar* Fritz Schmidt. In this sphere in particular the former *Gaupropagandaleiter* and party representative in the Reich Propaganda Ministry proved to be an able pupil of Joseph Goebbels. The 're-organisation' of the Dutch media, organised under Schmidt's responsibility, the *Gleichschaltung* in the cultural sphere and the establishment of a Dutch Propaganda Ministry – all were impressive indications of the effectiveness of the *General-kommissar zur besonderen Verwendung* (General Commissioner for Special Affairs).

By comparison, Seyss-Inquart's strategy of self-nazification turned out to be a political miscalculation. The majority of the Dutch parties, Trade Unions and other institutions made known, indeed repeatedly, their interest in co-operating with the occupation authorities, and some of them were prepared to make the required concessions regarding personnel and organisation; but they refused the radical ideological committment envisaged by the *Reichskommissar*. But even though this policy of the 'gentle hand' (Himmler) was already showing signs of failure in the late autumn of 1940, Seyss-Inquart at first continued to hold fast to his original concept. This was partly due to the fact that he had clearly over-estimated the initial success of establishing a bour-geois-national unification movement, the *Nederlandse Unie* (Netherlands Union). Because of its heterogeneous structure and the ambivalence of its policy, the membership of this organisation had reached proportions previously unknown in the Netherlands. The 'unity movement' was finally dissolved after it became apparent that, despite some rather dubious statements and highly controversial actions by its leaders, it refused to agree to every single step the occupying power intended to take.[8]

Seyss-Inquart's strategy was further handicapped by his cautious tactics towards the native Fascist groups, as it were, the second leg of the collaboration policy. But his desire 'to keep several irons in the fire' at the same time led to increased distrust amongst the Dutch public and ultimately meant that his policy, supposedly based on broad agreement, was rejected.

In contrast to this, *Generalkommissar* Schmidt, whose department was formally in charge of all propaganda activities, set his sights above all on the Dutch National Socialist Party (NSB) – though certainly not without ambitions of his own. Its leading members, and particularly its *Leider*, Anton Mussert, proved to be useful tools for German policy. Above all, in the *Gleichschaltung* of public life the German authorities could count on the co-operation of opportunist and ambitious members of the NSB. Dutch National Socialists also played a leading role in

liquidating traditional associations and organisations as well as in establishing replicas of the Reich's institutions, such as the 'Netherlands
Winter Help', the 'Voluntary Labour Service' or the 'Netherlands
Labour Front'. Admittedly, the Mussert-movement did not succeed in
forming a Dutch Fascist government, despite numerous attempts by its
leader and his closest supporters, but on the other hand, in order to
implement their measures, the occupation authorities were constantly
forced to seek the co-operation and support of the NSB.

According to the decree issued on 3 June 1940 *Generalkommissar*
Schmidt was to be 'responsible for all matters relating to the formation
of public opinion',[9] i.e. propaganda. He was in charge of the so-called
Hauptabteilung Volksaufklärung und Propaganda, an institution modelled on the Reich Propaganda Ministry. The staff of the propaganda
department, comprising ten 'sections', consisted of former members of
the Press and Cultural Department of the German Embassy in the
Hague and of some members of the Reich propaganda offices, while the
majority were employees of the Reich Propaganda Ministry.[10] These
had come directly to the Netherlands with the German troops as the
Propaganda-Staffel-Holland, or else were specially assigned from Berlin.
The press and radio sections, later expanded into departments, were the
most heavily staffed, which emphasised the significance the Germans
placed on these spheres. They were responsible, above all, for directing
and controlling Dutch journalism.

The Nazi idea was that the press, seen by Goebbels as 'an enormously important and significant instrument for influencing the
masses', should serve state propaganda exclusively. The occupied
Netherlands were no exception to this. The assurance by the German
military authorities directly after the capitulation on 15 May 1940 that
the indigenous press would not be censored, soon proved to be an
empty promise. Instead of direct censorship 'general guidelines' were
issued and the newspaper editors were required to present the first
three printed copies of any issue for inspection by the *Reichskommissar*'s press department. At daily press conferences the editors were given
compulsory 'recommendations' regarding the choice of subjects and the
type of reports to be printed. The press conferences were initially
conducted by *Generalkommissar* Schmidt personally and later by the
head of the press department, Willi Janke; among those present were
representatives of various institutions and organisations and, initially,
also military censors. The themes dealt with most frequently were, in
the field of foreign affairs, the Allies' policy and war conduct, especially their bombardments of the Netherlands; in the domestic field there

was the question of food supply, especially rationing, the employment
of Dutch workers in Germany, the NSB and Mussert, as well as measures against Dutch Jews.[11] The central Dutch news agency (*Algemeen
Nederlands Persbureau*), which controlled the news service of all Dutch
newspapers, was taken over by the Germans as early as 15 May. The
establishment of a Dutch Propaganda Ministry (*Department van Volksvoorlichting en Kunsten*) in November 1940 seemed finally to set the
scene for the intended 'comprehensive reorganisation' of the Dutch
media. As regards its structure, sphere of responsibility and duties, the
new ministry under the Dutch Nazi Dr Tobie Goedewaagen, a lecturer
in philosophy, turned out to be an exact replica of Goebbels' Reich
Propaganda Ministry. Among its responsibilities were surveillance of the
press, radio, films, as well as control over 'non-academic literature,
music, creative arts including architecture and sculpture, theatre, ballet,
exhibitions and the combat of filth and smut'.[12] The competences and
responsibilities were so extensive that even the staff of the *Reichskommissariat* were impressed: 'These measures cut quite substantially
into the hitherto state-run machinery and into all matters of spiritual
life . . . since a state institution for a deliberate popular enlightenment
and for directing public opinion was unknown in the Netherlands'.[13]

In particular the press department of the ministry, run by Max
Blokzijl[14] − a man as eager and bustling as he was naïve − proved to be
a suitable instrument for furthering the *Gleichschaltung* of the press.
Before the war Blokzijl had been the Berlin correspondent of the liberal
Amsterdam daily, *Algemeen Handelsblad*, and had quickly been converted into a firm adherent of Fascist ideas. He played a significant role in
occupation measures against liberal and socialist newspapers and then
in June 1941 − due to his good relations with the Berlin press office −
was nominated as Director of the press department. His regular 'radio
chats' on the Hilversum Radio station soon created for Blokzijl the
reputation of a 'Dutch Goebbels', although he certainly did not have
the latter's brutal cleverness or gift for propaganda. Blokzijl now jointly
conducted the daily press conferences with the *Reichskommissar*'s
press chief. The 'press directives' and 'language regulations' laid down
there for Dutch journalists soon turned out to be so extensive that it
became necessary to compile all the prohihibitions or 'recommendations' for editors in a special pamphlet. This contained instructions on
the inclusion of photos ('no pictures of the Royal Family!'), linguistic
decrees ('it is forbidden to use English names . . . also applies to advertisements etc.'), numerous regulations regarding topics ('Any mention
of treason is forbidden') and manipulation of current events ('Nothing

may appear in the newspapers on the Hess tragedy, neither photo nor commentary, except the official German material').[15]

The concrete pretext for the 'reorganisation' of the Dutch press was an increasing shortage of paper for the printing industry caused by the war. Within one year a *Kommission zur Pressereorganisation* (Commission for reorganising the press), set up by *Generalkommissar* Schmidt and led by Max Blokzijl, had reduced the number of Dutch newspapers and periodicals by more than two thirds. Of the 710 daily and weekly newspapers that were on the market in the summer of 1940, only 184 remained a year later after the commission had done its work. Of around 4,000 journals 2,800 had ceased publication and of more than 2,000 religious pamphlets only 200 remained.[16] As a result presses were shut down and liquidations and mergers enforced in 200 enterprises in this branch; more than 4,000 people lost their jobs. The scope of those papers still in existence was curtailed to such a degree that during the last two years of the war most of the daily newspapers consisted of only two to four pages, which normally carried instructions for rationing and orders from the occupation authorities. Additional problems of supply, as well as the shortage of manpower caused by the *Arbeitseinsatz*, the deportation of workers to Germany, and the ever-increasing police raids, made the situation even worse. The end of the occupation period also saw the end of the non-Nazi press in the Netherlands. The consequences of war and occupation policy had simply 'organised it away'.[17]

Control and diversion of the Dutch press were by no means the only Nazi initiatives in the sphere of journalistic propaganda. Virtually from the start of the occupation the occupation force had a political mouthpiece of their own, the *Deutsche Zeitung in den Niederlanden* (German Newspaper in the Netherlands), DZN for short.[18] The DZN was one of 27 occupation newspapers issued in the whole of Europe during the war. In the Government-General of Poland alone there were four German newspapers. They were all published by the *Europa Verlag GmbH*, a sister-enterprise to the NSDAP's own *Eher-Verlag*. Apart from the propaganda effect, the initiators of this enterprise also anticipated a certain financial reward, especially since the occupation authorities generally guaranteed to sell a large proportion of each edition. There were 30,000 copies of the first issue of the DZN in June 1940; two years later this had already risen to 55,000. The newspaper had a permanent staff of ten, who were employed until the end of the war. The last issue, a duplicated sheet containing the final *Wehrmachtsbericht* was published on 5 May 1945. Apart from the permanent staff, the newspaper also had a large number of freelance contributors from Germany, the Netherlands and other occupied areas, who were used primarily for the extensive political leader articles. Among these were Joseph Goebbels and Arthur Seyss-Inquart. As regards language, style and format the *Deutsche Zeitung in den Niederlanden* aimed at a certain solidarity, reminiscent of the *Frankfurter Zeitung* or the weekly *Das Reich*. Despite all this the DZN had only a very meagre non-German readership. Most of the Dutch people rejected it from the outset as a propaganda organ. The majority of its readers were German troops stationed in the Netherlands, the staff of the *Reichkommissariat* and, last but by no means least, the staff of the allied intelligence services in London and Washington. Indeed, the German newspapers in the occupied European countries 'frequently yielded more information of value than the German home press. They were a primary source for the actions and policies of the German occupation officials.'[19]

In many respects German press policy in the occupied Netherlands reflected the general political development. It is, however, surprising that the press was spared the rivalries and 'trench warfare' between the competing occupation authorities, as well as the ideological and power-political disputes conducted within the Dutch Nazi party. Contrary to expectation, press policy remained the domain of the *Reichskommissar* and his press chiefs. Various attempts by the German SS and their Dutch auxilliaries to establish themselves within the indigenous press were carried out only half-heartedly and without the necessary persistance. This must also be an indication of the insignificance the German SS had come to attach to Dutch journalism. The *Generalkommissar für das Sicherheitswesen* (General Commissioner for Security), Hanns-Albin Rauter, Himmler's 'plenipotentiary' in the Netherlands, concentrated his propaganda efforts on recruiting SS volunteers and on proclaiming the 'Greater Germanic Reich' in the notorious *SS Kampfschriften* (fighting pamphlets). Examples of these would be the Dutch-language journals *Storm* (*Kampfblatt* of the Dutch SS), *SS-Vormingsbladen* and *Germanische Leithefte* (indoctrination for SS volunteers), as well as the organs for promoting the 'Germanic racial community' *Hamer* and *Volksche Wacht*. The last two contained mystic racialism and pseudo-scientific discussions, primarily concerned with eugenics and theories of evolution and genealogy as propagated by Nazi scientists. The number of copies printed of these SS pamphlets was certainly surprisingly high – for example, about 42,000 copies of *Storm* in 1944 – but they were hardly ever distributed beyond the circle of native SS supporters and fanatical Nazis.[20]

It is a well-known fact that films were particularly important as a mass-medium in Nazi propaganda. Goebbels' conviction that the film was one of the 'most modern and most important scientific means of influencing the masses' resulted in his demand that 'a government should not leave films to themselves'.[21] This was even more true of the film industry in the German-occupied countries of Europe. But in contrast to the wholesale confiscations which took place in the East, the film industry in the West was left in the possession of its owners, unless they were Jews, with the intention that after the war they should continue to operate in a kind of 'common market' that was heavily biased in Germany's favour.[22] Dutch film production was already linked with Germany through the *Tobis* syndicate before the war and studios in Amsterdam and The Hague were frequently used by German companies. As production continued the entire film industry was put under the control of *Generalkommissar* Schmidt's propaganda department and the existing film censorship replaced by a *Staatsfilmprüfstelle*, based on German censorship legislation and led by a Dutch Nazi. Cinema-owners were instructed to show 'certain films because of their great enlightening, educational and cultural value'.[23] Amongst these, for example, were such infamous anti-semitic productions as Fritz Hippler's pseudo documentary *Der ewige Jude* (The Eternal Jew) and Veit Harlan's *Jud Süss*, both dubbed into Dutch. There was also an 'obligation to show' short propaganda films such as *With Germany against Bolshevism*, *With Germany for a new Europe* or *With Germany for Free Netherlands* (all from 1941), as well as films publicising all the various Nazi organisations.[24] The majority of the other films, however, were supposedly apolitical entertainment films, either German, Dutch or Italian productions. Compared with the pre-war period, film-going actually increased, which would seem to suggest that the Dutch people's desire for entertainment far exceeded the revulsion against Nazi propaganda. All the same, the Propaganda Ministry decreed that no one was allowed to enter or leave the cinema during the newsreels and propaganda films and that while these films were showing there was to be no laughing, coughing or any other expressions of scorn or derision. 500 paid controllers were posted in cinemas all over the country with orders to catch and denounce the offenders.[25] Evidently the Nazi propagandists were not quite certain of the effectiveness of their products and campaigns.

Parallel to the process of *Gleichschaltung* in the sphere of the media, Dutch art and culture were also regularised and 're-organised'. Here again the initial political and organisational ambitions of the occupation authorities and the Dutch Nazis were largely identical: the establishment of an organisation of professions along the lines of the *Reichskulturkammer* (Reich Chamber of Culture), of which anyone engaged in the cultural sector had to become a member. Until an institutional framework like the *Kulturkammer* was created, various other 'cultural organisations' attempted to lend emphasis to their demands by propaganda. Thus the *Niederländisch-Deutsche Kulturgemeinschaft* (Dutch-German Cultural Association) tried, by means of concerts, operas, plays, exhibitions and lectures, to convey to the Dutch bourgeoisie an offer of *Kraft durch Freude* (strength through joy) for elevated tastes. The relatively large number of voluntary members (from 700 when it was founded in February 1941 to almost 20,000 in July 1944) is explained by the fact that this association never developed into a purely Nazi organisation.[26] On the other hand the *Nederlandse Kultuurkring* (Dutch Circle of Culture), constituted on 28 September 1940 in the presence of *Reichskommissar* Seyss-Inquart, was a more or less closed society of intellectuals who were all prepared to collaborate with the occupying power on the basis of a 'new order' for Europe.[27] The chairman of the society was the art historian and Professor of Archaeology at the University of Amsterdam, G.A.S. Snijder. However, the appointment of the subsequent *Obersturmführer* of the Dutch SS to culturally rejuvenate the Netherlands and to remind his people of their 'völkisch characteristics' hardly paid off. In the course of 1941 the 'Circle of Culture' was disbanded and in November of that year another institution, the *Nederlandse Kultuurraad* (Dutch Council for Culture), was founded.[28] After a long search, 22 Dutchmen eventually proclaimed their willingness to belong to the country's 'cultural conscience' (Seyss-Inquart), among them the leader of the famous Amsterdam symphony orchestra, Professor Willem Mengelberg. The other members of the council were hardly known outside the Netherlands for any significant artistic or intellectual achievements. Wisely looking ahead, Seyss-Inquart warned them at their 'inauguration' that 'for taking on such a responsibility . . . they would probably receive no thanks for a long time'.[29] The chairman of the council was, once again, Professor Snijder whose high position – he was directly responsible to the *Reichskommissar* – was an indication of the significance attached by the Germans to the 'Council for Culture'. As far as Seyss-Inquart was concerned, its formal independence, as it were, the marked separation from the Mussert-movement, made it a splendid propaganda instrument and, moreover, a 'tool' for the *Reichskommissar*'s own cultural policy. But the idea did not work: the Council did not play a role of any importance.

Its members met five times in all, and discussed nothing but minor items. The significance of the 'Council of Culture' was further reduced by the founding of a second representative cultural body, the *Neder-landse Kultuurkamer* (Dutch Chamber of Culture).[30] This organisation, set up after a year's preparation by the Dutch Propaganda Ministry and the *Reichspropagandaministerium*, corresponded almost exactly to the German *Reichskulturkammer*, the only difference being that its various sections were given the mediaeval name of 'guilds'. There were six 'guilds': for the press, for films, for music, for literature, for the theatre and dance and finally for architecture and applied arts. The 'guild leaders', almost exclusively Dutch Nazis, took up their new (honorary) posts on 30 May 1942. The actual administrative work, co-ordinating the sub-groups and sections and the various programmes, was the responsibility of the (professional) 'guild administrators', who, in their turn, could enlist the support of the so-called 'guild councils'. Dutch cultural life was to be made more regionalised and decentralised by means of regional agencies of the 'Chamber of Culture'. In addition, these were to carry out the necessary propaganda activities on the spot.[31]

Figure 8.1: The Reorganisation of Dutch Culture

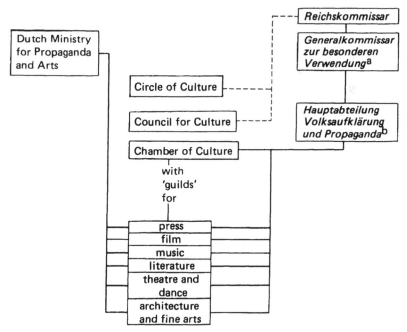

a. General Commissioner for Special Affairs; b. Department for Popular Enlightenment and Propaganda.

The guidance (or rather supervision) of the members was also the responsibility of the regional bodies and in this the selection process was facilitated enormously by the fact that membership was made compulsory. Jewish artists and organisations were excluded, but everyone else was required to register with the respective 'guild' before continuing work as an artist, journalist, actor, musician, bookseller, state-manager, art-dealer etc. In an article in the 'Chamber's' fortnightly periodical, *De Schouw*, its President, Dr Goedewaagen, declared that refusal by any cultural organisation to join the 'Chamber' was tantamount to signing its own 'death warrant'.[32] This extreme situation was the reason for the high membership (42,000) and for the co-operation — albeit often reluctant — of the majority of Dutch cultural groups and associations. Most of them acquired collective 'block' memberships, without taking the rights of the individual members into consideration. Moreover, the concept of 'culture' was extended to such a degree that even café owners who had music on their premises had to join the 'Chamber'.[33] Numerous people involved in some sort of cultural activity were forced to join, simply because of the desperate financial situation they would have fallen into as a result of the threatened *Berufsverbot* and their dependence upon public contracts. In fact, however, the majority of the population considered the *Kultuurkamer* to be just as much a typically German institution as the *Kultuurraad* — documented, apart from anything else, by the German *K* in *Kultuur* instead of the Dutch *C*.[34]

The contrasts and controversies exemplified in the two 'rival enterprises' in the sphere of Dutch culture are merely a reflection of the principal conflict between the German bodies and the native organisations dependent upon them. The controversy between the *Reichskommissar*, on the one hand, and the Reich Propaganda Ministry and its 'off-shoot' in the Netherlands — the *Department van Volksvoorlichting en Kunsten* — on the other, flared up, above all, over the question of adopting the model of the *Reichskulturkammer*. Seyss-Inquart, following his idea of 'self-nazification', called for greater participation by the Dutch people in establishing a 'national culture', while the representatives of Goebbels' ministry insisted that the Netherlands should be radically orientated towards the cultural model of the Reich.

It is impossible to say whether there was any decisive victory for one or the other. Even the cultural section of the Propaganda Department, the representative of the Reich Propaganda Ministry in the Netherlands, did not manage to win through, although it did gain some ground because the 'Chamber of Culture' it supported had a higher degree of organisation. The employees and officials of the Dutch Propaganda Ministry and the 'Chamber of Culture' had hardly got used to their new jobs and for this reason alone were no match for their German 'colleagues'. For example, all Dutch spheres of responsibility notwithstanding, surveillance and control of the cultural organisations and their members remained in the hands of the German security services (the Gestapo), who also saw to the political supervision of their respective publications.[35]

Neither the 'Council for Culture' nor the 'Chamber of Culture' became generally accepted bodies, nor did they manage to have any great spiritual influence on cultural life. The vast majority of Dutch writers, musicians and painters lived largely 'privately', having first of all formally registered with one of the 'guilds', and then waited to see what would happen. Only a minority became involved in organised resistance and in illegal work, for example in producing and distributing underground publications (*De Vrije Kunstenaar* – the Free Artist).[36] So, especially in the later years of the occupation there were two recognisable cultural systems in the Netherlands: an official one, which made great use of propaganda but had little respect from the populace, and a hidden one, the one underground, which in many respects, however, was surprising and, according to experts, greatly influenced post-war cultural development in the Netherlands.[37]

German propaganda activities in the occupied Netherlands were not restricted to the *Gleichschaltung* of Dutch media and cultural life, though this was certainly where Nazi propaganda had its most forcible and destructive results. But alongside all this organisational restructuring, remodelling and enforced adjustment there was also day-to-day propaganda, reflected in the vast amount of material that found its way into Dutch public life. *Aktivpropaganda*, (active propaganda), as it was called, consisted largely of posters, banners, leaflets and public announcements, as well as propaganda pamphlets and brochures. Their themes were constantly readapted to the changing needs of occupation policy and to shifts in the conduct of the war.[38] During the first year of the occupation, in view of the 'self-nazification' strategy, stress was put on the obvious malfunction of the pre-war political system in the Netherlands: the 'unhealthy' party-political and social segmentation of the country, the unresolved economic crises of the thirties, and the inability of the former government to protect the Dutch people. Propaganda emphasised the inevitability of a German victory and the fact that the only chance for survival lay in close co-operation with the Third Reich.[39] 170,000 copies of a brochure portraying the 'real' Adolf

Hitler and dismissing the 'false' democratic pre-war propaganda about the German Führer were distributed amongst the Dutch public.[40]

During the Battle of Britain the violent attacks against the 'pirate state England' dominated by 'plutocrats and Jews' were intensified. After British air raids, in which there were Dutch casualties, the Germans released a poster with the caption 'English fliers have no pity on peaceful citizens', which evoked much sarcastic comment among a population familiar with the German bombardment of Rotterdam.[41] The German attack on Russia in June 1941 was the occasion for a long-prepared propaganda barrage which again lent some measure of ideological cohesion to Nazi propaganda against the Bolsheviks.[42] Drawing on undoubtedly existing anti-Communist fears and sentiments in Dutch society, the *Reichskommissar* frequently stressed the need for a general 'crusade' against Soviet Russia, to save European civilisation from the horror of Bolshevik domination. An infamous portrait of a Russian soldier, looking like a cross between robot and Neanderthal man, with blood dripping from his bayonet as he went about his business of killing women and children, became a familiar sight in Dutch streets and public places. The German authorities, and especially the SS, appealed to young Dutchmen to join their German comrades in the defence of Europe against Bolshevism.[43] The highlight of the various propaganda campaigns during the summer of 1941 was the so-called V-action, which was supposed to counteract the earlier British victory-propaganda campaign specially orientated towards the German-occupied territories in Europe. Under the slogan 'V = Victory, Germany wins for Europe on all Fronts', the propaganda department of the *Reichskommissariat* launched a series of actions involving Dutch and German Nazis with the intention of repossessing the Victory sign. Amongst other things, three million sticky labels were ordered 'to be put on cars, trams, fences, walls etc.'. Apart from their Nazi emblems, party members were requested to wear an orange-coloured V-badge, and Dutch and German radio stations were to introduce their programmes with the appropriate signal in morse code.[44]

Various other propaganda campaigns followed which tried, above all, to persuade the Dutch people to join Nazi organisations of all sorts. Improving the food situation and the fight against the black market became major issues. By and large it seemed that economic and administrative considerations had replaced the political persuasion and agitation of the first period of occupation. Nazi propaganda became increasingly defensive, while, on the other hand, orders and prohibitions went along with the total nazification of the country. The defensive theme was also behind the concept of 'Fortress Europe' which developed after the German defeat at Stalingrad and the Allied successes in the Mediterranean. The more the military situation deteriorated, the more the Nazi occupation force became brutal and callous, revealing its true nature and the essence of its *Weltanschauung*. The persecution and annihilation of the Dutch Jewry, the exploitation of the country's economy and the displacement of native workers for the enforced *Arbeitseinsatz* were milestones on this road towards total aggression and destruction. The breakdown of the economy and the transport system caused catastrophic shortages in food supply, which reached a peak during the winter of 1944-5, the 'Hunger Winter'. More than 20,000 people starved to death or died of malnutritional diseases. Economic and social deprivation and the expectation of an Allied advance led to an increase in active resistance and underground activities. The terrorism of the German police and security forces, which included torturing and beating prisoners, shooting hostages and reprisal murders, caused a deep emotional revulsion against the regime.[45]

There was certainly no room for political manoeuvre or any chance of active political propaganda. It is therefore not surprising that the only significant campaigns, apart from the continuous attempts to recruit more Dutch volunteers for the 'Germanic SS', consisted of counter-propaganda and subversive actions designed to exploit the fears and anxiety of the population still further. Thousands of faked clandestine papers were distributed in order to make the underground press look ridiculous. The propaganda department of the *Reichskommissariat* produced these imitations by forcing inmates of the Vught concentration camp to typeset and print them. To maintain the illusion that the papers were genuine, most of the original copy was reproduced faithfully, merely replacing the anti-German passages by anti-Allied ones.[46]

All in all, active propaganda did not play the decisive role originally intended for it by the Nazi occupation force. As regards the widespread 'collaboration' in most sectors of the Dutch bureaucracy and industry, by social groups and organisations, including several parties and trade unions, the decision to co-operate with the German authorities was not influenced to any great degree by Nazi propaganda.[47] It was only in the ranks of the native fascist movement, and especially in Anton Mussert's Nazi party and its affiliated organisations and groups, that this propaganda fell on fertile soil.

As far as the occupied Netherlands were concerned, Nazi propaganda did not prove to be 'the war that Hitler won'.[48]

Notes

1. See K. Kwiet, *Reichskommissariat Niederlande. Versuch und Scheitern nationalsozialistischer Neuordnung* (Stuttgart, 1968), pp. 46, 49-50; L. de Jong, *Het Koninkrijk der Nederlanden in de Tweede Wereldoorlog* (10 vols., The Hague, 1969-81), vol. IV, no. 1, pp. 24-31.

2. A. Seyss-Inquart, 'Erster Bericht über die Lage und Entwicklung in den besetzten niederländischen Gebieten, Berichtzeit 29. Mai bis 19. Juli 1940', *International Military Tribunal*, vol. XXVI, Doc. 997-PS, pp. 413-29.

3. A.E. Cohen, 'Opmerkingen over de notitie van dr. De Pater over het doel van het Duitse civiele bestuur in Nederland' in A.H. Paape (ed.), *Studies over Nederland in Oorlogstijd* (The Hague, 1972), vol. 1, pp. 50-1; Kwiet, *Reichskommissariat*, pp. 93-4.

4. Text in A. Seyss-Inquart, *Vier Jahre in den Niederlanden. Gesammelte Reden, 1940-1944*, (Berlin/Amsterdam, 1944), pp. 7-12.

5. Letter from H. Himmler to A. Seyss-Inquart (7 January 1941) in N.K.C.A. In't Veld (ed.), *De SS en Nederland. Documenten uit SS-Archieven, 1935-1945*, (2 vols., The Hague, 1976), vol. 1, p. 532.

6. H. Picker (ed.), *Hitlers Tischgespräche im Führerhauptquartier 1941-1942* (Bonn, 1951), p. 254.

7. Quoted in H.-A. Jacobsen, *Der Zweite Weltkrieg. Grundzüge der Politik und Strategie in Dokumenten* (Frankfurt am Main, 1964), p. 181; idem, 'Nationalsozialistische Kriegsziele' in *Anatomie des SS-Staates* (Olten/Freiburg, 1965), vol. II, pp. 163-4.

8. Cf. G. Hirschfeld, 'Collaboration and Attentism in the Netherlands 1940-41', *Journal of Contemporary History* vol. 16 (1981), pp. 467-86, also in W. Laqueur (ed.), *The Second World War. Essays in Military and Political History* (London/Beverly Hills, 1982), pp. 101-20.

9. *Verordnungsblatt für die besetzten niederländischen Gebiete* (5 vols., The Hague, 1940-5), Verordnung (VO) 4/1940, para. 7.

10. Cf. G. Hoffmann, *Nationalsozialistische Propaganda in den Niederlanden* (Munich/Berlin, 1972), pp. 105-7.

11. Ibid., pp. 114-19; W. Janke, 'Regungen des neuen Geistes' in M. Freiherr du Prel (ed.), *Die Niederlande im Umbruch der Zeiten. Alte und neue Beziehungen zum Reich* (Würzburg, 1941), pp. 48-52.

12. *Verordnungsblatt für die besetzten niederländischen Gebiete*, VO 211/1940, para. 3.

13. Janke, 'Regungen des neuen Geistes', p. 52.

14. For biographical details see Rijksinstituut voor Oorlogsdocumentatie (RvO), Amsterdam, *Max Blokzijl. Zijn berechting en zijn veroordeling* (The Hague, 1946); de Jong, *Het Koninkrijk*, vol. V, no. 1, pp. 327-36.

15. *Niet voor Publicatie* (Not for Publication), ed. by the Press Department of the *Reichskommissariat* and the *Departiment van Volksvoorlichting en Kunsten* and collected by A. de Graaf (Amsterdam, 1943), 'Press regulations', nos. 304, 477, 414.

16. See the figures given by M. Blokzijl, 'Persorganisatie in Nederland' in H.A. Goedhart (ed.), *De Pers in Nederland (onder auspicien van het Departiment von Volksvoorlichting en Kunsten)* (Amsterdam, 1943), p. 48; Hoffmann, *Nationalsozialistische*, pp. 228-9.

17. Cf. J.B.Th. Spaan, 'Pers en Propaganda' in *Onderdrukking en Verzet. Nederland in Oorlogstijd* (Amsterdam/Arnhem, 1950), vol. II, *passim*; de Jong, *Het Koninkrijk*, vol. V, no. 11, pp. 282-324; A.J. van der Leeuw, 'La Presse néerlandaise sous l'occupation Allemande', *Revue d'histoire de la deuxième Guerre Mondiale*, no. 80 (October 1970), pp. 29-44.

18. See Hoffmann, *Nationalsozialistische Propaganda*, pp. 78-93.

19. O.J. Hale, *The Captive Press in the Third Reich* (Princeton, NJ, 1964), p. 282.

20. See In't Veld, *De SS en Nederland*, vol. I, pp. 263-82.

21. Extracts from Goebbels' address to a meeting of *Filmschaffende* in the Berlin 'Krolloper' on 10 March 1939 are quoted in J. Wulf (ed.), *Theater und Film im Dritten Reich. Eine Dokumentation* (Gütersloh, 1964), pp. 319-20.

22. See M.S. Phillips, 'The German Film Industry and the New Order' in P. Stachura (ed.), *The Shaping of the Nazi State* (London/New York, 1978), pp. 257-81, here pp. 270-1.

23. *Verordnungblatt für die besetzten niederländischen Gebiete*, VO 132/1941.

24. See Hoffmann, *Nationalsozialistische Propaganda*, pp. 245-6.

25. Cf. Spaan, 'Pers en Propaganda', pp. 173-4; E.G. Groeneveld, 'The Muses under Stress. Dutch Cultural Life during the German Occupation' in C. Madajczyk (ed.), *Inter Arma non silent Musae. The War and Culture 1939-1945)* (Warsaw, 1977), pp. 343-65, here p. 358.

26. See *Documentatie: status en werkzaamheid van Organisaties en Instellingen uit de tijd der Duitse Bezetting van Nederland, samengesteld ten behoeve van de Bijzondere Rechtspleging op last van de Procureur Fiscaal bij het Bijzonder Gerechtshof* (Amsterdam, 1947), pp. 263-4.

27. Ibid., p. 166; Groeneveld, 'The Muses', p. 349.

28. *Verordnungsblatt für die besetzten niederländischen Gebiete*, VO 211/1941; *Documentatie*, p. 168; de Jong, *Het Koninkrijk*, vol. V, no. 1, pp. 271-82.

29. Seyss-Inquart's address to the *Kulturrat* in the 'Studio Pulchri' (The Hague) on 11 February 1942 in Seyss-Inquart, *Vier Jahre in den Niederlanden*, p. 100.

30. *Verordnungsblatt für die besetzten niederländischen Gebiete*, VO 211/1941.

31. See *Documentatie*, pp. 141-3; Hoffmann, *Nationalsozialistische Propaganda*, pp. 184-91.

32. *De Schouw*, 16 March 1942, p. 5.

33. Cf. de Jong, *Het Koninkrijk*, vol. V, no. 2, p. 786.

34. Ibid., vol. V, 1, p. 276-7. Despite Dutch reservations (Snijder/Goedewaagen) about the German orthography, the cultural department of the *Reichskommissariat* had spoken out in favour of it – a further indication of the occupying power's claim to leadership, which was not hampered by any social-psychological considerations.

35. See Hoffmann, *Nationalsozialistische Propaganda*, p. 193.

36. *De Vrije Kunstenaar, 1941-1945. Facsimile herdruc van alle tijdens de bezetting verschenen afleveringen* (Amsterdam, 1970). For the resistance by artists see J. Boot, 'Het Kunstenaarverzet' in *Onderdrukking en Verzet*, vol. II, pp. 523-32; de Jong, *Het Koninkrijk*, vol. V, no. 2, pp. 759-90; Groeneveld, 'The Muses', *passim*.

37. Cf. *Delta – A Review of Arts, Life and Thought in the Netherlands*, vol. VIII (Amsterdam, 1965); 'War Poetry from Occupied Holland', in *Poetry Review*, vol. XXXV, no. 4 (London, 1944), pp. 225-38; *War Poetry from Occupied Holland* (London, 1945); B.H. Wabeke, 'Dutch Underground Publications' in *The Library of Congress Quarterly Journal of Current Acquisitions* (Washington DC, 1947), pp. 3-7; A.E. Simoni, *Dutch Clandestine Printing, 1940-1945* (London, 1972); D. Dooijes, 'Untergrunddrucke in den besetzten Niederlanden', *Buchhandelsgeschichte* vol. I, no. 2 (1979), pp. 3-21.

38. A.F.G. Hoesel (see Spaan, 'Pers en Propaganda', p. 133) distinguishes between three phases of propaganda, reflecting the changing influences and policies of the occupation force: (1) phase of promises – indirect propaganda/ campaigning; (2) phase of orders and prohibition – direct propaganda; (3) phase of terror – indirect propaganda/subversion.

39. See W. Warmbrunn, *The Dutch under German Occupation, 1940-1945* (Stanford and London, 1963), p. 51.

40. The brochure *Wilt U de waarheid weten? Hitler zoals men hem aan U getoond heeft en zoals hij in werkelijkheid is* was published in November 1940.

41. See Warmbrunn, *The Dutch*, p. 51.

42. Cf. J.W. Baird, *The Mythical World of Nazi War Propaganda, 1939-1945* (Minneapolis, 1974), esp. pp. 147-65.

43. Warmbrunn, *The Dutch*, p. 51. See for example Z. Zeman (ed.), *Selling the War. Art and Propaganda in World War II* (London, 1978), pp. 100-3.

44. See Hoffmann, *Nationalsozialistische*, pp. 252-3.

45. Cf. Warmbrunn, *The Dutch*, p. 264; H. van der Zee, *The Hunger Winter. Occupied Holland 1944-5* (London, 1982).

46. See P. Rijser, 'Nazi Propaganda in bezet Nederland' in Z.A.B. Zeman (ed.), *De propaganda van de Nazi's* (Hilversum/Antwerpen, 1966), p. 197-8.

47. For the phenomenon of 'collaboration during the Nazi occupation see G. Hirschfeld, *Die Kollaboration mit der deutschen Besatzungsmacht in den Niederlanden während des zweiten Weltkriegs* (Stuttgart, 1983).

48. See R.E. Herzstein, *The War that Hitler Won. The most infamous propaganda campaign in history* (London, 1979).

9 NAZI FILM PROPAGANDA IN OCCUPIED FRANCE

François Garçon

On 22 June 1940 France signed the Armistice. In five weeks she had just suffered the worst military defeat of her history. Germany occupied three-fifths of the country, and to the 100,000 soldiers killed were added three million prisoners; families were scattered and murdered and the economic activity of the country was disrupted.

And yet, on 15 June, that is the day after the German troops entered Paris, the Pigalle cinema opened its doors.[1] Four days later 20 cinemas were in business again; by the beginning of July there would be 100.[2] Despite the traumatic experiences of May and June the world of entertainment, especially the cinema, was again welcoming the public. It should be pointed out that the Occupying Power benefited from the renewal of leisure activities. They were aware that their decisions would be more acceptable if the occupied people could enjoy themselves as in peacetime. What better, then, than the world of entertainment to forget present troubles? And so the authorities in Berlin, who saw entertainment merely as another outlet for their propaganda, decided to develop their *Filmpolitik* in two directions: First, the Occupying Power was to distribute its own films in the part of the country it controlled (the Occupied Zone – ZO). This brought two benefits; financially, through the box-office receipts, and ideologically, thanks to the corrosive effect of the films from the Berlin-Neubabelsberg, studios. Secondly, the Nazis decided to help re-establish the French cinema, albeit, of course, on a different economic, racial and ideological base.

Amusement Propaganda: The Impact of German Feature Films

The *Wehrmacht* brought to France not only a large number of intellectuals who were to take charge of the institutions which would promote Franco-German *rapprochement*, they also brought cultural products for immediate consumption by the general public. The feature film occupied an important place in this ideological arsenal. Made in

161

Berlin, often with foreign actors, these films were quickly shown on the Champs-Elysées and the Grands Boulevards before conquering the provinces. In order to make the distribution of its films even easier, Germany took three steps:

1. The day after the Armistice, Germany banned all British films that had been freely circulating up until then; in September 1942 the ban would be extended to American films.

2. Closely following this, the occupation authorities also proscribed certain French films; thus all the pre-October 1937 films were withdrawn from distribution − guilty of 'poor quality'. To these, which numbered approximately 300, were added more recent films made between 1937 and May 1940, and judged to be hostile to Germany. Films such as *Marthe Richard au service de la France* (*Marthe Richard at the Service of France*, Raymond Bernard, 1937), *Sœurs d'armes* (*Sisters in Arms*, Léon Poirier, 1937) and 14 other feature films were affected by this measure.[3] This double censure had a serious effect on the French film industry, but on the other hand, and this was the aim envisaged, it stimulated the German cinema. In fact the ensuing shortage of films led to cinema-owners stocking up at the German distributors, if only to break even at the box-office. For Berlin, the operation had succeeded.

3. Finally, as the last step in imposing their films on France, Germany, in confiscating all Jewish property, seized a vast network of cinemas. For Tobis and ACE (the *Alliance Cinématographique Européenne*) this proved an excellent outlet to the best cinemas in Paris and the provinces.

The authoritarian elimination of English and French competition, the confiscation of the best distribution networks, the ban on certain French materials, like the 17.5mm format − show the extent to which Germany was able to exploit, in the realm of the cinema, her military victory of May 1940. The effects of this foreign domination on the French industry were immediate. French screens had never shown so many German films. In less than three months the Nazi cinema, which had been banned in France since the declaration of war in September 1939, re-installed itself throughout the country without encountering serious obstacles. Among the first films to figure in the trade weekly *Le Film*'s list of new releases were the most recent productions of Ufa, Terra and Wienfilm. 'The cinema season was inaugurated by ACE who presented *Es war eine rauschende Ballnacht* (*It was a Lovely*

Night at the Ball), exclusively at two cinemas – one on the Champs
Elysées and one on the Boulevards.'[4] Carl Froelich's film was followed
by Nunzio Malasomm's *Die Nacht der Entscheidung* (*The Night of
Decision*). During the month of October the Parisians were able to
enjoy *Die Drei Codonas* (*The Three Codonas*), Herbert Selpin's *Ein
Mann auf Abwegen* (*A Man Led Astray*) as well as *Weisser Flieder*
(*White Elder Trees*) by A.M. Rabenalt.

Were the French hostile to the invader? Not at all. On the contrary,
Parisian high society generously helped promote German new releases.
As for the press, they were not slow to praise these films. For example,
Der Postmeister (*The Postmaster*) received a reception that was more
than warm: 'There is no doubt that this is the cinematic event of our
present time' wrote *Paris-Soir*.[5] One of the capital's other dailies
commented that the film was 'received by the glittering audience of the
Colisée with a hearty ovation'.[6] *L'Oeuvre* (15 November 1940), *L'Illus-
tration* (16 November 1940) *Le Cri du peuple* (7 November 1940)
recorded similar reviews. In fact it would be difficult to detect even
slight reservations on the part of the Parisian press towards these Nazi
films. The release of *Bel ami* at the Biarritz in April 1941 'was the
greatest cinema evening of the year. The extremely eclectic audience
time and time again showed the enormous pleasure Willy Forst's film
was giving them by their enthusiastic applause. The last shots were
greeted with an ovation.'[7] But was not this public 'made-to-measure'?
Did not the 'enthusiastic applause' come from those who favoured an
alignment with Germany? Not at all. Those hurrying along to the
Biarritz were from the elite of the French cinema: Danièle Darieux,
Arletty, Simone Renault, Junie Astor, Marcel L'Herbier, Henri Decoin,
Christian Jaque, Pierre Véry, Jean Dréville, Georges Lacombe, Léo
Joannon, Le Vigan and many others.

Like a good demagogue, the Nazis did not neglect the underprivil-
eged. They varied their approach according to the sector of the public
being addressed. Thus, at the end of 1940, 'ACE is offering free cinema
to more than 5,000 children of prisoners and unemployed men' at the
Gaumont-Palace.[8] This attempt to woo the people was repeated two
months later, in the Normandie: 'On this occasion the ACE has donated
10,000 francs to the National Winter Aid programme.'[9]

In the first months of the Occupation, with battles raging over the
channel, the Germans assimilated themselves very skilfully into France.
This is borne out by the complete lack of resistance. Contrary to expectations, the films Berlin sent to Paris were not simplistic monuments of
propaganda glorifying the Reich and its leaders. Neither *Es war eine*

rauschende Ballnacht nor *Der Postmeister* contained speeches aimed at setting French opinion against the Jews, the Freemasons, Great Britain or any other direct enemy of Nazism. Film propaganda as seen on the screens of the Occupied Zone masqueraded under entertainment and comedy.

A closer analysis, however, reveals that the German programmes were far removed from innocent recreation. Short and medium-length documentary films intended for showing before the main feature film gave, for example, a disproportionate amount of attention to 'scientific' themes. The French considered Germany to be a war-mongering ogre, but Berlin reminded them of the extent to which the Germanic people had contributed to the development of modern sciences, particularly medicine. On 21 November 1940, for instance, 'before an élite audience', Paris celebrated *Robert Koch, Der Bekämpfer des Todes* (*Robert Koch Who Fought Death*), 'an admirable film dedicated to the memory of doctor Robert Koch, illustrious benefactor of humanity'.[10] Short- and medium-length documentary films were also used to highlight the merits of the Nazi regime. For this a more instructive, didactic form of propaganda was used. The facts reported to the French public were of course irrefutable. It was impossible to lie with this easily verifiable knowledge. And so, in December 1940, Ufa distributed a 17-minute documentary directed by Dr Rikli entitled *Radium*. A month later Terra showed *Au pays des microbes* (*In the Land of Germs*), a fourteen minute documentary dealing with micro-organisms. These 'scientific' films sum up all the obsessions with hygiene and health found at the core of Nazi ideology. This theme, whose ultimate aim was the destruction of inferior races, recurred again in 'The documentaries of social hygiene'. Out of many, we can mention *Air pur* (*Pure Air*), which described in detail the air-conditioning of German workshops in an attempt to expel industrial gases and vapours harmful to the health of the workers of the Reich.[11]

German film propaganda then was keen on feature films and hagiographies of German genuises (Friedemann Bach, Robert Koch etc.), but they did not forget to draw attention to a regenerated Nazi Germany. *Constructions dans la nouvelle Allemagne* (*Constructions in the New Germany*), directed by Walter Hege and produced by Ufa, showed, for example, a vast panorama of German architecture of the post-1933 period. With great attention to detail, Hege's camera described the Berlin Olympic Stadium, the Air Ministry, the Party Headquarters in Munich and Nuremberg, apparently with the sole purpose of instructing French cinema-goers.

At this stage the French could hardly complain about Nazi propaganda. Apart from the ban on English films and on about 20 French films too obviously anti-German, there was no real ideological difference to be noted on the cinema screens of the Occupied Zone, still less in the Non-occupied Zone. Where then was the Nazi barbarism referred to by the French authorities in order to stir an apathetic population before the defeat? In February 1941 a film event took place which clearly proved that Germany was no ordinary occupying power, wishing merely to entertain the conquered nation. With *Jud Süss (Jew Süss)*, which was premièred on 14 February 1941 at the Colisée, Germany suddenly revealed a face it had previously disguised – at least in the cinema. Unquestionably a product of the Nazi ideological machine,[12] this film was an excellent example of the receptiveness of the French public to an anti-semitic discourse. *Jud Süss* beat all box-office records. In Paris as in Marseilles, Bordeaux or Lyons, where it 'provoked a veritable revolution',[13] the people rushed to see the specially prepared French version of Veit Harlan's film. According to the experts:

It constitutes a real triumph of technique . . . At the head, Monsieur Rognoni, of the Comédie-Française, who has been dubbing Heinrich George. We must also mention Monsieur Francoeur, who dubbed Ferdinand Marian [Jew Süss], Monsieur Blondeau and Maurice Lagrenée. In fact to everyone, we must offer sincere congratulations and thanks. For it is to their tireless work that we have the opportunity of seeing A.C.E.'s masterpiece on all of France's cinema screens'.[14]

Jud Süss was not an isolated incident. In the following months similar Nazi propaganda films would be seen in the cinemas of both zones.[15] *Die Rothschilds, Ohm Krüger (Uncle Krüger), Der Fuchs von Glenarvon (The Fox of Glenarvon), GPU, Titanic*, etc. In defence of the French audience, it should be pointed out that these films never achieved a success equal to that of *Jud Süss*. In fact, as Table 9.1 demonstrates, Ufa films were to suffer more and more as a direct result of the competition from the French cinema that had been relaunched by the Nazis themselves at the beginning of 1941.

While it may be true that overall the French public began to desert the products of Ufa and Terra, it must be remembered that in certain areas, notably in the east of France, the German cinema remained extremely popular up to the Liberation.[16] This is partly explained by the quasi-monopoly which the Occupying Power held over programmes in this area, but it was also due to the predominantly German culture which prevailed in these regions.

Table 9.1: Films Distributed in France, 1936-44

Year	Total films distributed	Number of German films distributed in France	Percentage of German films
1936	331	16	5
1937	331	20	6
1938	343	17	5
1939	255	12	5
1940	167	24	14
1941	98	55	56
1942	128	39	30
1943	125	28	22
1944	55	8	15

Source: Le Film Français (Winter 1956), nos. 611-12.

French Propaganda: the Re-establishment of the French Cinema

Berlin did not rest on its laurels after its victory over France. Nor did it leave affairs to its own propaganda alone. Since the summer of 1940, the Nazis had decided to re-establish the French cinema industry amidst all the chaos wrought by the war. Of course, they intended to maintain control of the industry, but they quickly appreciated that their own propaganda was not enough to satisfy the French. Therefore, as soon as the guns were silenced, Germany did all it could to re-establish film production in a weak and exhausted France. In the autumn of 1940, Berlin appointed Alfred Greven head of a new film company, *Continental*, which would be based in Paris. *Continental* was set up with a capital of one million francs and would produce, sell and distribute films in France. Assisted by R. Langenscheidt and Richard Ehrt,[17] Greven managed to persuade many of the professionals, who were for the most part unemployed, to work for *Continental*. People like Henri Decoin, Léo Joannon, Jean Dréville, Henri-Georges Clouzot, André Cayatte, many of whom would be considered celebrities in the 1950s. To a few, like Clouzot and Cayatte, *Continental* even offered the opportunity of directing their first full-length film. *Continental* would also be responsible for exporting French films and as such was a major company, indeed it was the most prolific film company of the occupation. When it was dissolved after the Liberation, it left behind no less than 30 films, that is, 14 per cent of the total films produced between August 1940 and May 1944. *Continental*'s catalogue is full of prestigious titles such as *Le Corbeau* (*The Raven*), *Les Inconnus dans la maison* (*Strangers in the House*), *L'Assassinat du Père Noel* (*The Killing of Father Christmas*), and *Premier rendez-vous* (*First Meeting*).

There is a fundamental question raised by *Continental*'s film production, for the directors recruited by Greven have frequently been accused of collaborating with the Nazis. On a business level this criticism is justified, for the people concerned did in fact work thanks to German capital. Paradoxically, however, from an ideological point of view the accusation is unfounded. *Continental*'s films, at least certain ones, are the most subversive if this word could be said to have any meaning between 1940 and 1944. They are certainly the most offensive towards Vichy ideology. Films financed by German capital were the only ones to severely criticise the family, social taboos, and the pillars of social order like the Church, doctors and the old. Furthermore, Nazi funds sponsored the most overtly nationalistic film of the period – *La Symphonie fantastique* (*The Fantastic Symphony*, 1941), a film glorifying Berlioz and directed by Christian Jaque. For anyone doubting the patriotic nature of *La Symphonie fantastique* here is what an emminent propaganda specialist had to say:

The film is of excellent quality and amounts to a first class national fanfare. Unfortunately, therefore, I cannot release it for public showing. I am very angry to think that our own offices in Paris are teaching the French how to represent nationalism in films. This lack of political instinct can scarcely be surpassed. But that's how we Germans are. Whenever we go into another country, our first task seems to consist in putting it in order, regardless of the fact that in a few years or decades it may go to war against us. This lack of political instinct among Germans is the result of their passion for work and their idealistic enthusiasm. One must constantly be aware so that this state of affairs does not bring about disastrous repercussions. I am going to have Greven come to Berlin to give him clear and precise instructions: at the moment I want only superficial, amusing, but unsophisticated films made for the French market. The French will probably be satisfied with this. There is absolutely no reason why we should cultivate their nationalism.

These thoughts are Joseph Goebbels'.[18] They reveal a strange paradox to do with propaganda. The Nazis, who saw themselves as experts in this field, tried manifestly to control the French cinema, just as they scrutinised and tamed the French press[19] and radio.[20] As far as the cinema was concerned, control was centred on film production in accordance with Goebbels' instructions that 'we should not encourage the French to develop a new film art which would compete too fiercely with ourselves on the European market. Consequently I will do all that is necessary to see that the particularly gifted actors of the French cinema are gradually attracted to the German film industry.'[21] From the ideological point of view, Nazi manipulation was an obvious failure, in so far as none of their objectives were achieved. How then can we explain such a failure? In his Diary Goebbels speaks of 'the unsurpassed lack of political instinct' of his compatriots, their 'lack of political experience'. In this context there can be no doubt that Greven was not the diabolical French censor that so many feared. All witnesses agree on what he was like as a person. In reality, the explanation for *Continental*'s ability to produce most of the best films of the Occupation lies more in the contradictions to be found in French society, rather than in the failure of the Nazis' approach and methods. One simply cannot analyse Nazi propaganda in France without reference to the National Revolution. Whichever way you look at it, the politics of Pétainism was ideologically retrogressive;[22] anti-industrial, rural, pro-Church, family, and the values of the past. To Vichy we owe some of the most oppressive literature and films of the twentieth century. This conservatism was extremely active. The regime's spokesmen hailed from the *Légion Française des Combattants* (French Legion of Soldiers) and the *Commissariat Général de la Famille* (Central Office for Family Affairs) under police jurisdiction and they were involved in most aspects of censorship — particularly those that dealt with questions of morality in the cinema. As far as French-financed films were concerned, the Pétainist censors were implacable. It was forbidden, for example, to make fun of the police, the army, or to discuss adultery, abortion, etc . . . However, the censors were more sympathetic when it came to *Continental*'s films — films made by the Nazis' own company and controlled by one of Goebbels' trusted men. It was because *Continental* enjoyed a privileged position and a certain degree of freedom, that we can detect in their films anti-establishment themes aimed at the family and a general impudent attitude towards hallowed traditions which were forbidden elsewhere. In fact the only shots of naked women to be seen on the French screens between 1940 and 1944, were produced not by French film companies but by *Continental.*[23]

The extent to which even the National Socialist code of morality was less restrictive than that of Vichy France can be gauged by the fact that a number of Ufa's films actually shocked the French public! In 1943 cinema-goers wrote to the Censor demanding that scenes judged permissive in Veit Harlan's *Die Goldene Stadt (The Golden State)* be cut.[24] On the other hand, the Nazis were occasionally forced to intervene to protect French films which had fallen victim of the Parisian Censors. Thus *La Bête humaine* (1938) was banned by the French Censor only to be re-distributed by the Occupying Power.[25] The most controversial incident involving film censorship during the Occupation was over *Le Corbeau* (1943) and once again *Continental* was involved. Rejected by most of the critics,[26] this film, which described the ignomy of provincial people, was painfully close to the French experience. However *Le Corbeau* (which was produced by Greven) was, with *Les Enfants du Paradis* (1944) the masterpiece of those dark years.

Taking fictional film propaganda as a whole, the Nazis failed. They failed because, contrary to Goebbels' designs, they were unable to either attract and keep the most distinguished French film people in Germany, or to render the French cinema so insipid that the French public turned to Ufa's films. This brings us back to the paradox mentioned earlier; precisely because of its special legal and political status which left it immune to Vichy's restrictions, *Continental* kept alive a specifically French spirit of derision, irony and provocation. To go by French-produced films alone, these themes may well not have existed at all between 1940 and 1944 if *Continental* had not embraced them and to some extent protected them.

But are we not missing the point in speaking of failure? Did not Germany commit this error of judgement on the feature film because at the time it was focusing most of its attention on a more fundamental propaganda weapon? Surely it was because it was keeping strict control on the cinema newsreels, which it considered essential for shaping peoples' thoughts and ideas, that Germany seemed so indulgent towards the feature film?

Classic Propaganda: Film Newsreels

The film newsreels were the principal area in which the Nazis intervened. Because of the importance of controlling information in a conquered country always liable to turn on its invader, Germany used newsreels like real weapons of war. Therefore, every week, from 30 May to 4 August 1944, Berlin addressed itself directly to the 39 million French people.

In order to appreciate fully the extent of the German control following the defeat of 1940, we must go back to the months prior to the onset of the conflict in 1939. Five firms shared the French and colonial market — and three French firms, *France-Actualités Gaumont, Eclair-Journal* and *Pathé-Journal*, and two American companies, *Fox-Movietone* and *Actualités Paramount*. The fall of France interrupted the activity of the five companies, and talks between the Occupying Power and the new French authorities on restarting the film industry proved tortuous.

In the course of the summer of 1940, the *Alliance Cinématographique Européenne* (ACE), a French company funded by German capital, took up once more its activity in the Occupied Zone. Helped by French technicians, ACE distributed a special edition of *Deutsche Wochenschau* (the Nazi newsreel). However, Nazi propaganda was clearly too obvious. In Number 13, for example, the French narrator on the bombing of Mers-El-Kébir by the Royal Navy had a very strong German accent.[27] Conscious of the failure of such imported propaganda, the Nazis decided in September of the same year to attract French assistance. To this end, the company *Les Diffusions Modernes* was requested to set up a cinema news agency funded mainly by German capital. Negotiations were at an advanced stage, but the Nazis reckoned without the Vichy authorities. Although hardly thought of as hostile towards Nazi Germany, they were, however, swift to react against what they believed was an attack on French sovereignty. For the French, the only negotiable solution lay in an inter-governmental agreement for the creation of a company in which the French had the major interest. It would seem that Vichy politicians desperately tried to prevent the Nazis from controlling film news in the Non-occupied Zone. Negotiations were undoubtedly being frustrated. On 14 November 1940, the Nazis, clearly exasperated by these procrastinations, sent an 'important personality'[28] to Paris. Having decided to act swiftly, the Occupying Power then demanded absolute control of the news over the whole of French territory. In this way they hoped to introduce ACE newsreels in the Non-occupied Zone. But here again German pressure was ineffective. Instead of inundating the south of the country with their pictures, the Nazis only succeeded in antagonising those they were addressing, even though they were in a strong position. Talks were once again held up. Jean-Louis Tixier-Vignancourt resigned from *Le Service du Cinéma* to become Vice-President of the Council at Vichy. The bone of contention between the Nazis and the French was always the nature of the film company responsible for making the newsreels. On the one hand Berlin was desperate to replace American newsreels with their own in the Non-occupied Zone. On the other hand, Vichy was eager to re-establish contact with the French of the Occupied Zone and wished to secure the free circulation of their newsreels throughout the whole of the country.

Finally, on 17 November 1941, a law was signed by Admiral Darlan, Philippe Pétain and Yves Bouthillier, Secretary of State at the Ministry of Finance, which allowed an unnamed company[29] 15 years' exclusive rights to the shooting, editing and distribution of film newsreels in France and the territories under the sovereignty of the French state'. On 4 May 1942, *France Actualités*, saw the light of day. With a capital of 12 million francs made up of 1,200 shares each worth 10,000 francs, it was directed by a council of five members — three French and two Germans. Its President, Henri Clerc, was French; the Vice-President, Wilhelm Knothe, was German.

In comparison with the pre-war companies, *France Actualités* was different in various ways: firstly it was different because of the large amount of time allotted to Nazi propaganda in each newsreel. In all there were 104 newsreels and each issue was approximately 440 metres long. Of this, sections dealt with sport, geography, the arts, day-to-day affairs and more specific matters. In reality, more than half of this information came directly from the specialised film units of the *Wehrmacht*. But what did these German shots refer to? To be brief, let me say that they formed the backbone of the newsreels. In fact the German contribution dealt exclusively with the war. Following on from the credits, or at the end of the reel, the section *La Guerre* (*The War*) showed the French the only visible images of the battles taking place in the North Atlantic, Tunisia, on the Eastern front and in the Pacific. The records show that the public was not indifferent to these views of the war. In May 1941, Ernst Junger reported on a performance in a Parisian cinema in his *Journal*:

While the newsreel was being shown, the cinema was lit up, doubtlessly to prevent demonstrations. Then, the offensives in Africa, Serbia and Greece wwere screened. The sight alone of the means of destruction provoked startled cries. The way they appeared to move of their own accord, gliding by under their steel plating, the gradual consumption of the shining bullets as the shooting went on, the caterpillar tracks, the slits of the periscopes, the movement of the

armoured vehicles, the arsenal of living forms which had hardened
like crustaceans, or tortoises, crocodiles and insects — it is just like
a Bosch painting. To be studied: the ways in which propaganda is
related to terror![30]

Once the French had borne the German accounts, they could enjoy
the real French news, which concentrated in a superficial and malicious
way on day-to-day life. For example, *Madeleine-Bastille en patins à
roulettes* (*Madeleine-Bastille on Roller Skates*),[31] *Paris: Mise en service
du 'trolleybus'* (*Paris: the Introduction of the Trolleybus*),[32] *Raimu à
la Comédie Française dans 'Le Bourgeois Gentilhomme* (*Raimu at the
Comédie Française in the 'Bourgeois Gentilhomme*).[33]

Another difference from the pre-war newsreels was that those made
during the Occupation were longer. Despite the scarcity of film, the
average newsreel was 440 metres long — whilst it was never more than
350 metres before 1940.[34] The extended length was in keeping with
the importance the Nazis attached to the newsreels, for they were
always anxious to prove to the French their military superiority. It
would take some time before the scarcity in raw film material effected
the length of *France Actualités*, but it had a marked affect on the
number of copies made. Before 1940, 600 copies were made of each
newsreel, but this was reduced to 500 copies during the Occupation.
This reduction would have a number of consequences. As cinema-
owners were obliged to screen the newsreel before the feature film,
certain local cinemas who could only show third-run films were forced
to screen newsreels which could be over a month old. In the latter half
of 1943 such delays began to have unexpected ideological repercussions
for Germany. Although they were intended to terrorise the audience,
the newsreels were increasingly revealed as outdated, and thus a rather
vulgar tool of propaganda — especially when they were compared with
the more immediate information provided by the press and the radio.
Therefore, since it failed to keep pace with the amount of information
possessed by the average person, the propaganda in the newsreels often
turned against its masters. The earlier fear of the newsreels was now
replaced with laughter.[35]

The last important difference from pre-war newsreels was that
France Actualités, thanks to the legislation of 17 November 1941,
possessed a monopoly over all Metropolitan France as well as North
Africa and those colonies still under Vichy control. Moreover, these
newsreels were obligatory and sanctions would have been taken against
any distributor who attempted to avoid circulating this propaganda.[36]

So much for the rules. But what of the ideological content of these newsreels during the four years of Occupation? I have already alluded to this. The most important part of each edition was the German section, both from the point of view of the quality of the pictures and of their emotional impact. The main thrust of Nazi propaganda was the exaltation of the New Order which had arrived in France with Guderian's Panzers and was maintained by Laval and the Collaborators. Like *Actualités Mondiales* (World-Wide News),[37] *France-Actualités* stressed the 'marriage' between Paris and Berlin every week. In Number 5, which came out on 23 January 1943, there was an item on 'the professional training of the Relief Troops' (*Formation professionnelle pour la Relève*), 15 days later, in Number 5 of 5 February, the New Order featured in two film articles: *A Vichy: le Président Laval et la Milice Francaise* (*At Vichy: President Laval and the French Militia*), then in *Anniversaire historique: 10 ans de national-socialisme* (*Historic Anniversary: Ten Years of National Socialism*). Regularly, French prisoners were shown becoming free men again by working in Germany and, similarly, contingents of French volunteers were filmed departing for the Russian front.

The second thrust of Nazi propaganda was the war. This proved particularly convincing, at least up until the end of 1943: 'Here the scenes are not faked – we see only the naked truth, with not the slightest artifice. Its terrible eloquence comes from itself, and no amount of clever speeches could prevail over such a testimony.'[38] Every newsreel contained a section with an apparently neutral title, for example, *Le Monde en guerre* (The World at War), *La Guerre* (*The War*), *Sur les Divers fronts* (On the Different Fronts), *La Guerre dans le monde* (*War in the World*). In fact, it was under these headings that the newsreels described scenes of violence unprecedented in the world conflict. What effects could these images have had on French audiences? There seems no doubt that, shocked by the disaster of May 1940, the French found, in these reports, a further reason for not offering resistance against the Nazi tyrant. And so Nazi propaganda was not without its successes. By reminding those who were not at war of what they were escaping, these brutal images paralysed the French and helped create an atmosphere of calm in the *Wehrmacht*'s rearguard. In this respect Nazi propaganda freed German soldiers to be employed on the battle fronts.

However, have I not inferred that the French sometimes greeted the newsreels with demonstrations and derision? This is indeed true. For example, in the period immediately following the defeat of June 1940, the newsreels, which were rightly suspected of coming directly from Berlin, were badly received by French audiences. Constantly urged to rally to the new conqueror, many Frenchmen protested by shouting and whistling as the newsreels were being screened. The invasion of the Soviet Union of course strengthened the cause of those dissatisfied Frenchmen:

> In certain cinemas, when the news comes on, the public ostentatiously leave their seats and ignore the faked images disseminated by the dwarfish Goebbels. In other cinemas the public loudly boos Hitler's 'ugly mug' whenever he shows it. Good for you, French public.[39]

These demonstrations against Nazi propaganda grew to such proportions that the authorities in both the Occupied and the Non-occupied Zones were quick to insist that while newsreels were being projected some auditorium lights should remain switched on so that the agitators could be more easily identified. The existence of such agitators cannot be denied. We also know that many patrons would leave their seats when *France-Actualités* appeared. The Prefects' Reports — hardly to be suspected of sympathy for the trouble-makers — are quite definite on this point. A report in January 1941 from the prefect of the Landes stated: 'In Dax, the French public's appreciation of the *Actualités Mondiales* seems to be no more than moderate, and we noted that eighty to ninety per cent of the patrons left the cinema during the screening.'[40] All the same, these examples, which have been assimilated into the historiography of the Occupation where they have assumed the proportions of a popular anti-German resistance, were limited both in time and space.

In terms of the time-span, the rejection of Nazi news seems to have been strongest during the first months of the Occupation. The wounds of May 1940 were still exposed and the fate of French prisoners did not encourage collaboration with Berlin. Under such conditions Franco-German relations were naturally affected by mistrust, even anger. But appeasement came gradually so that the Occupying Power, whose behaviour was 'correct' according to general opinion,[41] became on the whole bearable. We can safely say, then, that apart from those who implacably opposed the Germans, Nazi propaganda, at least up until 1943, provoked very little hostile reaction from the French public.

In terms of location, the extent and the manner with which Nazi propaganda was accepted varied enormously, according to whether or not the French audience had been affected by the war and whether they could receive counter-information from foreign broadcasts. Coming from London or some neutral country (e.g. Switzerland or Spain), this counter-information tended to cancel out Nazi rhetoric. For example, the prefects of the South-west and L'Ain (a department on the Swiss border) stressed in their twice-monthly reports the extent of the resistance to Nazi propaganda, precisely because the French were listening to information which challenged German propaganda claims.

However, it was the change in Germany's military fortunes on the eastern fronts that really heralded the decline of Nazi propaganda. The growing difficulties of communications in France — disruptions in the distribution of the film reels due to the running down of the railway system and then, finally, the increasingly inevitability of an Allied victory — began to undermine the credibility of the reports compiled by *France-Actualités*. If the French public was still going to the cinema it was by now only for the feature film and no longer to marvel at the prowess of the *Luftwaffe* or the *Wehrmacht*. In its last issue of 4 August 1944, *France-Actualités* featured the following six reports: 'New methods of teaching in Bohemia-Moravia'; 'Fire practice in Germany'; 'Providing Paris with supplies'; 'Mass at the Houcke arena'; 'The variety of tasks falling to German women'; 'Masks of the world in Geneva' — all this on a newsreel reduced by 216 metres. It was a far cry from the triumphant *Actualités Mondiales* of July 1941 which were 721 metres in length.

Propaganda: Between Collaboration and Resistance

Germany deployed numerous means of controlling the conquered nation: censorship, an unrelenting desire to gain free access to the cinema screens of both zones for their newsreels, purging the French film catalogues and banning all film production except under strict supervision. This suggests that Germany *was* concerned about the sort of images circulating within France.

But did the Nazis achieve their objectives? This raises the difficult question of the efficiency of political propaganda. Not only do we lack the instruments for measuring such a phenomenon (obviously there were no opinion polls or any other reliable indicators), but the German occupation of France only lasted four years. Although for some this period seemed interminable, it was of little consequence as far as changing French attitudes. In such a short time it is inconceivable that indoctrination, however well adapted to a French context, could have produced tangible and lasting results. All the more so in a country whose own culture was so lively and firmly woven into the fabric of its society. It was unlikely that this culture would dissolve as a result of the Occupation, however powerful the Nazis may have been from the military point of view. At the very best (or worst), some pro-German tendencies should, perhaps, have been discernable on the part of the French, but this was not the case.

In the absence of a brutally enforced assimilation into Nazi culture (*acculturation*), are there any indications of changes in the traditional moral and aesthetic values that had been associated with the French cinema? None at all. As far as feature films were concerned, there was total *indifference* towards Nazi Germany. This is borne out by several factors: not a single French director attempted to emulate the style to be found in the Nazi cinema. Indeed, during the height of the Occupation, with Germany the overlord of Europe, the French cinema remained theatrical, producing mainly light comedies. As far as foreign influences could be discerned, Paris and Nice looked to Hollywood more than Ufa. No aspect of the cinematic craft — be it staging, acting or even historical reconstruction — bore any evidence of the victor's culture. A further indication of the resistance against German propaganda can be highlighted by comparing the pre-war situation with the experiences of the French cinema industry under the Occupation. It is a fact that between August 1940 and May 1944, no German technician, director, actor, musician or the like figured in the production of French films. The Occupation, therefore, strangely enough, brought about the elimination of German professionals from the French studios. The French worked only with each other at this time. This distancing of themselves from Nazi culture is also shown by the sources of their inspiration for feature films. While up to 1939 French film makers had no hesitation in producing films on Beethoven[42] or Franz Schubert,[43] not a single feature film between 1940 and 1944 was based on the great German geniuses. Christian Jaque stressed with his *Berlioz* that the French were the geniuses and, especially after the humiliating disaster of June 1940, authors of both stage and screen would take up this call.

Such a spontaneous rejection of anything German by the film world should be considered as proof of a resistance, albeit symbolic, against the Occupying Power. One becomes convinced of this upon recalling how generously the French film makers depicted Germany up until the declaration of war in 1939. At the very moment that the French cinema was denouncing Great Britain as plutocratic, imperialistic and 'riddled with Jews', this same cinema was displaying extraordinary friendliness towards a Germany that was ostentatiously rearming and mobilising for war. This *volte face*, unexpected and contrary to official government policy and diplomacy, provides more evidence of the relative autonomy of culture as opposed to politics. It also shows that, despite a particularly restrictive creative environment, French film makers did resist Nazi propaganda.

How can we account for this resistance? Was it Nazi incompetance? Or was it the strength of French culture? Before we can criticise the Occupying Power for failing to disseminate its ideology, we must remember that their views reigned supreme in the French newsreels. For four years Berlin terrorised even the most sceptical French cinema patrons. Perhaps it was their relative success in this area which explains the Nazis' indifference towards feature films which they believed should entertain and not instruct. Their concentration on news at the expense of feature films warrants further attention. It stems from their basic conception of propaganda directed towards occupied territories. Clearly, politics, in the narrow sense of maintaining order, was the only aspect which really concerned Berlin. As for feature films, since they were considered a minor genre – an unimportant activity – Berlin did not demand such strict supervision. Such priorities reveals that Germany's strategy was based on disuasive measures (for example, weekly demonstrations of their military strength), and thus on the short term rather than on persuasive, long-term indoctrination which could have gradually convinced the conquered people to pledge their allegiance to the thousand-year Reich.

And so, in conclusion, the persistant contradiction between the desire to control the French cinema and the paucity of the results shows, in Goebbels' own words, that he never found amongst his entourage any real *Gauleiters* for France. Whether the failure was attributable to the Propaganda Ministry or to the specific nature of the cinema, the basic fact remains: Nazi propaganda failed to change the composition of the French cinema, or even to modify it superficially. The only presence of Nazi propaganda to be seen on French screens between 1940 and 1944, came directly exported from Berlin.

Notes

1. *Le Film*, 12 October 1940.
2. Ibid.

3. *Archives Nationales* (Paris), note VAA 2227, AJ 41.62.

4. *Le Film*, 12 October 1940.

5. *Paris-Soir*, 14 November 1940.

6. *Le Matin*, 8 November 1940.

7. *Le Film*, 12 April 1941.

8. Ibid., 15 January 1941.

9. Ibid., 1 March 1941.

10. Ibid., 1 December 1940.

11. Ibid., 7 March 1941.

12. F. Garçon, 'Les Trois discours Juif Süss', *Annales, E.S.C.*, (July-August, 1979), pp. 694-720.

13. *Le Film*, 7 June 1941.

14. Ibid.

15. Richard Grunberger showed that only a small percentage of films made in the Third Reich were overtly political. R. Grunberger, *A Social History of the Third Reich* (London, 1971), pp. 376-89.

16. Thus, in Nancy in 1943, of the 122 films to be shown, only 70 were of French origin; most of the others came from Germany. *Le Miroir de l'écran* (February 1944).

17. *Le Film*, 1 November 1940.

18. H. Goebbels, *Le Journal du Dr Goebbels* (Paris, 1948), pp. 201-2.

19. C. Bellanger, J. Godechot, P. Guiral and F. Terrou, *Histoire générale de la presse française* (Paris, 1975), vol. 4, pp. 7-91.

20. A. Lefébure, 'Le Rôle et l'influence politique de la radio en France pendant la seconde guerre mondiale', Unpublished Masters dissertation, University of Paris, 1972, 103 pp.

21. Goebbels, *Le Journal*, p. 199.

22. Recent studies have shown that the bases of a modern economy were being installed when the ideology was fiercely opposed to such a move. Cf. R. Kuisel, 'Vichy et les origines de la planification économique, 1940-6', *Le Mouvement Social*, no. 98 (January-March 1977), pp. 77-101.

23. *Le Dernier des Six* (*Last of Six*), directed by Georges Lacombe, 1941) with its six fixed shots of entirely naked female dancers in the scene on the Tabarin in Paris and *Le Corbeau* (directed by Henri-Georges Clouzot, 1943) with the bare shoulders of Ginette Leclerc are, in fact, the two films in which nakedness was shown most during the whole of the Occupation. Both are products of *Continental*.

24. *Archives Nationales* (Paris), AG II. 55

25. The German Order of 9 September 1940, which was reinforced on 27 May 1942, forbad French administrative and religious authorities from preventing the showing of films which had been authorised by the German Censorship Board. *Archive Nationales* (Paris), AJ 41. 336.

26. The Communist critique written by Georges Sadoul, *Le Cinéma pendant la guerre* (Paris, 1954), the fascist critique, *Je Suis Partout*, of 8 October 1943, and the Catholic review, *Réagir*, 10 December 1943, all criticise the film which an official at the *Commissariat Général à la Famille* described as 'particularly disgusting'. *Archives Nationales*, (Paris), AG II. 159

27. *Actualités Mondiales*, no. 13 (23 October 1940, 480 metres).

28. *Archives Nationales*, (Paris), F 42. 133.

29. *Journal Officiel de l'Etat Français*, 21 November 1941.

30. E. Jünger, *Journal de guerre et de l'Occupation, 1939-48* (Paris, 1965), p. 104.

31. *France-Actualités*, no. 5 (18 September 1941, 407 metres).

32. *France-Actualités*, no. 3 (22 January 1943, 421 metres).

33. *France-Actualités*, no. 13, (23 March 1944, 397 metres).

34. In 1944, as a result of various difficulties – the destruction of chemical factories, shortage of electricity, film material, etc. – the length of *France-Actualités* was reduced to 250 metres.

35. The following was written by H. Clerc (President of *France-Actualités*) to Von Weyrauch in April 1943' 'If the spectator is not interested by the film he thinks about something else while the scenes are shown, and the intended propaganda effect is lost. If the film is boring and scenes are too long, we even risk provoking a hostility that is shown not by noisy demonstrations, but by fidgeting and whisperings. *The film then becomes counter-propaganda.*' (Author's italics.) *Archives Nationales* (Paris), AG II. 555.

36. 'To go into operation from 11 July 1941 in the Non-occupied Zone, all film programmes are now legally required to show newsreels.' *Décision No. 5 du Comité d'Organisation de l'Industrie Cinématographique*, Paris, 8 July 1941.

37. *Actualités Mondiale* was a version of the German newsreel (*Deutsche Wochenschau*) intended for use in Occupied France. The first edition appeared on French screens on 39 May 1940 (350 metres long) and was edited and distributed by ACE. All in all, there were 107 editions of *Actualités Mondiale*. The last one was on 14 August 1942. A week later (21 August) the first edition of *France-Actualités* appeared.

38. *Ciné-Mondial*, 9 January 1942.

39. *L'Humanité*, 7 August 1941.

40. *Archives Nationales* (Paris), FIC III. 1160.

41. In May 1944, the prefect of the Marseilles region wrote once more: 'The conduct of the Occupation troops continues, on the whole, to be correct.' *Archives Nationales* (Paris), FIC III. 1200.

42. *Un Grand Amour de Beethoven* (*A Great Love of Beethoven*), directed by Abel Gance, 1936).

43. *Sérénade* (directed by Jean Boyer, 1939).

10 HOW EFFECTIVE WAS NAZI PROPAGANDA?

Ian Kershaw

A great deal has been written about Nazi propaganda. The bulk of it has concentrated overwhelmingly on the organisation, production and output of propaganda – domestic and foreign – in the press, the arts, through the film medium and through numerous other channels. This literature is in good measure a reflection of the importance which the Nazis themselves, beginning with Hitler and Goebbels and extending to the lowest ranks of the Nazi Party, attached to propaganda as the indispensable means of mobilising, manipulating, controlling, directing and (re-)educating the population. Especially in the hey-day of totalitarianism theories, the presumption was strong among Western scholars that the propagandistic exploitation of modern technology was one of the key features of the 'totalitarian state'[1] and that the inevitable succumbing of the population to such unremitting and relentless manipulative techniques formed one of the hallmarks of the 'totalitarian society'. Belief in the power of Nazi propaganda, with its monopoly hold over a largely defenceless population, has not, however, been confined to 'totalitarianism' theorists. From an entirely different theoretical position, East German scholarship has also stressed the extent to which the bulk of the population – outside the 'progressive' sections of the working class – was manipulated by clever propaganda techniques and Nazi demagogy into support for the regime.[2] Studies of propaganda have generally been premised upon the implicit or explicit notion that Nazi propaganda, from the regime's point of view, was a success story. A recent book, for instance, speaks of Nazi propaganda as 'the war that Hitler won'. Its author, Robert Herzstein, who did a presentable job in illustrating (once more) the nature and techniques of Nazi propaganda, wrote: 'The greatest success of the Goebbels propaganda apparatus was reflected in the continuation of the struggle by the German people into 1945 . . . '; and 'the German people fought on to the end. Thus Hitler and Goebbels won their war against the "shame" of 1918'.[3] Indeed, when one looks at the impressive output of Nazi propaganda, feels the visual impact of striking posters, old newsreels, or scenes from *Triumph of the Will*, hears the roars of acclamation on old records of speeches by Goebbels and Hitler, appreciates the cleverness of machiavellian technique and remembers the notion of the 'big lie', and not least when one reflects upon how important – and successful – the Nazis imagined their propaganda to be, then one is almost compelled to conclude that such a propaganda apparatus *must* have been successful, *must* have been highly effective.

Yet this is the view which I would like to challenge here. Trying to assess the reception of propaganda is of course an exercise considerably more difficult than the description of propaganda output. In the absence of public opinion surveys and other means of quantifying reactions to propaganda, accurate measurement is naturally impossible. Nevertheless, I believe there is sufficient evidence – much of it of an indirect nature – to attempt some broad assessment of the effectiveness of Nazi propaganda. In questioning the generalised (and doubtless oversimplified and overdrawn) picture of the success of Nazi propaganda which I have outlined, I am anxious to avoid looking simply for 'failures' and arguing that Nazi propaganda was wholly or even largely ineffective. Rather, my aim is to arrive at a more balanced picture of Nazi propaganda's effectiveness – something both desirable and possible – and one which can accommodate areas both of success and of failure in coming to an overall assessment of 'the power of Nazi propaganda'. I should emphasise that I am concerned here only with propaganda directed at the Germans themselves, with the period of the dictatorship and not the rise to power[4] and that I exclude from consideration propaganda within specific organisations such as the SS, the *Wehrmacht*, or Party formations, which is best regarded under the rubric of 'ideological training'.

An immediate problem is by what criteria to measure the effectiveness of propaganda. One approach has been to adopt a comparative basis, assessing the effectiveness of the German propaganda system relative to that of the British during the Second World War.[5] Such a comparison (in which by and large the British propaganda machine did better than the German one, without at all altering the course of the war) is in my view of limited value because of the radically different aims and ambitions of the two systems. Though of course the maintenance of wartime morale was an aim common to both systems, the task of the British propaganda apparatus was markedly simpler. Building upon the general acceptance of a just and necessary war in defence of existing values and one which, with all its setbacks, could be viewed with increasing optimism, the job of British propaganda in maintaining both civilian and military morale was a relatively easy and straightforward one. German propaganda, on the other hand, was far more ambitious. From the very beginning of the Third Reich it had set itself the task of educating the German people for a new society based upon a drastically restructured value system. The 'revolutionary' task of German propaganda contrasts starkly with the 'conservative' basis of British propaganda aims. Furthermore, German propaganda was faced with a military situation worsening gradually from late 1941 onwards to a point of despair for Germany. Its task in upholding morale in these circumstances was incomparably greater than that of British propaganda. All this suggests that assessments of the effectiveness of propaganda cannot be carried out either on the basis of a notional absolute scale of what is 'effective' or on a comparative basis with dissimilar systems. It can be attempted only by evaluating differentiated responses to propaganda in the context of the specific aims of that propaganda. The dominant aim of Nazi propaganda was so extraordinarily ambitious – amounting to the reconstruction of a value-system in what, because of the immanent dynamic of the armaments race, was an impossibly short time – that the attempt might be thought to have been doomed to failure from the start. This makes it, in fact, all the more surprising that the 'propaganda machine' has commonly been regarded as so successful.

The overriding and interlocking Nazi propaganda aims can be broken down into the simple schema laid out in Figure 10.1.

Figure 10.1: Nazi Propaganda Aims

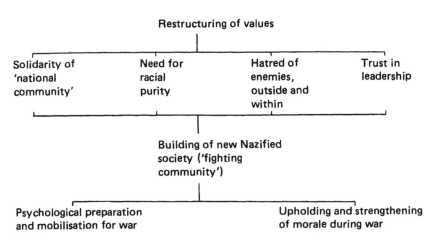

According to such a conceptualisation, the overriding goal of Nazi propaganda was the mobilisation of the population for war and, once in war, the continued psychological mobilisation and maintenance of fighting morale among both troops and civilian population.[7] This central goal was attainable in the form and to the extent desired by the Nazi leadership only through a restructuring of values based especially upon four interlocking spheres of socio-political consciousness: (1) the need to remove class, sectional, regional, denominational and party political loyalties and replace them by the ideal of selfless service to a united 'national community'. (2) The need for recognition of the indispensability of racial purity as the cornerstone of this 'national community'. This meant the eradication of any 'liberal', 'humanistic' or 'Christian' feelings towards the Jews, the main racial enemy, and towards all those social drop-out, mis-fit, or non-conformist minorities deemed unfit to belong to the 'national community' – the 'community aliens' (*Gemeinschaftsfremde*) as they came to be called.[8] (3) The need to instil in the population the hatred both of internal enemies – political, racial and 'anti-social' – and of foreign enemies through a madly heightened chauvinism and sense of 'Germanness'. (4) Cementing all this together was the need for a trust in the leadership going way beyond conventional respect for the authority of the head of a government and demanding unthinking adulation and obedience towards a leader wrapped up in a cult of almost deified infallibility who would unquestionably do what was right for people and nation. The successful linkage of these four aims provided the necessary base for the building of the new nazified society, what Nazi jargon called the 'fighting community', which in turn was the guarantor of the required psychological state of mobilisation for waging a war of national survival.

I want in what follows to retain the notion of the four pillars of restructured socio-political consciousness on which the new society was to be built, but to break down further the aims of propaganda into specific themes and leitmotivs and to consider them within the framework of four distinct spheres of propaganda influence. These can be broadly defined as: (a) areas where propaganda could readily build upon already generally accepted values, ideological predisposition and dominant opinion; (b) areas where propaganda encountered no preexistent consensus and had to try to manufacture one; (c) areas of heavy prejudice premised on widespread ignorance, where propaganda largely functioned in a vacuum; and (d) areas where propaganda ran up against strong counter-opinion and disbelief. Though the first and third and second and fourth areas overlap to some extent, this scheme of differentiation provides a useful framework for the brief treatment of each area which follows.

Building upon Existing Values

Three areas where Nazi propaganda coincided with and could reinforce what might be regarded as the dominant ideology (as it existed outside the ranks of organised labour) can be singled out as particularly important: (i) anti-Marxism and the need felt for a powerful counter to the forces of the Left — the most crucial prop of bourgeois ideology since the Imperial era; (ii) deep hostility towards the Weimar Republic — arising partly from a principled rejection of democracy but even more from the recognition that the democratic system had failed — coupled with the growing belief that strong leadership was needed to transcend class and sectional interests and provide Germany with a new start; and (iii) an even wider consensus, extending into sections of the Left, that Germany had been wronged in the Versailles settlement and was surrounded by a ring of hostile nations. These areas of pre-existing wide consensus offered the potential for a strong basis of support for a government which could appear to embody the need for inner unity and outward strength. They provided the foundation upon which Nazi propaganda could score its most notable successes.

Where Nazi propaganda before 1933 was undoubtedly successful was in persuading large sections of the German people that only a large, powerful, and dynamic anti-Marxist force — the NSDAP — stood a chance of succeeding in the fight against Marxism. Building upon the deep-rooted and wide-ranging virulent anti-Marxism in the German bourgeoisie, the Nazis had no difficulty in manufacturing and exploiting the anti-Communist hysteria following the burning of the Reichstag in order to emphasise the polarisation of politics into the Marxist Left and the nationalist Right. The wave of terror unleashed against the Left in the first months of the Nazi government counted without doubt among the most popular actions of the regime in its early phase, functioning as one of its leading integratory elements at this date.[9] Nazi propaganda was highly effective here, therefore, in bolstering existing anti-Marxist sentiment and in establishing a negative integration around the notion of the enemies of the State, the *Staatsfeinde*. In 1936-7 Nazi propaganda again seems to have scored considerable success in channelling anti-Left feeling in an outward direction through its massive anti-Bolshevic campaigns. Even anti-Nazi sources such as the reports of the *Sopade* (the Social Democrats' exile organisation) testify that these campaigns were effective, penetrating even into sections of the working class.[10] The success nevertheless rested plainly upon the exploitation by Nazi propaganda of long-standing ideological preconceptions and reinforcement of existing sentiment among substantial sections of the German population.

There is much to be said for Goebbels' own reported view that his most notable propaganda success was the creation and consolidation of extraordinary bonds of loyalty to Hitler surpassing any 'normal' level of trust in political leadership.[11] Here, too, the effectiveness of propaganda depended heavily upon the predisposition of wide sections of society to believe in such a form of leadership as Hitler offered, and it has been rightly pointed out that the Hitler image was just as much a creation of the masses as it was imposed upon them.[12] Ideas of heroic leadership were present in rightist circles before the First World War and formed a common component of right-wing thought throughout the 1920s. The qualities of the coming leader were seen as reflecting struggle, conflict, the values of the trenches. The leader would be hard, ruthless, resolute, uncompromising and radical — ruler, warrior and high-priest alike.[13] The weaker the Weimar Republic became, the more attractive such qualities appeared to be. There was, therefore, nothing specifically Nazi about belief in heroic leadership. But where Nazi propaganda proved highly effective was, first, in making such leadership the organisational premise of the Nazi Party from the mid-1920s onwards, secondly, in portraying Hitler as not just another Party leader but as *the* Leader for whom Germany had been waiting — a man of incomparably different stature to that of Germany's ordinary 'politicians' — and thirdly, and most important of all, in the successful extension of the Hitler image from that of party leader to that of national leader, accomplished in 1933. Following the 'seizure of power', one of the most significant successes of the propaganda construction of the Hitler cult was, in fact, in separating Hitler from the increasingly negative image of the Nazi Party itself. The full-blown Hitler cult, as it developed from 1933 onwards, was a genuinely integratory force in German society. Hitler's popularity even extended into sections of the working class who otherwise left no doubt about their distaste for Nazism. His positive image as profiled by propaganda, bearing scant resemblance to reality, proved extraordinarily resilient and fell apart only gradually during the war. Whatever negative sentiments were expressed towards the Party and the subordinate leadership of the Reich, Nazi propaganda was at its most effective in creating an astonishing degree of personal loyalty to Hitler.[14]

Much of Hitler's popularity derived, of course, from the scale of his 'achievements' after 1933 as portrayed by the propaganda apparatus. The most spectacular of all his 'achievements' occurred in the realm of foreign policy. The massive acclamation for these 'achievements' rested, however, upon the wide preexisting consensus favouring the overthrow of the Versailles settlement and revised German territorial borders. Nazi propaganda had a remarkably easy task in the foreign policy arena before 1938. For one thing it could simply play on the belief, prevalent in practically all sections of the population, that Germany had been maltreated by the Allies at the end of the war, and on the equally generally held fear that Germany was threatened by a ring of hostile nations. And secondly, propaganda was generally given the task — at least before the Sudetenland crisis in 1938 — of justifying successful *faits accomplis* such as the withdrawal from the League of Nations, the reintroduction of military service and the reoccupation of the Rhineland. As long as foreign policy appeared to be no more than revisionist in intent, and above all as long as it was accomplished without bloodshed and involvement in war, propaganda effectiveness was guaranteed.[15] Propaganda on foreign policy aims and actions contained, however, an immanent incompatibility: while it was vital to appear to be preaching peace and making no more than revisionist claims, it was difficult to reconcile this with the chief aim of producing the required degree of psychological mobilisation of the population for war. And precisely on this point —whether German demands warranted war — propaganda could rely on no ready-built consensus, and without that consensus propaganda effectiveness was severely limited. As is well known, the prolonged crisis in the summer of 1938 — the first time that the propaganda machine had been faced with upholding morale for several months in the likely expectation of war — produced feelings bordering on panic about the likelihood of war and even expressions of unwillingness to fight for the Sudetenland.[16] Hitler's speech to the leaders of the press in November 1938 brought out forcefully the inbuilt incompatibility of a propaganda which for years had preached peace but was meant to mobilise the population for war.[17] Little changed by September 1939 when, as is also generally known, the German people showed a distinct lack of enthusiasm for the opening of armed conflict with the invasion of Poland.[18] However, propaganda was certainly effective in persuading the bulk of the population that the war had been unavoidable and had been forced upon the Germans.[19] Resilience and determination were not lacking, even if there was scant enthusiasm. And in the light of early German successes, it was not difficult for propaganda to tighten still further the bond of identification of the overwhelming majority of the population with Hitler.[20]

In two of the four spheres of restructured socio-political consciousness with which we began our enquiry, it would be possible to conclude that Nazi propaganda enjoyed considerable success. Hatred of enemies, without and within, was heightened through an intensified emphasis on German identity. And an almost religious loyalty to the Führer surpassed all previous levels of trust in political leadership. In neither case, of course, were all sections of society convinced. But doubters and waverers were socially and politically isolated. In each case the effectiveness of propaganda was conditioned by the wide consensus (excluding the ranks of the formerly organised Left) on which propaganda could build. Quite plainly, however, propaganda had not produced by 1939 the required level of psychological mobilisation for war which, to that date, had been its prime underlying aim. There had been massive acclamation for Nazi successes in foreign policy which had fulfilled longstanding aspirations and revisionist hopes in a spectacular series of coups. But the prospect of war was a different story. Fear of war was a pervading trait of popular opinion during the 1930s in Germany. It was particularly pronounced in the generation which had experienced the Great War, and there was in the nature of things a higher level of effectiveness of militaristic propaganda among the young, where the formative influence of the Hitler Youth was considerable. Even among young Germans, however, an important feature of propaganda success lay not so much in its militarism as in its bolstering of the Hitler image in such a way that, perversely, the Führer appeared to act as a guarantor of peace not a bringer of war.[21]

The Need to Manufacture Consensus

The Nazi aim to mobilise the German people in the cause of the nation meant the displacement of all class, religious or regional allegiances through massively heightened national self-awareness and the release of national energies. It has been rightly said that what was intended was a permanent reproduction of the experience of 1914:[22] 'civil peace' at home and a united nation straining for the chance to destroy its enemies. The revolution in attitudes which was to condition the German people for the inevitable showdown with the nation's enemies was, of course, summed up in the main Nazi social idea, that of the 'national community' (*Volksgemeinschaft*). The creation of a 'national community' demanded the erasure of all loyalties which ran counter to or detracted from loyalty to the nation; it implied the transcending of social and class divisiveness by the harmony of a national unity which could only be achieved by the replacing at all times of sectional interest by the national interest. Since the cleavages in German society, in particular along class and denominational lines, were extraordinarily deep, the sense of 'national community' had clearly to be manufactured.[23] And given the nature of the social divisions, Nazi propaganda obviously faced one of its most difficult tasks in its attempt to manufacture the 'national community'.

As its basis for action, propaganda could at least rely on the fact that the idea of national and social harmony as the ideological obverse of class conflict had featured prominently in middle-class social culture since the Imperial period. There is some evidence, too, that the solidarity of the 'national community' was among the most important ideological drawing-cards in winning support for the Nazis before 1933.[24] And following the 'seizure of power' a vast amount of energy and initiative was poured into social propaganda of the most varied kinds and of the 'deed' as well as the word.[25] It would not be going too far to suggest that practically every aspect of the propagated image of the Nazi Movement could be subsumed under the heading of 'social propaganda'. Despite this massive effort — full analysis of which would have to consider not only the Goebbels propaganda machine, but also the impact of Nazi welfare services, the 'Strength through Joy' organisation and much of the work of the Party at the local level among other sides of 'social propaganda' — it seems clear that Nazi policies failed to break down objective class and social divisions and — more important for present considerations — that propaganda signally failed to destroy the awareness of these divisions. Nazi social propaganda seems, in fact, to have been far more effective in confirming the 'achievements' of the Third Reich to those who were already either committed followers or potential sympathisers than in winning over those groups which before 1933 had stood aloof from Nazism. The two most significant sectors of the German population which had proved relatively immune to Nazi propaganda before 1933 were the industrial working class and Catholics. And much evidence suggests that it was above all these sectors of the population which the 'national community' myth failed to convince after 1933.

Tim Mason's studies have vividly demonstrated the almost unmitigated failure of Nazi social propaganda among German industrial workers.[26] Even the undoubted propaganda impact of the tumbling unemployment figures in the early years of the Regime was arguably far greater among those not directly affected than among workers forced into unpalatable and back-breaking employment, often far away from their homes, and at rates of pay frequently lower than employment benefit, to whom eulogies of Nazi achievements in work creation could seem less than wholly convincing. 'Winter Aid', too, which undoubtedly did bring genuine belief to many during the first years of the regime before it simply poured in its entirety into the rearmament coffers, may well have been more effective as propaganda among the 'well-doing' middle class than among the poorer sections of society, from whom demands for a proper wage rather than the alms of winter relief could be heard. Even 'Strength through Joy' was only a qualified popular success among workers since, as was not infrequently pointed out, only the better-off among them could afford to go on the scheme's trips let alone on its foreign excursions. My own enquiry into subjective perceptions of social position in the Third Reich suggests in fact that not only among the working class, but also among the peasantry and the lower middle class, the 'national community' idea was little able to alter behavioural patterns and ways of thinking determined in the main by considerations of material self-interest.[27]

Just as class differences and status perception were left fundamentally unchanged by the empty rhetoric of Nazi social propaganda, so 'national community' exhortation could not replace religious loyalties to some extent even enhanced by the 'Church struggle'. The Nazi war of attrition against the Churches made the much vaunted unity of the 'national community' seem no more than a mockery as loyalties polarised around representatives of Church or Party. A report from a Protestant deanery in Franconia in 1939 provides one not untypical verdict on the effectiveness of 'national community' propaganda:

The growing discontent in the countryside and the accompanying increasing fear of the rulers among many people show another very unpleasant side of parish life: people's distrust of each other and the nasty conflict between entire households and families. Never was the 'national community' less of a reality than now.[28]

In Catholic communities the loyalties to the Church were, if anything, even firmer. Nazi authorities repeatedly pointed out in their reports the difficulties encountered by propaganda in staunchly Catholic districts. Comments of the sort that 'the influence of the Church on the population is so strong that the National Socialist spirit cannot penetrate', or 'these people much prefer to believe what the priest says from the pulpit than the words of the best speakers', are not uncommon.[29] Anti-clerical propaganda at the time of the 'immorality trials' of 1936-7 met with flat disbelief in Catholic circles, subscriptions to Nazi newspapers were cancelled, and fervent denunciations from the pulpit of 'the lying Nazi press' drew applause from congregations.[30]

Nazi attempts to manufacture a consensus where one did not exist through the propaganda of the 'national community' were largely a failure long before 1939. And far from class or sectional interests being overcome through a strengthened sense of 'national community' during the war, the perception of social divisions and injustices became sharper than ever under the strains of wartime civilian life. The gap between social myth and social reality in the Third Reich grew ever wider.[31] And the gap could not be closed, however much the Regime's propaganda stressed the value of belonging to a 'national community' and the need for self-sacrifice in the interests of the nation.

The solidarity of a 'national community', in which the placing of the nation first was axiomatic, was a central pillar of the new value system on which psychological mobilisation for war and during war was to rest. In Nazi eyes, the strength of the nation as a 'fighting community' depended upon its social unity. Yet the evidence points to the conclusion that Nazi propaganda on this point was at its least effective.

Propaganda in a Vacuum: Prejudice and Ignorance

The third sphere of propaganda effectiveness to consider relates to issues which emanated from the dominant socio-political culture discussed earlier but seldom affected the lives of the mass of the population in any tangible, direct or material way and where existing prejudice and extensive ignorance, unchallenged by any significant countervailing 'education', allowed propaganda to act in a vacuum. The central question here concerns the effectiveness of racial propaganda, an issue dominated by the 'Jewish Question' but embracing also the racial-eugenic components of 'social policy' and the racial stereotype images of Germany's enemies. The Nazi Regime set great store by racial propaganda to instil in the population the need for racial purity — the fourth pillar of the restructured value system of the intended new society. Yet even here, close to the core of Nazi ideology, the evidence — difficult though it often is to evaluate and seeming to run in conflicting and unclear directions — suggests that propaganda was by no means as effective as has frequently been assumed.

The Jew was clearly the number one hate target for Nazi propaganda thoughout the Third Reich. Propaganda could depend upon the pre-existence of extensive latent anti-Jewish feeling for its campaigns (with their high points in 1933, 1935 and especially 1938), quite apart from the activist hatred of the already mobilised sectors within the Nazi organisations. Prejudice against Jews derived in no small measure from ignorance. Only a small percentage of the German population actually came regularly in contact with Jews or had much directly to do with them. Antagonism based upon trading rivalries and economic grievances did of course, in the climate of the Third Reich, lead to terrible out-breaks of anti-Semitic violence and countless horrific attacks on indivi-dual Jews. But for most Germans, 'the Jew' was seldom equated with a real, living person. Extensive prejudice coexisted with widespread ignor-ance about the Jews, who scarcely impinged directly upon the lives of most Germans.

Nazi propaganda found it difficult, in fact, in the first years of the Third Reich to persuade Germans to break off commercial or profes-sional dealings with Jews. The disgust of party anti-Semites at the reluctance of people to avoid Jewish shops and department stores and at the stubbornness of farmers in continuing trafficking with Jewish cattle-dealers was expressed with nauseating regularity. Propaganda evidently had a hard time convincing people that ideological correct-ness must be put before material self-interest if Jewish prices were better than 'Aryan' prices. Despite the propaganda barrage – in the forefront the obnoxious *Stürmer* – on the need to boycott and ostracise the Jews, the economic (and increasingly social) exclusion of the Jews from German life was the result of terror and legal discrimination, not propaganda.[32]

Where propaganda on the 'Jewish Question' *was* effective, was in spreading the conviction that there was such a thing as a 'Jewish Ques-tion'. Even the anti-Nazi reports of the *Sopade*, the Social Democrats' exile organistion, reluctantly accepted by the mid-1930s that the regime had been successful in persuading people that there was indeed a 'Jewish Question',[33] A huge increase in the circulation of the *Stürmer* was one ominous indication of this development.[34] The greatest success of anti-Semitic propaganda was, however, in the advancing depersonal-isation of the Jew which accompanied the progressive elimination of Jews from German society and their reduction to little more than an abstract ideological anti-symbol. The result was rather the creation of a fatal degree of indifference than of dynamic hatred towards the Jews.

The negative reactions towards the violence of the pogrom of November 1938 — and the overwhelming rejection of Goebbels' propaganda claim that it arose from the 'justified anger of the German people' — pointed to a lasting residue of humanitarian and Christian values which Nazi propaganda was penetrating and breaking down only with enormous difficulty (though it is true that rejection of the pogrom also frequently stemmed from material and often base motives, and there seems to have been widespread acceptance of the 'legal' discriminatory measures taken against the Jews in the aftermath of the pogrom). As far as public interest went, the pogrom and its consequences were a short-lived phenomenon. And despite an increasing rather than diminishing volume of anti-Jewish propaganda during the war, anti-Semitism was for most Germans now so abstract and so routine that there was apparently difficulty in keeping alive a real interest in the 'Jewish Question'. The propaganda film *The Eternal Jew* was reportedly playing to low cinema audiences; workers were bored in 1943 by Robert Ley's monotonous anti-Semitic tirades; and a year later Party propagandists were admitting that for most young Germans the Jews amounted to little more than a 'museum piece', left-overs from a bygone age.[35]

The effectiveness of propaganda aimed at building stereotype images of Germany's external enemies, especially the 'Slav *Untermenschen*' east of the Reich, is difficult to assess. Given the extent of pre-existing anti-Polish and anti-Russian sentiment, the level of anti-Bolshevic propaganda, and the actual ignorance about the Polish and especially the Russian people, it is a fair assumption that Nazi propaganda was successful in confirming and reinforcing prevailing sterotypes.[36] In the period following the attack on the USSR in 1941 the propaganda picture of the primitive Asiatic and Slavic 'sub-humans' was of course unceasingly hammered home. Yet relations between Germans and Polish and Russian prisoners-of-war and 'foreign workers' — an area which has not yet been exhaustively researched — seem to demonstrate the difficulties encountered by propaganda in maintaining racial-national stereotypes when Germans were confronted with reality and, again, in breaking down Christian and liberal-humanitarian values as well as residual ideological sympathy and class solidarity among some German workers. By 1942 SD reports were pointing out that actual contact with Russian 'foreign workers' was not according with propaganda directives. People were seeing the Russian not as a member of an 'alien race' but as 'also a human being', and a tendency towards a 'strongly humane evaluation of the Russian' could be observed. Whereas propaganda had depicted Russians as bestial and primitive *Untermenschen*, people found them to be frequently intelligent, skilful, adaptable and quick at picking up the German language. The real live Russian was set against the stereotype Bolshevic monster, and the result was a propaganda failure. The SD concluded that ever more Germans were becoming aware 'that the earlier unified picture' of Bolshevic horror 'did not or does not any longer correspond to reality'.[37] By 1942, therefore, real contact with Russians and growing respect for their war performance was drastically altering the effectiveness of the stereotype propaganda which had earlier been successful because it had largely functioned in a vacuum. A year later in fact, according to the SD, the new respect for the Russians was leading, particularly among workers, to a re-appraisal of not only anti-Russian but also anti-Bolshevic propaganda. Willingly or not, the population had come to have closer dealings with Bolshevics as a result of the war

and thereby noticed differences between Bolshevism as portrayed by our propaganda and Bolshevism as the population has got to know it, in small part through the tales of those on leave, and especially through their own experiences from contact with Soviet workers. And so, as has been variously reported recently, propaganda is finding it increasingly difficult, especially in worker circles, to put across and illustrate with positively convincing arguments that Bolshevism really is the danger that it has always been painted.[38]

Here too, therefore, propaganda effectiveness was limited, and by factors over which Goebbels and the Nazi regime in general had little control. Success was once more conditioned by the ability to build upon prejudices already present and to work in a vacuum without any opposing propaganda of note. But propaganda lost its effectiveness as soon as it was confronted with the more complex picture presented by reality. Moreover, the difficulties of propaganda in altering rather than merely reinforcing existing values were reflected in the problems encountered in attempting to undermine Christian and humanitarian attitudes. This can be graphically seen in responses to a further deadly strand of Nazi racial-eugenic policy, the so-called 'euthanasia programme' of 1939-41.

As is well known, the 'euthanasia action' was carried out in secret — itself testimony to the fact that the Regime did not regard the population as ideologically prepared to welcome the 'action' — but the secret was an open one. Propaganda in this case was not given the task of 'educating' the population for the 'euthanasia programme', but was hurriedly required to provide justificatory backing (within the framework of the remaining official veil of secrecy) when things started to go wrong. One main product was the film *Ich klage an* (I Accuse), which attempted to portray an emotionally sympathetic case for 'mercy killing'. Though Goebbels hoped the film would prove a first step towards 'educating' the German people on this sensitive issue, he was forced to concede that it had been a failure and that, despite reasonably good attendance figures, there had been a strong tendency among cinema audiences to side with the Churches against the State on the 'euthanasia' issue.[39] In this instance, propaganda acted not in a vacuum, but in direct competition with the counter-propaganda of the Churches (especially of the Catholic Church, with its own firm hold over its adherents). Moreover, propaganda was not functioning here in an area which was of only tangential or indirect relevance to the bulk of the German population, but in an issue which could potentially affect any Germans and their families.

Counter-opinion and Disbelief

The anxieties of war made Germans keener than ever for reliable information. Yet the 'closed' and tightly-controlled information provided by the propaganda agencies gave rise in such circumstances – to a far greater extent than in wartime Britain – to the construction of a frequently powerful counter-opinion which contributed significantly to the growing general scepticism about the reliability of 'official' information. The part played by rumour – often started by foreign broadcasts which, despite draconian penalties, found ready listeners – in forming resilient counter-opinion and prompting scepticism about the 'official' version, was extraordinary. And stories told by eye-witnesses – soldiers home on leave or bombed-out evacuees – often conflicted directly with optimistic press reports and were listened to eagerly.[40] The veracity of German propaganda was in these and other ways increasingly called into question and general confidence in official information gradually undermined. Of course, there were certainly phases of propaganda success and themes which were undoubtedly highly effective, but the general picture of wartime propaganda which can be gleaned from sources such as press directives and especially SD reports is one of growing and eventually almost total propaganda failure long before the end of the war. The more propaganda seemed to conflict with reality, the more discredited it became. The process began even in the 'triumphant' phase of the war, before the invasion of the USSR.

Propaganda had a relatively easy task in the first years of the War in capitalising on the *Blitzkrieg* victories. However, the seeds of the later collapse in confidence in German propaganda were sown in this period. One difficult issue from the beginning of the war was the question of living standards, and on this German propaganda was largely hoisted with its own petard. Even in the early phase of the war, claims that the harsh impact of war on the civilian economy had been avoided encountered great scepticism in the light of the obvious difficulties and restrictions affecting the majority of the population. The more deeply rationing and shortages of various commodities bit, the more hollow the propaganda claims seemed.[41] The coal crisis in 1939-40 was also mis-handled by the propaganda machine. Frequent reports of the fuel diffi-culties of enemy countries but press silence or trivialisation of the domestic coal crisis provoked considerable resentment, especially among the working class, the chief sufferers.[42] The lauding of Nazi social 'achievements' met a cool response among the large numbers in big cities still living in overcrowded and sub-standard housing. And anti-British propaganda emphasising the enormous class differences in England boomeranged as workers pointed out the similarity of condi-tions in Germany.[43]

Another area in which propaganda credibility suffered from a rela-tively early stage was in its exaggerated claims about the strength of Germany's air defences. Though it was Göring's reputation which suffered most of all as a result of British bombing raids on German towns following his bravado claims that no enemy planes would get through, repeated propaganda threats of reprisals against Britain which failed to take place both fuelled popular anger and damaged propa-ganda credibility after 1940.[44] Propaganda was certainly effective in this first phase of the war in maligning Britain as the only major obstacle to peace. Building on a store of traditional anti-British feeling, enormous hostility to Britain was whipped up in the summer of 1940, though Goebbels realised that this was engendering a dangerous impat-ience and optimism about Germany's ability to steamroller Britain as it had done the rest of Europe, and the protracted build-up to the German offensive against Britain and the inability to force a victory again put strains on the confidence in German propaganda. Scenes of London ablaze during the 'Blitz' were popular, but as the bombing dragged on without conclusive results even admiration for the Londoners and the stubbornness of the British was recorded. More significantly, distrust of German reported losses of planes over Britain led to an increase in listening to broadcasts of the BBC, whose reports on the losses in the 'dog-fights' were apparently trusted more than those of German propaganda.[45]

By summer 1940, SD reports were commenting on popular criticism of propaganda and on diminishing interest in the press on account of its boring uniformity.[46] Doubts about the correctness of German military reports were frequently expressed.[47] Goebbels' propaganda was reportedly scorned by army officers.[48] What people were looking for in radio and press reports were above all hints that the war would soon be over.[49]

A great embarrassment for German propaganda occurred in May 1941 with the flight of Deputy Führer, Rudolf Hess, to Britain. The official explanation that Hess was mentally ill, which emerged after a lapse of three days following the flight, met with a combination of flat disbelief and — even worse for the regime's image — the response that Germany must be in a bad way if a man known to have been suffering for years with a serious mental disorder had nevertheless been allowed to continue holding high office. German propaganda was savagely criticised by all sections of the population:

> German press and radio reports of the Hess affair were from the working class to the intelligentsia described as very clumsy and bungling. These very reports have prompted people to concern themselves especially closely with the Hess case and have so shaken the confidence in German propaganda (the truthful press and radio reportage) that for the time being the whole press and radio reports will automatically be regarded as untrue.[50]

Goebbels himself took a sanguine view of the affair. He was surprised and relieved that Britain did not make more of the propaganda opportunity, and regarded the issue as a nine-days' wonder in which the criticism heaped upon German propaganda would not seriously endanger the long-term work of the propaganda ministry.[51] Even so, the year and a half following the invasion of the Soviet Union was a bad spell for German propaganda, as Goebbels himself realised, and reached its nadir in the catastrophic coverage of the battle for Stalingrad.

As the Russian war dragged on, it became increasingly plain that propaganda claims of the 'Russian giant with feet of clay' being easily overrun were madly optimistic, and worries grew that propaganda was hiding the plain truth of the situation from the people. The hurried collections for winter clothing for the troops at the end of 1941 again raised questions about the reliability of a propaganda which had hitherto been reassuring about the extensive provisioning of the army in Russia.[52] Already by spring 1942 Goebbels was moving towards the need to speak plainly and openly in propaganda about the grimness of the situation. The Propaganda Minister's change of tone and new realism were inseparable from his keen ambition to be in charge of a German 'total war' effort. Even so, his own statements in 1942, long before the Stalingrad disaster, provide an extraordinary indictment of the weakness and ineffectiveness of his own propaganda at that date. In one of his addresses to those in charge of the mass media towards the end of September 1942, Goebbels castigated

the inadequacies of German propaganda methods. Proceeding from a number of reports he had received, he explains that the public at home and also abroad is no longer accepting German propaganda because it has become so worn out and expressionless that it provokes a feeling of weariness among its listeners and readers ... The Minister gives all propaganda agencies such as press, wireless, newsreel, and speaker deployment the binding directive to refrain from this method of a stereotype and spiritless repetition of propaganda expressions and from now on to make more effort to prevent a further drop in public interest in information, reports, articles, speeches, and so on.[53]

Around the same time, Goebbels was berating the political immaturity of the German people in contrast with the inbuilt self-confidence, and therefore greater resilience, of the 'English' (i.e. British) people. He argued that German propaganda had of necessity to be so restrictive and offer only a single official opinion because the fickleness of Germans meant that, given a choice, they would instinctively go for the opinion least pleasant to the government. He pointed to the contrast between the lasting negative echo of Göring's exaggerated claims for German air defence and, despite numerous mistakes, the continuing respect for Churchill in England. He even stated that Churchill was well respected by the German people. He claimed, remarkably, that the English motto 'my country, right or wrong' was not practical for Germany, and that nine years after the Nazi 'revolution' the skin of the German people was so thin that it needed only to be scratched for the old wounds to be re-opened.[54]

Soon after Goebbels' admission of German propaganda deficiencies came Stalingrad — military defeat and propaganda débâcle of the first magnitude. The Stalingrad catastrophe occasioned a massive loss of confidence in the German leadership, even now directly including Hitler. This was in no small measure owing to the wholly misleading and irresponsible propaganda which came close to destroying credibility once and for all. As late as September 1942, newspapers were still prophesying the imminent defeat of the encircled Russian army in Stalingrad, arousing expectations that the city could fall to the Germans at any moment. As unease grew at the length of time the victory was taking, German propaganda spoke of the 'unexpected strength' of Russian resistance, but still made no mention as such of the Russian counter-offensive. And for weeks, radio and press said nothing whatsoever of the fact that not the Russians but the Germans had been encircled and trapped. Despite the propaganda silence, rumours to this effect, put into circulation by foreign broadcasts, were rife by late December 1942. It was only towards the end of January 1943 that German propaganda swung completely around to a sudden plaintive admission of the plight of the encircled German troops and the imminent end of the 'heroic epic' of Stalingrad. The terrible announcement that 'the fight in Stalingrad is over' came on 3 February. Even now, in order to sustain the myth of the heroic sacrifice of the Sixth Army, the capitulation and imprisonment of 90,000 Germans was not disclosed.[55] It was an astounding propaganda fiasco.

Though the new 'realism' as portrayed in Goebbels' 'total war' speech in February 1943 and in related propaganda was in the short-term effective, and though in the remaining period of the war there were still propaganda successes — such as exploitation of hatred towards the Western Allies stirred up by their terror bombing, the creation of hope in 'wonder-weapons' (rapidly dissipated when the V1 and V2 were actually deployed), the short-lived resuscitation of trust in Hitler following the failure of the 1944 plot against him, and the stimulation of intense fear of the Russians in the final months of the war as reports of Red Army atrocities spread — the final two years of the war were in general a period of decreasing propaganda effectiveness and culminating sense of failure. Interest in the press declined still further, despite keenness for news of the military front. Increasing numbers of people turned surreptitiously to foreign broadcasts, despite the heavy penalties if discovered. Weekly newsreels in the cinema, so popular in the early part of the War, now lost their attraction.[56] By early 1944, the loss of confidence in propaganda was widespread and general. The incompatibility of press and radio announcements with what people could judge of the situation from the witness of their own eyes and reports of others, and from foreign broadcasts (whose veracity was more trusted than that of the German media), became ever more acute. In April 1944 the SD office in Schweinfurt reported that 'our propaganda encounters rejection everywhere among the population because it is regarded as wrong and lying'.[57] And from Würzburg, two months later, came the devastating assessment:

> Propaganda: the opinion is widespread among the people that things are worse than we are told, and the comment can be heard: 'We're lied to in this War just as much as we were in the last one'. Above all, the many announcements of Dr. Goebbels in 'Das Reich', which up to now have never been followed by any action, have had an unsatisfactory effect in that they have for a long time aroused hopes and promised early fulfilment and now leave great disappointment in their wake. The people, also Party members, say it would be better if Dr. Goebbels didn't write anything more, since either he repeats what he has already said ten times or makes prophecies which are not fulfilled.[58]

Reporting on the reception of an article on the Führer which Goebbels had published in *Das Reich* at New Year 1945, the SD office at Stuttgart reported that 'a Goebbels article has probably never before stood so much in the forefront of attention as this one, but his articles have also probably never before been so criticized'.[59] And, according to another SD local agency, at Berchtesgaden, Goebbels' appeal for a heroic struggle 'to the last' for a new Europe, 'in order to go down in history', met with a stony response: 'The broad mass of the people could not care less what the future Europe looks like . . . and place not the slightest value on going down in history.'[60]

Already long before this, the Propaganda Minister had helped to get the production and circulation among leaders of the regime of central digests of the unpalatable SD reports stopped.[61] By the middle of the war, Goebbels had lost all patience with critical comments (other than his own) on propaganda, even from officials within the Propaganda Ministry and from Party propaganda offices. By this time, he was rapidly losing touch with reality. He wanted the reports to tell him only that which he hoped to hear.[62] His furious reactions to reports of the ineffectiveness of his propaganda were themselves, however, the best testimony to the ultimate failure of his work.

The effectiveness of propaganda, I have argued, was heavily dependent upon its ability to build on an existing consensus, to confirm existing values, to bolster existing prejudices. Its success was guaranteed wherever it could identify Nazi aims with values which were unquestioned.[63] It was particularly effective in constructing an extraordinary degree of loyalty of the German people to Hitler on the basis of a highly artificial 'Führer image' which corresponded in good measure to popular idealistic notions of leadership. It was effective, too, in reinforcing fears and prejudices about supposed enemies of Germany, internal and external. Pre-existing anti-Marxist and anti-Bolshevic sentiment was consolidated and extended. Propaganda was a qualified success in its attempt to persuade the German people of the need for racial purity. Depersonalisation of the Jews was effectively accomplished, and the notion that there was indeed an important 'Jewish Question' was established. On the other hand, as reactions to the 1938 pogrom showed, open maltreatment of Jews met with wide disfavour, even if discrimination was acceptable. Propaganda justification of the 'euthanasia programme' was largely a failure and, as in this case, the limits of effectiveness were reached where propaganda ran against existing values and norms, encountered more plausible counter-propaganda (or counter-prejudice) and contradicted obvious reality and the evidence of people's own eyes. Moreover, the notion of a solidly united people, built around the myth of the 'national community', was, taken all round, a notable propaganda failure and never likely to overcome the immanent contradictions of Nazi social policy. In some respects, the propaganda picture of a united German people totally behind its leadership was more convincing for the outside world than for the German public.

The central aim of German propaganda before 1939 had been to prepare the German people psychologically for war. In this aim it can be said to have partially, but not wholly, successful. It was effective in persuading people — who did not need much convincing anyway — that Germany's revisionist claims were justified, that Germany was threatened on all sides, and that should it come to war the fault would not be Germany's. A sense of grim determination, of being ready to fight if need be, was widespread in 1938-9 and had undoubtedly been furthered by the continued impact of Nazi propaganda. On the other hand, the obvious lack of enthusiasm for war (and longing for peace when war had broken out) was clearly painful to the Nazi leadership. Hitler's comments to the editors of German newspapers in November 1938, his reported annoyance at popular reactions to the Sudeten crisis and the elation when peace was secured at the Munich Conference, and his ambivalent comment in November 1939 that behind him stood the German people 'whose morale can only get worse',[64] all testify to the limited effectiveness of propaganda in what, in Nazi eyes, was its overriding task.

From September 1939 the chief aim switched to the preservation of morale during the war. And in this aim propaganda encountered growing failure. Distrust of German propaganda, coupled with boredom at its dull monotony, paved the way even in the period of German military triumph for the later drastic collapse of confidence. Miscalculations, errors of emphasis, and downright embarrassing blunders (as in the Hess case) did not help the wilting image of propaganda. By 1942, long before the major military defeats, the image was largely negative. Stalingrad was a propaganda disaster. Goebbels' 'realism propaganda' restored credibility for a while, but the downward spiral was inevitable. By 1944 the failure was all but total. If temporary and partial successes could still be registered, the general effectiveness of propaganda in this phase was minimal. The reasons why Germany fought on to the bitter end, why there was no repeat of 1918, are complex and cannot be entered into here. But these reasons have little to do with propaganda. Far more important than propaganda was its counterfoil, present since the beginning but now reaching its apogee: terroristic repression. The escalation of terror in the latter years of the regime was no incidental development. It denoted the collapse of any form of consensus in Germany except the one most unacceptable to the regime – a consensus for ending the war. And with the collapse of any popular base of support for the regime, the ultimate powerlessness of Nazi propaganda was complete.

Notes

1. This was implicit, for instance, in E.K. Bramsted's study, *Goebbels and National Socialist Propaganda 1925-1945* (Michigan, 1965); cf. esp. the conclusion, and in particular p. 450. See also the introductory remarks in Z.A.B. Zeman, *Nazi Propaganda*, 2nd edn (Oxford 1973), p. xvii. L. Schapiro, *Totalitarianism* (London, 1973) revises the earlier approaches (without fundamental alteration) of Carl Friedrich and others, and deals with the role of propaganda on pp. 53-4.

2. The theme of more or less successful manipulation runs through the nevertheless valuable works by Klaus Scheel, the foremost GDR historian of propaganda. See his *Krieg über Ätherwellen. NS-Rundfunk und Monopole 1933-45* (Berlin, 1970); 'Meinungsmanipulierung im Faschismus', *Zeitschrift für*

Geschichtswissenschaft, vol. 17 (1969); and 'Faschistische Kulturpropaganda im zweiten Weltkrieg. Ihr Einsatz zur Irreführung des deutschen Volkes während der ersten Kriegsjahre (1939-1941)', *Jahrbuch für Volkskunde und Kultur-geschichte*, vol. 21 (1979). At the same time, GDR writers pointed earlier and more clearly than many Western historians to aspects of the class-based nature of Nazi propaganda success and limits of its effectiveness. Cf. e.g. E. Paterna *et al.*, *Deutschland 1933-9* (Berlin, 1969), Ch. 3 Pt 2, esp. pp. 178ff.

3. R.E. Herzstein, *The War that Hitler Won* (London, 1979), pp. 22, 431. Chs. 11-12 of the book seem to me to provide evidence which casts serious doubt on the book's main argument. Cf. also Zeman, *Nazi Propaganda*, p. 177: 'In the six years of peace, the cumulative impact of Nazi propaganda on the Germans was tremendous', though he immediately adds that it is difficult to judge how divided or undivided Germany embarked on the war, and saw the war itself as a period of decline in the effectiveness of propaganda (Ch. VII).

4. For differing assessments of the role of propaganda in the rise of Nazism, cf. R. Bessel, 'The Myth of Nazi Propaganda', *Wiener Library Bulletin*, vol. 33 (1980), and my essay, 'Ideology, Propaganda, and the Rise of the Nazi Party' in P. Stachura (ed.), *Hitler's Machtergreifung, 1933* (London, 1983).

5. Cf. M. Balfour, *Propaganda in War, 1939-45* (London, 1979).

6. Hitler's own reported comments towards the end of the war, which emphasised the pressure of time on the creation of a new society, amounted practically to an admission of the failure of propaganda and indoctrination. He is reputed to have said that he had had no time in which to shape the people to his liking and would have required 20 years to bring to maturity an elite which would have imbibed the Nazi 'way of thinking' along with its mother's milk. See F. Genoud (ed.), *The Testament of Adolf Hitler*, 2nd edn (London, 1961), pp. 58-9.

7. Cf. esp. J. Sywottek, *Mobilmachung für den totalen Krieg. Die propagan-distische Vorbereitung der deutschen Bevölkerung auf den Zweiten Weltkrieg* (Opladen, 1976); and W. Wette, 'Ideologien, Propaganda und Innenpolitik als Voraussetzungen der Kriegspolitik des Dritten Reiches' in W. Deist *et al.* (eds.), *Das Deutsche Reich und der Zweite Weltkrieg* (Stuttgart, 1979).

8. The Nazis planned during the War to introduce a specific 'community aliens law' (*Gemeinschaftsfremdengesetz*), but were prevented from doing so by Germany's defeat. I am grateful for this information to Jeremy Noakes, who is engaged on what will be a valuable study of such social and racial 'outsiders' in the Third Reich.

9. Cf. I. Kershaw, *Der Hitler-Mythos. Volksmeinung und Propaganda im Dritten Reich* (Stuttgart, 1980), pp. 49-50.

10. See the sometimes conflicting reports in *Deutschland-Berichte der Sozial-demokratischen Partei Deutschlands (Sopade) 1934-1940* (7 vols., Zweitaus-endeins, Salzhausen and Frankfurt am Main, 1980), vol. 3 (1936), pp. 674-5, 1107-9, 1389-92, 1588-9; vol. 4 (1937), pp. 20-2, 317-19, 464-5, 1234-5.

11. Cf. R. Semmler, *Goebbels. The Man next to Hitler* (London, 1947), pp. pp. 56-7.

12. J.P. Stern, *Hitler. The Führer and the People* (London, 1975), p. 111.

13. K. Sontheimer, *Antidemokratisches Denken in der Weimarer Republik*, 4th edn (Munich, 1962), pp. 268-80.

14. I have tried to explore the features and development of Hitler's popular image in *Der Hitler-Mythos* (cf. n. 9), and more briefly in 'The Führer Image and Political Integration: The Popular Conception of Hitler in Bavaria during the Third Reich' in G. Hirschfeld and L. Kettenacker (eds.), *Der Führerstaat: Mythos und Realität* (Stuttgart, 1981).

15. Cf. my *Hitler-Mythos*, ch. 5.

16. See esp. Sywottek, *Mobilmachung*, pp. 162-6; Kershaw, *Hitler-Mythos*,

pp. 118-23; M. Steinert, *Hitlers Krieg und die Deutschen* (Düsseldorf, 1970), pp. 77-9; L. Stokes, 'The Sicherheitsdienst of the Reichsführer SS and German Public Opinion' unpublished doctoral disseration, Johns Hopkins University, 1972 (henceforth, Stokes, 'SD'), pp. 268-72.

17. An English translation of the central parts of Hitler's speech can be found in J. Noakes and G. Pridham (eds.), *Documents on Nazism* (London, 1974), pp. 549-50; cf. also Sywottek, *Mobilmachung*, pp. 162-6; Wette, 'Ideologien', pp. 133-4.

18. Wette, 'Ideologien', pp. 137-42; Sywottek, *Mobilmachung*, pp. 233-7; Steinert, *Hitlers Krieg*, pp. 91-2; Kershaw, *Hitler-Mythos*, pp. 123-6.

19. Stokes, 'SD', p. 472 and references in n. 5; W. Shirer, *Berlin Diary 1939-1941* (London, 1970), p. 138.

20. Cf. Kershaw, *Hitler-Mythos*, Pt II, Ch. 1.

21. Cf. I. McKee, *Tomorrow the World* (London, 1960), p. 27.

22. T.W. Mason, *Sozialpolitik im Dritten Reich* (Opladen, 1977), p. 26.

23. Nazism aimed to transform subjective consciousness rather than objective realities; cf. M. Broszat, *The Hitler State* (London, 1981), p. 18.

24. See P. Merkl, *Political Violence under the Swastika* (Princeton, 1975), pp. 453ff.

25. Cf. A.L. Unger, *The Totalitarian Party* (Cambridge, 1974), Chs. 2, 6-7.

26. See esp. T.W. Mason, *Arbeiterklasse und Volksgemeinschaft* (Opladen, 1975); *Sozialpolitik im Dritten Reich* and 'Labour in the Third Reich', *Past and Present*, vol. 33 (1966).

27. Cf. my *Popular Opinion and Political Dissent. Bavaria 1933-1945* (Oxford, 1983). Ch. 2 cites and summarises some of the evidence for statements in this paragraph. See also Mason, 'Labour', and Mason, *Sozialpolitik*, Ch. V.

28. M. Broszat *et al.* (eds.), *Bayern in der NS-Zeit* (6 vols., Munich and Vienna, 1977-83), vol. 1, pp. 411-12.

29. These examples, representative of many, are drawn from *Gendarmerie* reports from the Schrobenhausen district of Upper Bavaria: Staatsarchiv München, LRA 59595, Gend.-Station Karlskron, 29 April 1937; Gen.-Station Berg im Gau, 29 October 1938. For this and other evidence, cf. Ch. 5 of my *Popular Opinion*.

30. Cf. Kershaw, *Hitler-Mythos*, p. 108 and sources cited in n. 60.

31. See Chs. 7-8 of my *Popular Opinion* and also Steinert, *Hitlers Krieg*, and Stokes, 'SD', *passim.*. Stephen Salter's forthcoming doctoral dissertation will undoubtedly amplify this generalisation as regards the working class. Cf. in the meantime his contribution to the present volume.

32. I attempted to draw together the evidence for the above comments in 'The Persecution of the Jews and German Popular Opinion in the Third Reich', *Leo Baeck Institute Year Book*, vol. 26 (1981) and specifically for Bavaria in Ch. 6 of my *Popular Opinion*.

33. Cf. *Deutschland-Berichte der Sopade* vol. 3, pp. 26-7 (reports for Jan. 1936). One report cited from Berlin ended: 'In general terms one can say that the Nazis have indeed brought off a deepening of the gap between the people and the Jews. The feeling that the Jews are another race is today a general one.'

34. 'How popular was Streicher?' (no author), *Wiener Library Bulletin*, vols. 5/6 (1957), p. 48.

35. Steinert, *Hitlers Krieg*, pp. 243, 259; 'Aus deutschen Urkunden 1935-1945' unpublished documentation in Imperial War Museum, London, pp. 68-9 (reports of SD-Leitstelle Wien, 3 May 1943 and SD-Hauptaussenstelle Würzburg, 6 May 1943.

36. On Nazi propaganda regarding the Soviet Union, cf. in general J.W. Baird, *The Mythical World of Nazi Propaganda* (Minneapolis, 1974).

37. Staatsarchiv Bamberg, M30/1049, report of SD-Abschnitt Bayreuth, 20 July 1942; H. Boberach (ed.), *Meldungen aus dem Reich* (Neuwied, 1965), pp. 286-9; Steinert, *Hitlers Krieg*, p. 309.

38. Boberach, *Meldungen*, p. 421.

39. Herzstein, *The War that Hitler Won*, pp. 308-9, 427-8.

40. Cf. Steinert, *Hitlers Krieg, passim.*

41. Stokes, 'SD', p. 382.

42. Ibid., p. 392.

43. E.g. Staatsarchiv Neuburg an der Donau, unsorted NSDAP collection, reports of the *Kreisleiter* of Augsburg-Stadt, 10 October 1940, 10 November 1940.

44. Stokes, 'SD', p. 422 and n. 147.

45. Ibid., pp. 420-36, esp. p. 433; and for propaganda directives and popular reactions to them in summer 1940, cf. Steinert, *Hitlers Krieg*, pp. 138-40.

46. Boberach, *Meldungen*, pp. 82, 102.

47. Ibid., p. 154.

48. E.g. Staatsarchiv Würzburg, SD-Hauptaussenstelle Würzburg 2/16, report of SD-Aussenstelle Bad Kissingen, 24 January 1941.

49. Boberach, *Meldungen*, p. 153.

50. 'Aus deutschen Urkunden', p. 243; and cf. Steinert, *Hitlers Krieg*, pp. 193-5; Stokes, 'SD', pp. 508-12; and my *Hitler-Mythos*, pp. 147-8.

51. Steinert, *Hitlers Krieg*, p. 195.

52. Boberach, *Meldungen*, p. 202.

53. W.A. Boelcke (ed.), *'Wollt Ihr den totalen Krieg?' Die geheimen Goebbels-Konferenzen 1939-43* (Munich, 1969), p. 373. Baird (*Mythical World*, p. 178) points out Goebbels' plans in autumn 1942 to make a complete change in German war propaganda and his attachment of blame to Otto Dietrich for the fact that German newspapers had lost all their influence among the public.

54. Goebbels' comments, reportedly in a speech to about 60 German journalists in a meeting in the Propaganda Ministry in Berlin on 23 September 1942, are summarised in F. Nadler, *Eine Stadt im Schatten Streichers* (Nuremberg, 1969), pp. 47-53. Nadler provided no reference for his source and I have been unable to trace the speech. It may be that Nadler's date is inaccurate, though I see no reason to doubt the substance of the reported speech.

55. Cf. Kershaw, *Hitler-Mythos*, pp. 167-8; Bramsted, *Goebbels*, pp. 259-68; Steinert, *Hitlers Krieg*, pp. 325-8; W. Hagemann, *Publizistik im Dritten Reich* (Hamburg, 1948), pp. 259-63.

56. Cf. Herzstein, *The War that Hitler Won*, p. 425.

57. Staatsarchiv Würzburg, SD-Hauptaussenstelle Würzburg 22, report of SD-Aussenstelle Schweinfurt, 23 April 1944.

58. Ibid, 23, report of SD-Aussenstelle Würzburg, 6 June 1944.

59. 'Aus deutschen Urkunden', p. 66.

60. Staatsarchiv München, LRA 29656, report of SD-Aussenstelle Berchtesgaden, 7 March 1945 (cited in my *Hitler-Mythos*, p. 193).

61. Goebbels had managed in 1943 to have the format of the reports altered and the circulation restricted. It was Bormann's objections which finally brought the central SD report abstracts to a halt in summer 1944. Cf. Boberach, *Meldungen*, pp. XXVI-XXVIII.

62. Cf. Bundesarchiv Koblenz, R55/601, fols. 14-20 for an example of a weekly activity report (from 13 April 1943) of the head of the propaganda staff in the Ministry of Propaganda summarising reports from different parts of the Reich and heavily scored by Goebbels.

63. Balfour, *Propaganda in War*, p. 436, citing John Steinbeck.

64. See Noakes and Pridham, *Documents on Nazism*, p. 575, for Hitler's

comment on 23 November 1939, and N. Henderson, *Failure of a Mission* (London, 1940), pp. 161, 175, 179; and Stokes, 'SD', pp. 272-4 for his reactions at the time of the Munich Agreement in 1938.

GLOSSARY AND LIST OF ABBREVIATIONS

ACE	*Alliance Cinématographique Européene*
AEL	*Arbeitserziehungslager*, labour 'education' camp for 'asocial' elements within the workforce
Arbeitseinsatz	The deportation of workers to Germany
BA	Bundesarchiv, Koblenz
BBA	Berbauarchiv, Bochum
BDC	Berlin Document Center
BdM	*Bund deutscher Mädel* (League of German Girls), female branch of the Hitler Youth, for girls over 14 years of age
DAF	*Deutsche Arbeitsfront* (German Labour Front)
DFW	*Deutsches Frauenwerk* (German Women's Enterprise), the Nazi-led federation of women's groups from 1934 to 1945
Dienstverpflichtung	Civil conscription
DZN	*Deutsche Zeitung in den Niederlanden* (the German Newspaper in the Netherlands)
Filmprüfstelle	Film Censorship Office
Führerprinzip	The leadership principle
Gau	(Region), the major territorial division of the national NSDAP organisation
Gaufilmstellen	Regional Party Film Centres
Gauleiter	Regional Party leader
Gleichschaltung	(Co-ordination), the obligatory assimilation within the Nazi State of all political, economic and cultural activities
HA	NSDAP Hauptarchiv, the Party's own archival collection, started in January 1934 and now deposited in the Bundesarchiv, Koblenz.
HJ	*Hitlerjugend* (Hitler Youth), the Nazi Party's youth organisation
HSTAD	Hauptstaatsarchiv, Düsseldorf
IfZ	*Institut für Zeitgeschichte*, Munich
Jugendfilmstuden	Youth Film Hours
Jugendwert	A special distinction mark for a film considered 'valuable for youth'

Kampfzeit	Time of struggle
Kleinbürgertum	Petit-bourgeoisie
KPD	*Kommunistische Partei Deutschlands* (German Communist Party)
Kreis	(District), territorial unit of the NSDAP into which the Gaus were divided
Kreisbildstellen	District Picture Centres
Kreisfilmstellen	District Film Centres
Landesbildstellen	Regional Picture Centres
Lebensraum	Living space
LFS	*Landesfilmstellen*, Regional Film Centres
MA	Bundesarchiv-Militärarchiv, Freiburg
Mittelstand	Lower middle class
Neuordnung	The New Order
NSB	Dutch National Socialist Party
NSBO	Factory Cell Organisation
NSDAP	*Nationalsozialistische Deutsche Arbeiterpartei* (the Nazi Party)
NSF	*Nationalsozialistische Frauenschaft* (Nazi Women's Group), the monopoly Party organisation for women founded in 1931
NSV	*NS-Volkswohlfahrt*, the Nazi welfare organisation
Ordensburg	Finishing school for future Nazi leaders
Prädikate	The distinction marks awarded to films
Reichsarbeitsdienst	Reich Labour Service
RWU	*Reichsanstalt für Film und Bild in Wissenschaft und Unterricht* (Reich Institute for Film and Pictures in Science and Education)
Reichsjugendführung	Reich Youth Leadership
RFFg	*Reichsfrauenführung* (Reich Women's Leadership)
RKK	*Reichskulturkammer* (Reich Chamber of Culture)
Reichslichtspielgesetz	Reich Film Law
RMD	*Reichsmütterdienst* (Reich Mothers' Service), one of the sections into which the DFW's work was divided
RMVP	*Reichsministerium für Volksaufklärung und Propaganda* (Reich Ministry for Popular Enlightenment and Propaganda)
Reichsnährstand	Reich Food Authority

SA	*Sturm Abteilungen* (Storm Troopers), para-military formation of the NSDAP
SD	*Sicherheitsdienst der SS* (Secret Police Reports)
SPD	*Sozialdemokratische Partei Deutschlands* (German Social Democratic Party)
SS	*Schutzstaffeln*, Nazi elite paramilitary formation, under the leadership of Heinrich Himmler
Stadtbildstellen	Urban Picture Centres
Tendenzfilme	Films advocating themes and archetypes commonly associated with National Socialism
Thingstätten	An architectural term meaning 'national arenas'
völkisch	Originally a Germanisation of 'nationalist', it acquired racialist and mystical overtones which an English translation of 'folkish' fails to convey
volksdeutsch	(Ethnic Germans), used by the Nazis to describe people of German stock living outside the Reich
Volksgemeinschaft	(Community of the People), ie. a German society purged of 'alien' elements
Volkssturm	(People's Storm), the armed civilian militia
Vw/Hw	*Volkswirtschaft/Hauswirtschaft* (National Economy/Domestic Economy), one of the sections into which the DFW's work was divided
Wehrerziehungsfilme	Military educational films
Weltanschauung	(View of life), term used to describe the Nazis' all-embracing philosophy of Germany's destiny
Zeitfilme	Militarist feature films set in a contemporary context

SELECT BIBLIOGRAPHY

The bibliography is divided into various sub-headings which follow closely the individual essays contained in this volume. This should lead the reader to the sources that the authors have considered important and also to broader arguments associated with the subject of Nazi propaganda.

The Rise of the NSDAP

Allen, W.S., *The Nazi Seizure of Power. The Experience of a Single German Town, 1930-5* (Chicago, 1965)

Böhnke, W., *Die NSDAP im Ruhrgebiet 1920-33* (Bonn-Bad Godesberg, 1974)

Childers, T., 'The Social Bases of the National Socialist Vote', *Journal of Contemporary History*, vol. 11 (1976), pp. 17-42

Fischer, C., 'The SA of the NSDAP: Social Background and Ideology of the Rank and File in the Early 1930s', *Journal of Contemporary History*, vol. 17 (1982), pp. 651-70

Franz-Willing, G., *Ursprung der Hitlerbewegung 1919-22* (Oldendorf, 1974)

Hamilton, R.F., *Who Voted for Hitler?* (Princeton, 1982)

Milatz, A., *Wähler und Wahlen in der Weimarer Republik* (Bonn-Bad Godesberg, 1965)

Noakes, J., *The Nazi Party in Lower Saxony 1921-33* (Oxford, 1971)

Orlow, D., *The History of the Nazi Party 1919-33*, (London 1971)

Pridham, G., *Hitler's Rise to Power. The Nazi Movement in Bavaria 1923-33* (London, 1973)

Saldern, A. von, *Mittelstand im Dritten Reich* (Frankfurt/New York, 1979)

Schoenbaum, D., *Die braune Revolution* (Munich, 1980)

Steinbach, P. (ed.), *Partizipation als Mittel der Politischen Modernisierung* (Stuttgart, 1981)

Hitler

Baynes, N.H. (ed.), *The Speeches of Adolf Hitler* (2 vols. Oxford, 1942)

Bracher, K.D., *Die deutsche Diktatur* (Cologne, 1969)

—— *The German Dictatorship. The Origins, Structure and Consequences of National Socialism* (London, 1973)

Broszat, M., *Der Staat Hitlers* (Munich 1969), translated as *The Hitler State: The Foundation and Development of the Internal Structure of the Third Reich* (London, 1981)

Bullock, A., *Hitler. A Study in Tyranny* (London, 1962)

Carr, W., *Hitler: A Study in Personality and Politics* (London, 1978)

Dietrich, O., *12 Jahre mit Hitler* (Munich, 1955), translated as *The Hitler I Knew* (London, 1957)

Domarus, M. (ed.), *Hitler. Reden und Proklamationen 1932-45* (4 vols., Munich 1965)

Fest, J.C., *Hitler: Ein Biographie* (Frankfurt am Main, 1973), English translation (London, 1974)

—— *The Face of the Third Reich* (London, 1974)

Giesler, H., *Ein anderer Hitler* (Leoni, 1977)

Gordon, H.J. *Hitler and the Beer Hall Putsch* (Princeton, 1972)

Haffner, S., *Anmerkungen zu Hitler* (Munich, 1978)

Hanfstaengl, E., *Hitler: The Missing Years* (London, 1957)

Hauner, M., 'Did Hitler Want a World Dominion?', *Journal of Contemporary History*, vol. 13, no. 1 (January, 1978), pp. 15-32

Hesse, F., *Hitler and the English* (London, 1954)

Hildebrand, K., *The Foreign Policy of the Third Reich* (London, 1973)

—— *Das Dritte Reich* (Munich, 1979)

Hirschfeld, G. and Kettenacker, L. (eds.), *The 'Führer-State': Myth and Reality* (Stuttgart, 1981)

Hitler, A., *Mein Kampf* (Munich, 1937, London, 1939)

Hitler's Table Talk 1941-4, introduced and with a new Preface by H.R. Trevor Roper, (London, 1973)

Hoffmann, H., *Hitler was my Friend* (London, 1955)

Jäckel,E., and Kuhn, A. (eds.), *Hitler. Sämtliche Aufzeichnungen 1905-24* (Stuttgart, 1980)

James, J. and Barnes, P.P., *Hitler's 'Mein Kampf' in Britain and America* (Cambridge, 1980)

Kershaw, I., *Der Hitler-Mythos: Volksmeinung und Propaganda im Dritten Reich* (Stuttgart, 1980)

Peterson, E.N., *The Limits of Hitler's Power* (Princeton, 1969)

Picker, H.H., *Hitler's Tischgespräche im Führerhauptquartier 1941-2*

(Stuttgart, 1976)

Rauschning, H., *Hitler Speaks* (London, 1940)

Stern, J.P., *Hitler: The Führer and the People* (London, 1975)

Stone, N., *Hitler* (London, 1980)

Trevor Roper, H.R., *The Last Days of Hitler* (London, 1962)

Weinstein, F., *The Dynamics of Nazism: Leadership, Ideology and the Holocaust* (London, 1980)

Goebbels

Cloet, R., 'Les Directives de Goebbels', *Revue d'Histoire de la Deuxième Guerre Mondiale*, vol. 64 (1966), p. 1-6.

Ebermayer, E. and Roos, H., *Gefährtin des Teufels: Leben und Tod der Magda Goebbels* (Hamburg, 1952)

Goebbels, J., *Michael. Ein deutsches Schicksal in Tagebuchblättern* (Munich, 1929)

—— *Das eherne Herz. Reden und Aufsätze aus den Jahren 1941-2* (Munich, 1943)

—— *Vom Kaiserhof zur Reichskanzlei, Eine historische Darstellung in Tagebuchblättern* (Munich, 1934)

——*Der Kampf um Berlin. Der Anfang* (Munich, 1932)

—— *Die Zeit ohne Beispiel. Reden und Aufsätze aus den Jahren 1939-41* (Munich, 1943)

Heiber, H. (ed.), *The Early Goebbels Diaries. The Journal of Joseph Goebbels from 1925-6* (London, 1962)

—— (ed.), *Goebbels Reden* (2 vols., Düsseldorf, 1971)

——*Goebbels* (London, 1973)

Kotze, H., von (ed.), 'Goebbels' vor Offizieren im Juli 1943', *Vierteljahrshefte für Zeitgeschichte*, XIX (January, 1971), pp. 83-112

Lochner, L.P. (ed.), *The Goebbels Diaries* (London, 1948)

Manvell, R. and Fraenkel, H., *Dr. Goebbels* (London, 1960)

Martin, H.L., *Unser Mann bei Goebbels* (Neckargemünd, 1973)

Meisner, O., *Magda Goebbels* (London, 1979)

Moltmann, G., 'Goebbels Rede zum totalen Krieg', *Vierteljahrshefte für Zeitgeschichte*, XII (January, 1964), pp. 13-43

Oven, W. von, *Mit Goebbels bis zum Ende* (2 vols., Buenos Aires, 1949-50)

Reimann, V., *Dr Joseph Goebbels* (Vienna, 1973), translated in English as *The Man who Created Hitler* (London, 1977)

Riess, C., *Joseph Goebbels. A Biography* (London, 1949)

Semmler, R., *Goebbels. The Man Next to Hitler* (London, 1947)
Stephan, W., *Joseph Goebbels. Dämon einer Diktatur* (Stuttgart, 1949)
Taylor, F. (ed.), *The Goebbels Diaries 1939-41* (London, 1982)
Trevor Roper, H.R. (ed.), *The Goebbels Diaries: The Last Days* (London, 1978)
Wykes, A., *Goebbels* (New York, 1973)

Art and Architecture

Bischoff, R.F., *Nazi Conquest through German Culture* (Harvard, 1942)
Bosmajian, H.A., 'The Role of the Political Poster in Hitler's Rise to Power', *Print* (May, 1966), pp. 28-31
Brenner, H., *Die Kunstpolitik des Nationalsozialismus* (Hamburg, 1963)
Causton, B., 'Art in Germany under the Nazis', *London Studio*, vol. 12 (November 1936), pp. 235-46
Darkal, V., 'Adventures in Art under Hitler', *Horizon*, vol. 9 (March, 1944), pp. 192-204
Dreyer, E.A. (ed.), *Deutsche Kultur im neuen Reich. Wesen, Aufgabe und Ziel der Reichskulturkammer* (Berlin, 1934)
Dülffer, J., Thies, J. and Henke, J. (Eds.), *Hitlers Städte. Baupolitik im Dritten Reich* (Cologne, Vienna, 1978)
Hinz, B., *Art in the Third Reich* (Oxford, 1980)
Larsson, L.O. *Die Neugestaltung der Reichshauptstadt* (Stockholm, Stuttgart, 1978)
Lehmann-Haupt, H., *Art under Dictatorship* (Oxford, 1954)
Mosse, G., *Nazi Culture: Intellectual, Cultural and Social Life in the Third Reich* (London, 1966)
Schmidt, M., *Albert Speer: Das Ende eines Mythos* (Berne, Munich, 1982)
Schnell, R. (ed.), *Kunst und Kultur im Deutschen Faschismus* (Stuttgart, 1978)
Schönberger, A., *Die neue Reichskanzlei von Albert Speer* (Berlin, 1981)
Schroeder, R., *Modern Art in the Third Reich* (Dokumente, Offenburg, 1952)
Speer, A., *Inside the Third Reich* (London, 1971)
—— *Architektur Arbeiten 1933-42* (Frankfurt am Main, Berlin, Vienna, 1978)
Taylor, R., *The Word in Stone: the Role of Architecture in the National Socialist Ideology* (California Press, 1974)

Thies, J., *Architekt der Weltherrschaft. Die 'Endziele' Hitlers* (Düsseldorf, 1976)
—— 'Hitler's European Building Programme', *Journal of Contemporary History*, vol. 13 (1978), pp. 413-31
Wulf, J. (ed.), *Die Bildenden Künste im Dritten Reich. Eine Dokumentation* (Gütersloh, 1963)

Film

Albrecht, G., *Nationalsozialistische Filmpolitik. Eine soziologische Untersuchung über die Spielfilme des Dritten Reichs* (Stuttgart, 1969)
—— *Film im Dritten Reich* (Stuttgart, 1982)
Barkhausen, H., 'Die NSDAP als Filmproduzentin. Mit Kurzübersicht: Filme der NSDAP 1927-45' in Moltmann, G. and K.F. Reimers (eds.) *Zeitgeschichte im Film- und Tondokument* (Göttingen, 1970), pp. 145-76
Bauer, A., *Deutscher Spielfilm-Almanach, 1929-50* (Berlin, 1950)
Becker, W., *Film und Herrschaft* (Berlin, 1973)
Belling, C., *Der Film in Staat und Partei* (Berlin, 1936)
Blobner, H., and Holba, H., 'Jackboot Cinema. Political Propaganda in the Third Reich', *Film and Filming*, vol. 8, no. 3 (December 1962), pp. 14-18
Bredow, W. von and Zurek, R., (eds.), *Film und Gesellschaft in Deutschland. Dokumente und Materialien* (Hamburg, 1975)
Courtade, F. and Cadars, P., *Histoire du cinéma nazi* (Paris, 1972)
Eckert, G., 'Filmintendenz und Tendenzfilm', *Wille und Macht, Führerorgan der nationalsozialistischen Jugend*, vol. 4 (November 1938), pp. 19-25
Harlan, V., *Im Schatten meiner Filme. Selbstbiographie* (Gütersloh, 1966), translated into French as *Souvenirs ou Le Cinéma allemand selon Goebbels* (Paris, 1974)
Hollstein, D., *Antisemitische Filmpropaganda. Die Darstellung des Juden im nationalsozialistischen Spielfilme* (Munich, 1971)
Hull, D.S. *Film in the Third Reich* (Berkeley and Los Angeles, 1969)
Kalbus, O. *Vom Werden deutscher Filmkunst. Teil. 2: Der Tonfilm* (Altona-Bahrenfeld, 1935)
Kracauer, S., *From Caligari to Hitler. A Psychological History of the German Film* (Princeton, 1947 and 1973)
Kriegk, O., *Der deutsche Film in Spiegel der Ufa. 25 Jahre Kampf und*

Vollendung (Berlin, 1943)

Leiser, E., *Nazi Cinema* (London, 1974)

Phillips, M.S., 'The Nazi Control of the German Film Industry', *Journal of European Studies*, vol. 1 (March 1971), pp. 37-68

Riefenstahl, L., *Hinter den Kulissen des Reichsparteitagfilms* (Munich, 1935)

Spiker, J., *Film und Kapital* (Berlin, 1975)

Taylor, R., *Film Propaganda. Soviet Russia and Nazi Germany* (London, 1979)

Welch, D., 'The Proletarian Cinema and the Weimar Republic', *Historical Journal of Film, Radio and Television*, vol. 1, no. 1 (1981), pp. 3-18

—— *Propaganda and the German Cinema, 1933-45* (Oxford, 1983)

—— 'Nazi Wartime Newsreel Propaganda' in K.R.M. Short (ed.), *Film and Radio Propaganda in World War II: A Global Perspective* (London, 1983), pp. 201-19

Wulf, J., (ed.), *Theater und Film im Dritten Reich. Eine Dokumentation* (Gütersloh, 1964)

Press and Radio

Abel, K.D. *Die Presselenkung im NS-Staat* (Munich, 1968)

Eksteins, M., *The Limits of Reason. The German Democratic Press and the Collapse of Weimar Democracy* (Oxford, 1975)

Gombrich, E.H. *Myth and Reality in German Wartime Broadcasts* (London, 1970)

Hagemann, W., *Publizistik im Dritten Reich: Ein Beitrag zur Methodik der Massenführung* (Hamburg, 1948)

Hale, O.J., *The Captive Press in the Third Reich* (Princeton, 1964)

Heyde, L. *Presse, Rundfunk and Film im Dienste der Volksführung* (Dresden, 1943)

Kris, E. and Speyer, H., *German Radio Propaganda. Report on Home Broadcasts during the War* (London, 1944)

Koszyk, K. and Lindemann, M., *Geschichte der deutschen Presse, 1914-45* (Berlin, 1966-72)

Pohle, H., *Der Rundfunk als Instrument der Politik* (Hamburg, 1955)

Scheel, K., *Krieg über Ätherwellen. NS-Rundfunk und Monopole 1933-45* (Berlin, 1970)

Wulf, J. (ed.), *Presse und Funk im Dritten Reich* (Gütersloh, 1964)

Youth and Education

Aley, P., *Jugendliteratur im Dritten Reich* (Gütersloh, 1967)

Becker, H., *German Youth. Bond or Free?* (London,1946)

Belling, C. and Schütze, A., *Der Film in der Hitlerjugend* (Berlin, 1937)

Brandenburg, H.C., *Die Geschichte der HJ* (Cologne, 1968)

Ebeling, H., *The German Youth Movement* (London, 1945)

Eilers, R., *Die nationalsozialtische Schulpolitik* (Cologne, 1963)

Hagen, L., *Follow my Leader* (London, 1951)

Klönne, A., *Hitlerjugend. Die Jugend und Ihre Organization im Dritten Reich* (Hanover, 1960)

Klose, W., *Generation im Gleichschritt* (Oldenburg, 1964)

Koch, H.W., *The Hitler Youth: Origins and Development, 1922-45* (London, 1975)

Kuhn, H., *et al., Die deutsche Universität im Dritten Reich* (Munich, 1966)

Laqueur, W., *Young Germany, A History of the German Youth Movement* (New York and London, 1962)

Loewenberg, P., 'The Psychological Origins of the Nazi Youth Cohort', *American Historical Review*, vol. 76, no. 5 (December, 1971), pp. 1457-1502

McKee, I., *Tomorrow the World* (London, 1960)

Müller, G., *Ernst Krieck und die Nationalsozialistische Wissenschafts-Reform: Motive und Tendenzen einer Wissenschaftslehre und Hochschul-Reform im Dritten Reich* (Basle, 1978)

Sander, A.U., *Jugend und Film* (Berlin, 1944)

Schirach, B. von, *Die Hitlerjugend. Idee und Gestalt* (Berlin, 1934)

Schmidt, A., *Jugend im Reich* (Berlin, 1942)

Stachura, P.D., 'The Ideology of the Hitler Youth in the Kampfzeit', *Journal of Contemporary History*, vol. 8 (1973), pp. 155-67

—— *Nazi Youth in the Weimar Republic* (Santa Barbara, California, 1975)

—— *The German Youth Movement 1900-45* (London, 1981)

Steinberg, M.S., *Sabers and Brown Shirts: The German Student's Path to National Socialism 1918-31* (London, 1977)

Stephenson, J., 'Girls' Higher Education in Germany in the 1930s', *Journal of Contemporary History*, vol. 10, no. 1 (1975), pp. 41-69

Walker, L.D. *Hitler Youth and Catholic Youth 1933-36* (Washington, 1971)

Labour and the Economy

Auerbach, H., 'Arbeitserziehungslager 1940-4', *Gutachtern des Instituts für Zeitgeschichte*, vol. 2 (Stuttgart, 1966), pp. 196-201

Bessel, R. and Jamin, M., 'Nazis, Workers and the Uses of Quantitative Evidence', *Social History*, 4, 1 (1979) pp. 112-14

Broszat, M., Fröhlich, E. and Wiesemann, F. (eds.), *Bayern in der NS-Zeit. Soziale Lage und politisches Verhalten der Bevölkerung im Spiegel vertraulicher Berichte* (Munich and Vienna, 1977)

Broszat, M. et al. (eds.), *Bayern in der NS-Zeit III/IV. Herrschaft und Gesellschaft im Konflikt. Teil B/C* (Munich, Vienna, 1981)

Carroll, B.A., *Design for Total War. Arms and Economics in the Third Reich* (The Hague, 1968)

Erber, R., *Die nationalsozialistische Wirtschaftspolitik 1933-9 im Lichte der modernen theorie* (Zürich, 1958)

Farquharson, J.E., *The Plough and the Swastika. The NSDAP and Agriculture in Germany 1928-45* (London, 1976)

Fischer, W., *Deutsche Wirtschaftspolitik 1918-45* (Opladen, 1968)

Janssen, G., *Das Ministerium Speer* (Berlin, Frankfurt am Main, 1968)

Kele, M.H., *Nazis and Workers. National Socialist Appeals to German Labour 1919-33* (Chapel Hill, NC, 1972)

Klessman, C. and Pingel, F. (eds.), *Gegner des Nationalsozialismus* (Frankfurt am Main, 1980)

Mason, T.W., 'Labour in the Third Reich', *Past and Present* (April 1966), pp. 112-41

—— *Arbeiterklasse und Volksgemeinschaft. Dokumente und Materialien zur deutschen Arbeiterpolitik 1936-9* (Opladen, 1975)

—— *Sozialpolitik im Dritten Reich. Arbeiterklasse und Volksgemeinschaft* (Opladen, 1977)

—— 'The Workers' Opposition in Nazi Germany', *History Workshop Journal*, 11 (spring 1981), pp. 120-37

Milward, A.S., *The German Economy at War* (London, 1965)

Niethammer, L. (ed.), *Wohnen im Wandel. Beiträge zur Geschichte des Alltags in der bürgerlichen Gesellschaft* (Wuppertal, 1979)

Petzina, D., 'Soziale Lage der deutschen Arbeiter und Probleme des Arbeitseinsatzes während des Zweiten Weltkrieges', *Zweiter Weltkrieg und sozialer Wandel*, Dlugoborski, W. (ed.), (Göttingen, 1981), pp. 65-86

Petzina, D. Abelshauser, W. and Faust, A. (eds.), *Sozialgeschichtliches Arbeitsbuch III. Materialien zur Statistik des Deutschen Reiches 1914-45* (Munich, 1978)

Peukert, D., *Die KPD im Widerstand. Verfolgung und Untergrundarbeit an Rhein und Ruhr 1933 bis 1945* (Wuppertal, 1980)

Peukert, D. and Reulecke, J. (eds.), *Die Reihen fast geschlossen* (Wuppertal, 1981)

Reulecke, J. (ed.), *Arbeiterbewegung an Rhein und Ruhr* (Wuppertal, 1974)

Schoenbaum, D., *Hitler's Social Revolution. Class and Status in Nazi Germany* (London, 1967)

Schweitzer, A., *Big Business in the Third Reich* (London, 1964)

Women

Bajohr, S., *Die Hälfte der Fabrik. Geschichte der Frauenarbeit in Deutschland 1914 bis 1945* (Marburg, 1979)

Buresch-Riebe, I., *Frauenleistung im Kriege* (Berlin, 1942)

Evans, R.J., *The Feminist Movement in Germany 1894-1933* (London, 1976)

Gersdorff, U. von, *Frauen im Kriegsdienst 1914-45* (Stuttgart, 1969)

Kirkpatrick, C., *Woman in Nazi Germany* (London, 1939)

Koonz, C., 'Mothers in the Fatherland: Women in Nazi Germany' in R. Bridenthal and C. Koonz (eds.), *Becoming Visible. Women in European History* (Boston, 1977), pp. 445-73

McIntyre, J., 'Women and the Professions in Germany, 1930-40' in A. Nicholls and E. Matthias (eds.), *German Democracy and the Triumph of Hitler* (London, 1971), pp. 175-213

Mason, T.W. 'Women in Germany, 1925-40: Family, Welfare and Work', *History Workshop Journal* (spring and autumn 1976), pp. 74-113, 5-32

Rupp, L.J., *Mobilizing Women for War: German and American Propaganda 1939-45* (Princeton, 1978)

Scholtz-Klink, G., *Die Frau im Dritten Reich* (Tübingen, 1978)

Stephenson, J., *Women in Nazi Society* (London, 1975)

—— ' "Reichsbund der Kinderreichen": the League of Large Families in the Population Policy of Nazi Germany', *European Studies Review* (July, 1979), pp. 350-75

—— *The Nazi Organisation of Women* (London, 1981)

—— 'Middle-class Women and National Socialist "Service" ', *History*, vol. 67, no. 219 (1982), pp. 32-44

Winkler, D., *Frauenarbeit im 'Dritten Reich'* (Hamburg, 1977)

Nazi Propaganda

(a) General

Baird, J.W., *The Mythical World of Nazi Propaganda 1939-45* (Minneapolis, 1974)

Balfour, M., *Propaganda in War, 1939-45: Organisations, Policies and Publics in Britain and Germany* (London, 1979)

Boberach, H., *Meldungen aus dem Reich. Auswahl aus den geheimen Lageberichten des Sicherheitsdienstes der SS 1939-44* (Berlin and Neuwied, 1965)

Boelcke, W.A., *Kriegspropaganda 1939-41. Geheime Ministerkonferenzen im Reichspropagandaministerium* (Stuttgart, 1966)

—— *'Wollt Ihr den totalen Krieg?'. Die geheimen Goebbels-Konferenzen 1939-43* (Stuttgart, 1967, Munich, 1969), translated as *The Secret Conferences of Dr Goebbels 1939-43* (London, 1970)

Bramsted, E.K., *Goebbels and National Socialist Propaganda 1925-45* (Michigan, 1965)

Broszat, M., *German National Socialism* (Santa Barbara, California, 1966)

Burden, H.T., *The Nuremberg Rallies 1932-39* (London, 1967)

Cecil, R., *Myth of the Master Race. A. Rosenberg and the Nazi Ideology* (London, 1974)

Delmer, S., *Black Boomerang* (New York, 1962)

Driencourt, J., *La Propaganda, nouvelle force politique* (Paris, 1950)

Ellul, J., *Propaganda. The Formation of Men's Attitudes* (New York, 1973)

Farago, L. (ed.), *German Psychological Warfare. Survey and Bibliography* (New York, 1941 and 1972)

Fraser, L., *Propaganda* (London, 1957)

George, A., *Propaganda Analysis. A Study of Inferences Made from Nazi Propaganda in World War II* (Evanston, Ill., 1959)

Glaser, H., *The Cultural Roots of National Socialism* (London, 1978)

Grunberger, R., *A Social History of the Third Reich* (London, 1974)

Hadamovsky, E., *Propaganda und nationale Macht. Die Organisation der öffentlichen Meinung für die nationale Politik* (Oldenburg, 1973)

Herma, H., 'Goebbels' Conception of Propaganda', *Social Research*, vol. 10, no. 2 (May 1943), pp. 200-18

Herzstein, R.E., *The War that Hitler Won. The Most Infamous Propaganda Campaign in History* (London, 1979)

Kershaw, I., 'The Persecution of the Jews and German Popular Opinion in the Third Reich', *Year Book of the Leo Baeck Institut*, no. 26 (1981)

—— *Popular Opinion and Political Dissent in the Third Reich* (Oxford, 1983)

Kettenacker, L. (ed.), *Das Andere Deutschland im Zweiten Weltkrieg* (Stuttgart, 1977)

Kirwin, G., 'Waiting for Retaliation. A Study in Nazi Propaganda Behaviour and German Civilian Morale', *Journal of Contemporary History*, vol. 16 (July 1981), pp. 565-83

Klöss, E., *Reden des Führers. Politik und Propaganda Adolf Hitlers 1922-45* (Munich, 1967)

Lerner, D. (ed.), *Propaganda in War and Crisis* (New York, 1951)

Merkl, P., *Political Violence Under the Swastika* (Princeton, 1975)

Mosse, G., *The Crisis of German Ideology: Intellectual Origins of the Third Reich* (London, 1964)

Müller, G.W., *Das Reichsministerium für Volksaufklärung und Propaganda* (Berlin, 1940)

Münzenberg, W., *Propaganda als Waffe* (Paris, 1937)

Neumann, F., *Behemoth. The Structure and Practice of National Socialism* (London, 1942)

Paterna, E., *et al., Deutschland 1933-9* (Berlin, 1969)

Qualter, T., *Propaganda and Psychological Warfare* (New York, 1962)

Scheel, K., 'Faschistische Kulturpropaganda im zweiten Weltkrieg. Ihr Einsatz zur Irreführung des deutschen Volkes während der ersten Kriegsjahre (1939-41)', *Jahrbuch für Volkskunde und Kulturgeschichte*, vol. 21 (Berlin, 1979)

Shirer, W., *Berlin Diary 1934-41* (London, 1972)

Sington, D. and Weidenfeld. A., *The Goebbels Experiment. A Study of the Nazi Propaganda Machine* (London, 1942)

Speer, A., *Inside the Third Reich* (London, 1971)

Speier, H., 'Nazi propaganda and its decline', *Social Research*, vol. 10, no. 3 (September 1943), pp. 358-77

Stachura, P. (ed.), *The Nazi Machtergreifung, 1933* (London, 1983)

Stern, F., *The Politics of Cultural Despair: A Study in the Rise of the Germanic Ideology* (Berkeley, 1961)

Wedel, H. von, *Die Propagandatruppen der deutschen Wehrmacht* (Neckargemünd, 1962)

Wykes, A., *The Nuremberg Rallies* (New York, 1970)

Zeman, Z.A.B. *Nazi Propaganda* (2nd edn., Oxford, 1973)

—— (ed.), *Selling the War. Art and Propaganda in World War II* (London, 1978)

(b) In the Occupied Territories

Amouroux, H., *La Grande Histoire des Français sous l'occupation* (4 vols., Paris, 1977-9)

Aron, R., *Histoire de Vichy* (Paris, 1954)

Baudot, M., *L'Opinion publique sous l'occupation, l'example d'un départment français, 1939-45* (Paris, 1966)

Bazin, A., *Le Cinéma de l'occupation et de la Résistance* (Paris, 1975)

Bellanger, C., Godechot, J. and Guiral, P., *Histoire générale de la presse française*, vol. 4 (Paris, 1975)

Bertin-Maghit, J.P., *Le Cinéma français sous Vichy. Les films français de 1940 à 1944, signification, fonction sociale* (Paris, 1980)

Cremieux-Brilhac, J.L. and Bensimon, G., 'Les Propagandes radio-phoniques et l'opinion publique en France de 1940 à 1944', *Revue d'Histoire de la Deuxième Guerre Mondiale*, vol. 101 (January 1976), pp. 3-18

Farmer, P., *Vichy. Political Dilemma* (London, 1955)

Groeneveld, E.G., 'The Muses under Stress. Dutch Cultural Life during the German Occupation' in C. Madajczyk (ed.), *Inter Arma non silent Musae. The War and Culture (1939-45)* (Warsaw, 1977), pp. 343-65

Hirschfeld, G., 'Collboration and Attentism in the Netherlands 1940-41', *Journal of Contemporary History*, vol. 16 (1981), pp. 467-86

—— *Die Kollaboration mit der deutschen Besatzungsmacht in den Niederlanden während des zweiten Weltkriegs* (Stuttgart, 1983)

Hoffmann, G., *Nationalsozialistische Propaganda in den Niederlanden* (Munich, Berlin, 1972)

Jäckel, E., *Frankreich in Hitlers Europa* (Stuttgart, 1966)

Jünger, E., *Journal de guerre et de l'Occupation 1939-48* (Paris, 1965)

Kweit, K., *Reichskommissariat Niederlande. Versuch und Scheitern nationalsozialistischer Neuordnung* (Stuttgart, 1968)

Levy, C., 'L'Organisation de la propagande allemande en France', *Revue d'Histoire de la Deuxième Guerre Mondiale*, vol. 64 (1966), pp. 7-28

Levy-Klein, S., 'France 1940-44: le cinéma de Vichy', *Positif* (January, 1973), pp. 51-5

Meerloo, A.M., *Total War and Human Mind. A Psychologist's Experiences in Occupied Holland* (London, 1944)

Nobecourt, R.G., *Les Secrets de la propagande en France occupée* (Paris, 1962)

Novik, W., 'Four Years in a Bottle. A Critical Study of French Film Production under the Occupation', *Penguin Film Review*, vol. 2 (1947), pp. 45-53

Phillips, M.S., 'The German Film Industry and the New Order', in P.D. Stachura (ed.), *The Shaping of the Nazi State* (London, 1978), pp. 257-81

Sadoul, G., *Le cinéma pendant la guerre* (Paris, 1954)

Warmbrunn, W., *The Dutch under German Occupation* (Stanford and London 1963)

NOTES ON CONTRIBUTORS

David Welch is Lecturer in Modern History at the Polytechnic of Central London. He is the author of *Propaganda and the German Cinema, 1933-45* (Oxford, 1983) together with various articles and essays on German history. He is currently working on a biography of Joseph Goebbels and the history of propaganda in the twentieth century.

Lothar Kettenacker is Deputy Director of the German Historical Institute, London. His publications include *Nationalsozialistische Volkstumspolitik im Elsass* (Stuttgart 1973) and he edited *Das Andere Deutschland im Zweiten Weltkrieg* (Stuttgart, 1977). His study on British post-war planning for Germany is due to be published shortly.

Richard Taylor is a Lecturer in Politics and Russian Studies at University College, Swansea. He is the author of *The Politics of the Soviet Cinema, 1917-29* (Cambridge, 1979) and *Film Propaganda: Soviet Russia and Nazi Germany* (London, 1979), and is co-author of *Marxism in Russia: Key Documents 1889-1906* (Cambridge, 1983). He is at present researching into 'The Film Factory: Soviet Cinema in Documents, 1917-38'.

Jochen Thies is the author of *Architekt der Weltherrschaft. Die 'Endziele' Hitlers* (Düsseldorf, 1976) and editor, with J. Dülffer and J. Henke, of *Hitlers Städte. Baupolitik im Dritten Reich* (Cologne, 1978). After two years as speech-writer for Helmut Schmidt he is currently working as a political jouranlist.

Stephen Salter was, between 1979 and 1981, a Hanseatic Scholar from Oxford to the University of Hamburg. He is now Senior Germaine Scholar at Brasenose College, Oxford, where he is completing a doctoral thesis on the mobilisation of German labour during the Second World War.

Jill Stephenson is a Lecturer in History at Edinburgh University. Her publications include *Women in Nazi Society* (London, 1975), *The Nazi Organisation of Women* (London, 1980) and numerous articles and essays on National Socialism. She is at present working on a study of Württemberg in the first half of the twentieth century.

Gerhard Hirschfeld is a Research Fellow at the German Historical Institute, London. He is the author of a comprehensive study on Dutch collaboration with the Nazis during the Second World War, *Die Kollab-*

oration mit der deutschen Besatzungsmacht in den Niederlanden während des zweiten Weltkriegs (Stuttgart, 1983) and co-editor with L. Kettenacker of *'The Führer State': Myth and Reality* (Stuttgart, 1981) and with W.J. Mommsen of *Social Protest, Violence and Terror in the Nineteenth and Twentieth Century Europe* (London, 1982). He is currently working on a study of the emigration of German academics to Great Britain.

François Garçon is a Researcher at the Centre de l'Image et de la Recherche Audio-visuelle (CIRA). In 1981 he completed his history doctoral thesis on 'La société française dans son cinéma, 1940-4' and this is to be published shortly. He has written various articles on film as an historical source.

Ian Kershaw is Senior Lecturer in Modern History at the University of Manchester. His publications include: *Der Hitler-Mythos. Volksmeinung und Propaganda im Dritten Reich* (Stuttgart, 1980) and *Popular Opinion and Political Dissent in the Third Reich. Bavaria, 1933-45* (Oxford, 1983).

INDEX

224